SIGN REFERENCES
(signs used in the maps and diagrams)

Good footpath
(sufficiently distinct to be followed in mist)

Intermittent footpath
(difficult to follow in mist)

Route recommended
but no path
(if recommended one way only, arrow indicates direction)

Wall ∞∞∞∞∞∞∞∞   Broken wall °°°°°°°°°°°°°°°

Fence ++++++++++   Broken fence ''''''''''''''''''''

Marshy ground ↯↯↯↯↯   Trees 🌳🌳🌳🌳

Crags ⛰⛰⛰⛰   Boulders ⬠⬡◇△

Stream or River
(arrow indicates direction of flow)

Waterfall ⌇   Bridge ⌇

Buildings ▰▱   Unenclosed road ▓▓▓▓▓▓

Contours (at 100' intervals)
1900
1800
1700

Summit-cairn ▲   Other (prominent) cairns △

THE
NORTH WESTERN
FELLS

A PICTORIAL GUIDE

TO THE

LAKELAND FELLS

50TH ANNIVERSARY EDITION

being an illustrated account
of a study and exploration
of the mountains in the
English Lake District

by

a.Wainwright

BOOK SIX
THE NORTH WESTERN FELLS

Frances Lincoln Limited
4 Torriano Mews
Torriano Avenue
London NW5 2RZ
www.franceslincoln.com

Originally published by
Westmorland Gazette, Kendal, 1964

First published by Frances Lincoln 2003

50th Anniversary Edition with re-originated artwork
published by Frances Lincoln 2005

Printed and bound in Singapore

A CIP catalogue record for this book
is available from the British Library.

ISBN 978 0 7112 2459 9

9 8 7

50TH ANNIVERSARY EDITION
PUBLISHED BY
FRANCES LINCOLN, LONDON

THE PICTORIAL GUIDES

PUBLISHER'S NOTE

This 50th Anniversary edition of the Pictorial Guides to the Lakeland Fells is newly reproduced from the handwritten pages created in the 1950s and 1960s by A. Wainwright. The descriptions of the walks were correct, to the best of the author's knowledge, at the time of first publication and they are reproduced here without amendment. However, footpaths, cairns and other waymarks described here are no longer all as they were fifty years ago and walkers are advised to check with an up-to-date map when planning a walk.

Fellwalking has increased dramatically since the Pictorial Guides were first published. Some popular routes have become eroded, making good footwear and great care all the more necessary for walkers. The vital points about fellwalking, as A. Wainwright himself wrote on many occasions, are to use common sense and to remember to watch where you are putting your feet.

A programme of revision of the Pictorial Guides is under way and revised editions of each of them will be published over the next few years.

BOOK SIX

is dedicated to
those unlovely twins

MY RIGHT LEG and MY LEFT LEG

staunch supporters
that have carried me about
for over half a century,
endured much without complaint
and never once let me down

Nevertheless, they are unsuitable subjects for illustration

INTRODUCTION

Classification and Definition

Any division of the Lakeland fells into geographical districts must necessarily be arbitrary, just as the location of the outer boundaries of Lakeland must always be a matter of opinion. Any attempt to define internal or external boundaries is certain to invite criticism, and he who takes it upon himself to say where Lakeland starts and finishes, or, for example, where the Central Fells merge into the Southern Fells and *which* fells *are* the Central Fells and which the Southern and *why* they need be so classified, must not expect his pronouncements to be generally accepted.

Yet for present purposes some plan of classification and definition must be used. County and parochial boundaries are no help, nor is the recently-defined area of the Lakeland National Park, for this book is concerned only with the high ground.

First, the external boundaries.   Straight lines linking the extremities of the outlying lakes enclose all the higher fells very conveniently. There are a few fells of lesser height to the north and east, however, that are typically Lakeland in character and cannot properly be omitted : these are brought in, somewhat untidily, by extending the lines in those areas. Thus :

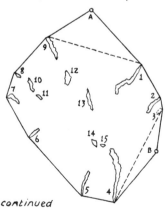

1 : *Ullswater*
2 : *Hawes Water*
3 : proposed *Swindale Resr*
4 : *Windermere*
5 : *Coniston Water*
6 : *Wast Water*
7 : *Ennerdale Water*
8 : *Loweswater*
9 : *Bassenthwaite Lake*
10 : *Crummock Water*
11 : *Buttermere*
12 : *Derwent Water*
13 : *Thirlmere*
14 : *Grasmere*
15 : *Rydal Water*
A : *Caldbeck*
B : *Longsleddale* (church)

continued

Classification and Definition

continued

The complete Guide is planned to include all the fells in the area enclosed by the straight lines of the diagram. This is an undertaking quite beyond the compass of a single volume, and it is necessary, therefore, to divide the area into convenient sections, making the fullest use of natural boundaries (lakes, valleys and low passes) so that each district is, as far as possible, self-contained and independent of the rest.

This division gives seven areas, each with a well-defined group of fells, and each will be the subject of a separate volume

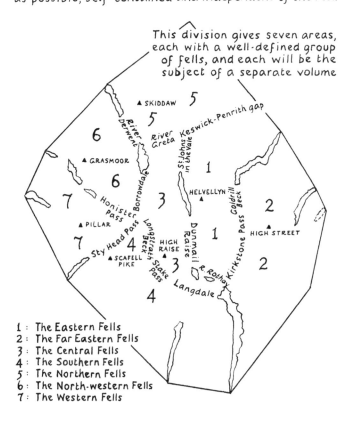

1 : The Eastern Fells
2 : The Far Eastern Fells
3 : The Central Fells
4 : The Southern Fells
5 : The Northern Fells
6 : The North-western Fells
7 : The Western Fells

Notes on the Illustrations

THE MAPS.................. Many excellent books have been written about Lakeland, but the best literature of all for the walker is that published by the Director General of Ordnance Survey, the 1" map for companionship and guidance on expeditions, the 2½" map for exploration both on the fells and by the fireside. These admirable maps are remarkably accurate topographically but there is a crying need for a revision of the paths on the hills: several walkers' tracks that have come into use during the past few decades, some of them now broad highways, are not shown at all; other paths still shown on the maps have fallen into neglect and can no longer be traced on the ground.

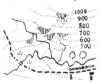

The popular Bartholomew 1" map is a beautiful picture, fit for a frame, but this too is unreliable for paths; indeed here the defect is much more serious, for routes are indicated where no paths ever existed, nor ever could — the cartographer has preferred to take precipices in his stride rather than deflect his graceful curves over easy ground.

Hence the justification for the maps in this book: they have the one merit (of importance to walkers) of being dependable as regards delineation of *paths*. They are intended as supplements to the Ordnance Survey maps, certainly not as substitutes.

THE VIEWS............... Various devices have been used to illustrate the views from the summits of the fells. The full panorama in the form of an outline drawing is most satisfactory generally, and this method has been adopted for the main viewpoints.

THE DIAGRAMS OF ASCENTS.................. The routes of ascent of the higher fells are depicted by diagrams that do not pretend to strict accuracy: they are neither plans nor elevations; in fact there is deliberate distortion in order to show detail clearly: usually they are represented as viewed from imaginary 'space-stations.' But it is hoped they will be useful and interesting.

THE DRAWINGS....... The drawings at least are honest attempts to reproduce what the eye sees: they illustrate features of interest and also serve the dual purpose of breaking up the text and balancing the layout of the pages, and of filling up awkward blank spaces, like this:

Thirlmere

THE
NORTH WESTERN
FELLS

The North Western Fells occupy a compact area, elliptical in plan, with clearly defined boundaries formed by the Rivers Derwent and Cocker. Only at one point, Honister Pass, is there a link with other high country, but even here, quite obviously, one mountain system ends and another begins. In all other places around the perimeter of the area deep valleys sever the North Western Fells from the neighbouring heights.

The Cocker is a tributary of the Derwent, and it follows, therefore, that the North Western Fells are wholly within the catchment of a single river — which further illustrates the geographical unity and separate identity of the group. Elsewhere, no combination of fells of similar extent is so neatly defined.

In size, the area is not very extensive on the map of Lakeland, but because its slopes rise immediately and steeply from the deep surrounding valleys, nothing is wasted: all is mountain country, first-class fellwalking territory. The hills tend to crowd together in the confined space available, but not in confusion and disarray, for connecting links bridge the tops in a pattern of high crests and scarped aretes that are a joy to explore. Indeed, here is to be found some of the finest ridge-walking in the district, smooth going for the most part, none of it difficult, none of it dangerous with ordinary care, all of it very pleasant and providing views of unsurpassed beauty.

THE THREE SECTORS

N

0
1
2
3
4
MILES

Bassenthwaite Lake

Northern

River Cocker

WHINLATTER PASS

Derwentwater

Central

NEWLANDS HAUSE

Crummock Water

Buttermere

SouthEastern

River Derwent

HONISTER PASS

Two motor roads cross the area, attaining their highest points at Whinlatter Pass and Newlands Hause and conveniently making three sectors.

The northern sector may be classed under the general title of Thornthwaite Forest. Slate is the underlying rock of the low rounded foothills comprising the region, but is not much in evidence, being well covered with vegetation and timber. A large part is occupied by the Forestry Commission, and here are being developed the most extensive plantations in the district. Perhaps because of this activity, the sector is less favoured by walkers than used to be the case, but it still offers many routes of unusual interest and charm.

The central sector contains the highest fells, all of them steep-sided and shapely, making arresting and exciting skylines. These, too, are of slate, and in the vicinity of Grasmoor particularly the steep slopes are excessively eroded and exhibit the most extensive wastes of scree in the district. These stony inclines are rarely climbed, but the summits and ridges above are very much frequented by walkers. The western flanks, rich in flora, are a happy hunting-ground for botanists. This sector is bisected by a foot-pass at Coledale Hause.

The south-eastern sector, too, is a place of fine ridges and shapely summits, and a great favourite of discerning walkers. The slate persists, but towards Borrowdale gives place to coarser, rougher volcanic ash.

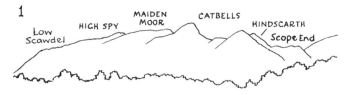

1

Low
Scawdel • HIGH SPY • MAIDEN MOOR • CATBELLS • HINDSCARTH • Scope End

The North Western Fells, as seen from The Heads, Keswick

This geological change is noticeable on the ground and manifests itself in the only tarns amongst the North Western Fells. Rock-climbers appreciate the change and here find their only major interests in the area.

Accommodation is available at several places around the perimeter, being in plentiful supply in Borrowdale, where it is a local industry, but less easy to find at Buttermere and Lorton in summer. Braithwaite is a good jumping-off place, but the finest centre for a fellwalking holiday is Newlands, the only populated valley *within* the area.   All the fells in this book may, however, be visited, with the help of the local bus services, from Keswick. It is worth noting that the best approaches to the area are from the north-east, the gradients being easier and the ascending ridges longer in this direction.

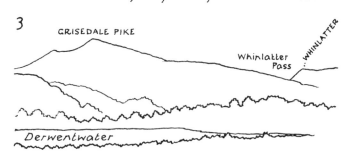

3

GRISEDALE PIKE • Whinlatter Pass • WHINLATTER

Derwentwater

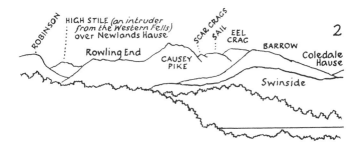

The main watershed lies close above the Cocker, and ascents from the southwest, in consequence, are short, abrupt and steep.

The North Western Fells, with riparian rights in four beautiful lakes, and sharing the proprietorship of the two lovely valleys of Borrowdale and Buttermere, can not be described as characteristic of Lakeland, the underlying slate tending to a smoothness of outline and an absence of tarns, but for walkers who prefer rather easier progression than is to be found amongst the more rugged volcanic fells, even at some sacrifice of romantic scenery, there are none better than these.

THE WATERSHED
south of
Whinlatter Pass

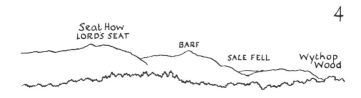

The North Western Fells, as seen from The Heads, Keswick

THE NORTH WESTERN FELLS

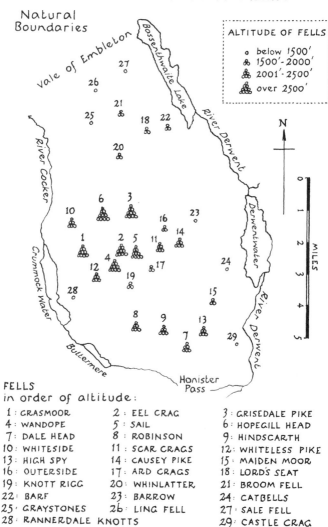

Natural Boundaries

Vale of Embleton

Bassenthwaite Lake

River Derwent

River Cocker

River Derwent

Derwentwater

Crummock Water

Buttermere

Honister Pass

N

ALTITUDE OF FELLS

- ○ below 1500'
- ⛰ 1500' - 2000'
- ⛰ 2001' - 2500'
- ⛰ over 2500'

0 1 2 3 4 5 MILES

FELLS
in order of altitude:

1 : GRASMOOR	2 : EEL CRAG	3 : GRISEDALE PIKE
4 : WANDOPE	5 : SAIL	6 : HOPEGILL HEAD
7 : DALE HEAD	8 : ROBINSON	9 : HINDSCARTH
10 : WHITESIDE	11 : SCAR CRAGS	12 : WHITELESS PIKE
13 : HIGH SPY	14 : CAUSEY PIKE	15 : MAIDEN MOOR
16 : OUTERSIDE	17 : ARD CRAGS	18 : LORD'S SEAT
19 : KNOTT RIGG	20 : WHINLATTER	21 : BROOM FELL
22 : BARF	23 : BARROW	24 : CATBELLS
25 : GRAYSTONES	26 : LING FELL	27 : SALE FELL
28 : RANNERDALE KNOTTS		29 : CASTLE CRAG

THE NORTH WESTERN FELLS

in the order of their appearance in this book

Reference to map opposite (over 2500' / 2001-2500' / 1500-2000' / below 1500')			Altitude in feet
17	. .	ARD CRAGS	. .	1860
22	. .	BARF	. .	1536
23	. .	BARROW	. .	1494
21	. .	BROOM FELL	. .	1670
29	. .	CASTLE CRAG	. .	985
24	. .	CATBELLS	. .	1481
14	. .	CAUSEY PIKE	. .	2035
7	. .	DALE HEAD	. .	2473
2	. .	EEL CRAG	. .	2749
1	. .	GRASMOOR	. .	2791
25	. .	GRAYSTONES	. .	1476
3	. .	GRISEDALE PIKE	. .	2593
13	. .	HIGH SPY	. .	2143
9	. .	HINDSCARTH	. .	2385
6	. .	HOPEGILL HEAD	. .	2525
19	. .	KNOTT RIGG	. .	1790
26	. .	LING FELL	. .	1224
18	. .	LORD'S SEAT	. .	1811
15	. .	MAIDEN MOOR	. .	1887
16	. .	OUTERSIDE	. .	1863
28	. .	RANNERDALE KNOTTS	. .	1160
8	. .	ROBINSON	. .	2417
5	. .	SAIL	. .	2530
27	. .	SALE FELL	. .	1170
11	. .	SCAR CRAGS	. .	2205
4	. .	WANDOPE	. .	2533
20	. .	WHINLATTER	. .	1696
12	. .	WHITELESS PIKE	. .	2159
10	. .	WHITESIDE	. .	2317

6 8 8 7

29

Each fell is the subject of a separate chapter

Ard Crags

1860'
approx.

from Rigg Beck

Rigg Beck •

EEL
CRAG ▲   ▲ ARD CRAGS

KNOTT
RIGG ▲   • Keskadale

⚡ Newlands Hause

• Buttermere

MILES
0   1   2   3

There is one point on the path alongside Rigg Beck where the defile ahead is occupied by the shapely pyramid of Ard Crags, its appearance suggesting a complete isolation from other fells. At the top of Rigg Beck, however, a high pass forms a bridge with the greater mass of the Eel Crag range; nevertheless, a clear identity is maintained by the ridge of Ard Crags as it runs southwest over Knott Rigg to Newlands Hause.

Both flanks are rough and exceedingly steep. Erosion on the south side — facing Newlands — has been halted by a plantation to protect the road and farmstead of Keskadale at its foot.

MAP

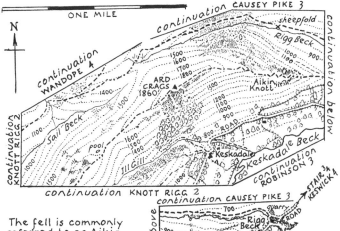

The fell is commonly referred to as Aikin Knott, which is more properly the name of a rocky excrescence on the 1500' contour. This latter name has wrongly appeared as Atkin Knott on some older Ordnance maps.

Rigg Beck

The sharp bend carrying the road over Rigg Beck is comparatively new. Formerly the road crossed at a ford lower down (still to be seen). Nearby, but now vanished, was a place of call, the Mill Dam Inn.

Higher up the road, at a wooded bend west of Gillbrow, the ruins of Bawd Hall can be seen, and, a little further, Aikin House, now a barn. Keskadale is the only inhabited dwelling on the four miles of road between Gillbrow and Buttermere, and there is no place of rest and refreshment for travellers.

ASCENT FROM RIGG BECK
1350 feet of ascent : 1½ miles

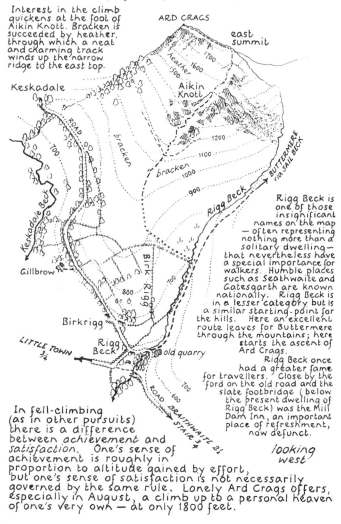

Interest in the climb quickens at the foot of Aikin Knott. Bracken is succeeded by heather, through which a neat and charming track winds up the narrow ridge to the east top.

ARD CRAGS

east summit

Aikin Knott

Keskadale

bracken

bracken

BUTTERMERE VIA SAIL BECK

Rigg Beck

Gillbrow

Birk Rigg

Birkrigg

Rigg Beck

old quarry

LITTLE TOWN 3/4

ROAD BRAITHWAITE STAIR 2½

Rigg Beck is one of those insignificant names on the map — often representing nothing more than a solitary dwelling — that nevertheless have a special importance for walkers. Humble places such as Seathwaite and Gatesgarth are known nationally. Rigg Beck is in a lesser category but is a similar starting-point for the hills. Here an excellent route leaves for Buttermere through the mountains; here starts the ascent of Ard Crags.

Rigg Beck once had a greater fame for travellers. Close by the ford on the old road and the slate footbridge (below the present dwelling of Rigg Beck) was the Mill Dam Inn, an important place of refreshment, now defunct.

looking west

In fell-climbing (as in other pursuits) there is a difference between achievement and satisfaction. One's sense of achievement is roughly in proportion to altitude gained by effort, but one's sense of satisfaction is not necessarily governed by the same rule. Lonely Ard Crags offers, especially in August, a climb up to a personal heaven of one's very own — at only 1800 feet.

THE SUMMIT

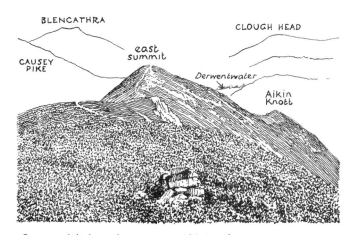

Save a visit here for a warm still day in August, and envy not the crowds heading for Great Gable. This is easier, more rewarding, and solitary. The narrow crest is a dense carpet of short springy heather, delightful to walk upon and even better as a couch for rest and meditation. But slumber is a hazard, for crags fall away sharply below one's boots to Keskadale. The highest point, marked by a cairn, has no official altitude, the surveyors having preferred to adopt the eastern end of the summit, at 1821', for their use.

DESCENTS : *For Newlands,* follow the ridge over the east summit and Aikin Knott. *For Buttermere,* traverse Knott Rigg and aim for Newlands Hause. The flanks of the fell are too rough for descent.

The summit crags

looking down to Keskadale from the summit

THE VIEW

The highlight of the view is the beautiful detail of Newlands, a picture of bright pastures intermingled with heathery ridges, backed by the Helvellyn range, which is seen end to end in the distance. In other directions, nearby higher fells seriously curtail the view, and this is especially so between west and north, where the massive wall of the Eel Crag range towers above, impressively close. Eel Crag itself impends on the scene overpoweringly. Also of interest is the regular pattern of aretes descending from the long summit of Scar Crags just across the deep valley of Rigg Beck.

Principal Fells

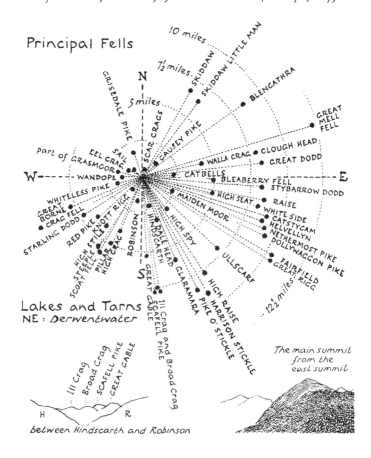

Lakes and Tarns
NE: Derwentwater

between Hindscarth and Robinson

The main summit from the east summit

RIDGE ROUTE

To KNOTT RIGG, 1790': 1 mile : SW
Depression at 1660'
130 feet of ascent

This is the natural continuation of the line of ascent over Aikin Knott. From the cairn a thin track in heather skirts the rim of a gully with a view downwards to Keskadale, and goes on to a depression. The heather is here left behind and a short climb up the facing grass slope leads to a definite ridge with Knott Rigg's cairn at the end of it.

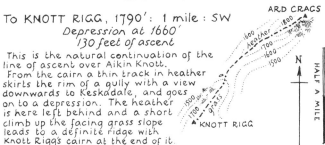

looking southwest along the ridge to Knott Rigg

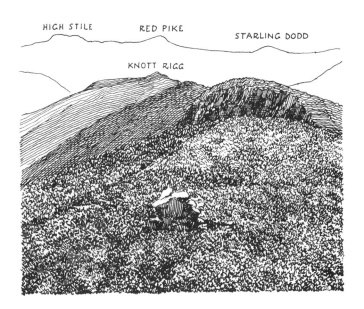

HIGH STILE   RED PIKE   STARLING DODD

KNOTT RIGG

Barf

1536'

from the main road near Beckstones

NATURAL FEATURES

Insignificant in height and of no greater extent than half a mile square, the rugged pyramid of Barf near the head of Bassenthwaite Lake yet contrives to arrest and retain the attention of travellers along the road at its base. Its outline is striking, its slopes seemingly impossibly steep; the direct ascent from its foot appears to be barred by an uncompromising cliff. There are few fells, large or small, of such hostile and aggressive character, for unrelenting steepness is allied to unstable runs of scree and outcrops. The rough ground is masked by bracken and heather, both enemies of smooth walking and rhythmical progression.... Passers-by look up at Barf with no thought of climbing it.

Barf is really a shoulder of Lord's Seat, which rises beyond but is unseen from the road. The neighbouring fells on both sides are densely planted with trees, but not so Barf. Crags and steep slopes do not normally deter the forestry workers but significantly they have not acquired any rights on Barf. This little rogue mountain cannot be tamed.

A unique feature that catches the eye from miles distant is the upstanding pinnacle long known as the Bishop of Barf, a venerable figure whose spotless vestments result from regular applications of whitewash by volunteers from the little community centred on the Swan Hotel directly below. This is a task not lightly to be undertaken, for the stiff climb to his pulpit up shifting scree is a bad enough scramble without the grave added responsibility of balancing a bucket that must not be spilled. But the job must be done from time to time: the Swan Hotel bereft of the benign presence of its old-established and effective publicity agent is quite unthinkable. The two go together, even more so than love and marriage.

The Bishop of Barf

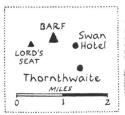

BARF

Swan
Hotel

LORD'S
SEAT

Thornthwaite

MILES

0   1   2

Barf 3

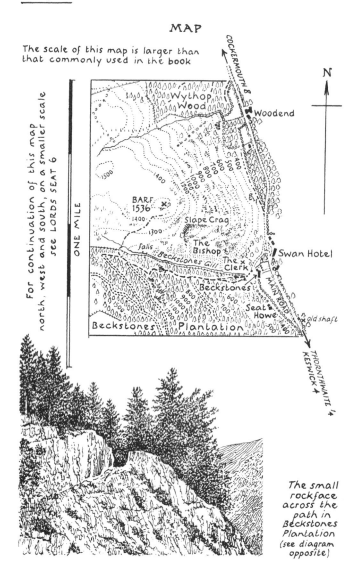

MAP

The scale of this map is larger than that commonly used in the book

N

For continuation of this map north, west and south, on a smaller scale see LORDS SEAT 6

ONE MILE

COCKERMOUTH 8

Wythop Wood

Woodend

1500

1400

1300

1200

1000

900

800

700

600

500

400

BARF 1536

Slope Crag

The Bishop

falls

Beckstones Gill

The Clerk

Swan Hotel

Beckstones

MAIN ROAD

Seat Howe

old shaft

Beckstones   Plantation

900

800

700

600

500

400

THORNTHWAITE ¼

KESWICK 4

The small rockface across the path in Beckstones Plantation (see diagram opposite)

ASCENT FROM THORNTHWAITE
1220 feet of ascent : 1 mile (from the Swan Hotel)

Above the tree-line, easier
slopes lead up to Lord's Seat

USUAL ROUTE

The path loses itself below the top.
The highest point is above a white
(quartz) rock

Blasted out of crags,
this road is a considerable
engineering achievement

new forest road

1200

1100

Beckstones
Plantation

900

800

old forest road

700

old path in groove →
– new track
alongside

600

500

Take the path
rising through
the wood.

400

BARF

1400

1300

50 yards beyond the terminus
of the forest road turn off the
path continuing distinctly up
through the wood, branching to
the right and scaling the fence
with the help of a few stones
piled there for the purpose.

The route is in doubt at a
small rockface. Climb this by
a ledge running right and then
left to a clear continuation of
the path above.

The lower (and older) plantings
are mainly larch ; higher, spruce.

The Bishop

The Bishop is conspicuous
from the road, appearing as
a detached pinnacle only for
a short distance 55-60 yards
north of the bus stop.

Beckstones Gill

bracken

MAIN ROAD → PHEASANT INN 3¾
COCKERMOUTH 8½

Beckstones

looking
west

THORNTHWAITE 2
KESWICK 4¼

bus stop

Swan Hotel
*Bus route 34 (Keswick–Whitehaven)
or 37 (Keswick–Thornthwaite terminus)*

Once a popular ascent, this route has fallen
from favour, and the path has been disturbed by
forestry operations. Nevertheless, it remains one
of the very best of the shorter Lakeland climbs.

The Clerk

In comparison with the commanding figure of the Bishop, the Clerk is a poor drooping individual who attracts little attention to himself. He stands amidst bracken at the foot of the slope. Once he too wore white vestments (which are sadly in need of renewal, a few ragged traces only remaining).

A visit to the Bishop discloses that, behind the spotless raiment he displays to the road below, his rear quarters are shamefully and indecently naked. Nor is he as tall as may be imagined: seven feet on the shortest side. Nevertheless it is to his credit that he has maintained his stately presence, for all around is the debris of shattered and eroded slate; the Bishop is slate, too, although obviously cast in a sterner mould. The time will come, however, when a collapsing pulpit will topple him down the screes.

The Bishop — rear view, looking down to the Swan Hotel

ASCENT FROM THORNTHWAITE
1200 feet of ascent : ¾ mile (from the Swan Hotel)

DIRECT ROUTE

BARF

looking west·north·west

Notes arranged from the bottom upwards

1500

grass

second false summit : true summit in view

first false summit : sudden, dramatic view of Bassenthwaite Lake below

heather

1400

Easier slopes now; difficulties over.

track

sheep

upper escarpment. Ignore track going up to it from end of traverse.

pinnacle

The traverse revives lurid memories of Jack's Rake on Pavey Ark, but is short and easy.

steep heather

1200

Round the escarpment on the left, at base of pinnacle

Slape Crag

This obstacle can be safely negotiated at one point only. Bear left at its base, across scree, to a rock traverse above an oak and a rowan together.

traverse

Oak tree (a surprise!) and a rowan growing together on crags.

steep heather

1000

At last, a few yards of level walking

Slape Crag is now in view

solitary rowan tree

heather

By the time the rowan tree is reached the feeling that one is pioneering a new ascent, treading where no man has trodden before, is very strong, and consequently it is mortifying to find the slender trunk of the tree elaborately carved with the initials of countless earlier visitors.

900

Escape left over loose rock to a small arête then go up an easier heather slope above

800

The scree gully is unpleasant. Its walls of rotten rock cannot be trusted for handholds and fall apart at a touch. The 'tiles' here pull out like drawers.

scree

700

The Bishop

The Bishop stands on a remarkable pulpit built of small flat tiles (of slate) lying horizontally.

Scramble up to the Bishop and pass behind him to a scree gully beyond

gorse

600

This wide scree slope, although not dangerous, is arduous to ascend, the feet often slipping down two steps for every step up —— from which it should not be supposed that better progress will be made by going up backwards. Keep to the scanty vegetation (gorse and bracken) where it exists.

In June, foxgloves make a colourful display here.

scree

500

Look out for the Clerk, an insignificant figure almost hidden amongst bracken in a clearing at the foot of the slope

400

The Clerk

MAIN ROAD → PHEASANT INN 3¾
COCKERMOUTH 8½

Beckstones

Bus routes 34 or 37

Swan Hotel
bus stop

THORNTHWAITE 2
KESWICK 4¼

Not a walk.
A very stiff scramble, suitable only for people overflowing with animal strength and vigour.

THE SUMMIT

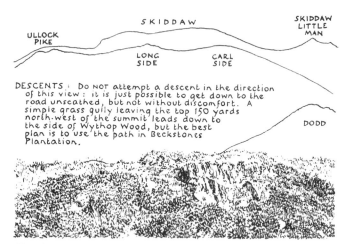

SKIDDAW

SKIDDAW
LITTLE
MAN

ULLOCK
PIKE

LONG
SIDE

CARL
SIDE

DODD

DESCENTS : Do not attempt a descent in the direction
of this view : it is just possible to get down to the
road unscathed, but not without discomfort. A
simple grass gully leaving the top 150 yards
north-west of the summit leads down to
the side of Wythop Wood, but the best
plan is to use the path in Beckstones
Plantation.

Heather encroaches almost to the bare top, a small platform
with grass growing thinly on underlying rock, which, in places,
shows through to form a pavement.   There is no cairn, nor
facilities for making one.   The summit breaks away in an
unseen crag on the side facing Skiddaw, a fact to bear well
in mind if there are children in the party.

The top of Barf

THE VIEW

The summit of Barf is the one place above all others for appreciating the massive build-up of Skiddaw, here seen, at mid-height, piling up from the shore of Bassenthwaite Lake in three great leaps to the summit 1500 feet above the viewpoint. The lake, too, is exceptionally well displayed directly below — a sensational surprise for those who reach the top from 'behind'. There is a pleasing view of the Vale of Keswick and Derwentwater and an extensive prospect seawards.

Principal Fells

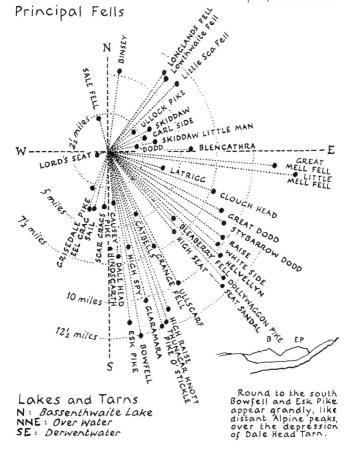

Lakes and Tarns

N : Bassenthwaite Lake
NNE : Over Water
SE : Derwentwater

Round to the south Bowfell and Esk Pike appear grandly, like distant Alpine peaks, over the depression of Dale Head Tarn.

RIDGE ROUTE

To LORD'S SEAT, 1811′ : ¾ mile : W
Depression at 1400′ : 420 feet of ascent

The objective is clear enough, but the route is a matter of choice. Intermittent tracks are a help. It is generally better to prefer the bracken to the wide tracts of thick heather, where walking is rough. In mist, it is advisable to go down to the fence and, without crossing it, follow it up, skirting some swampy patches in the hollow.

Lord's Seat from Barf

Barf, south side, from a forest road in Beckstones Plantation

Barf, north side, from a dead forest above Wythop Wood

Barrow

from Outerside
Stile End in the middle
distance; Stonycroft Gill
mine road down on the right

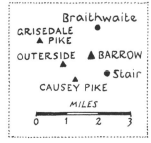

Braithwaite •

GRISEDALE
▲ PIKE

OUTERSIDE   ▲ BARROW
▲

• Stair

CAUSEY PIKE
▲

MILES

0   1   2   3

*from
Newlands Beck*

NATURAL FEATURES

Barrow occupies an enviable position overlooking a scene as fair as any in the kingdom. In shape a long narrow ridge, rooted in Braithwaite, it rises to present a broad flank to the valley of Newlands before curving west, bounded by Stonycroft Gill, to join the mass of Outerside across the gap of Barrow Door. A great scar on the Newlands face marks the site of the once-famous Barrow Mine; on the opposite flank facing Coledale is another great scar, this one a natural formation, at a point where Barrow Gill, after an uneventful meandering from Barrow Door, is suddenly engulfed in a remarkable ravine, a gorge of amazing proportions for so slender a stream and deeper even than Piers Gill, which continues down, becoming wooded, to the cottages of Braithwaite. Bracken clothes the lower slopes of Barrow, but a dark cap of heather covers the higher reaches.

At Stonycroft Bridge an old water-cut (now dry) can be traced up, first carved in the rock and then following the contour of the fellside, with the gorge steeply below. The old level illustrated, half-hidden by gorse, is alongside the cut in its top part.

This is the setting of the old Stonycroft Mine

Under Stonycroft Bridge. The beck enters the picture from the left. The dry watercut comes down on the right.

Barrow is 'the shivering mountain' of Lakeland. The great fan of spoil from the old mines on the Newlands face sweeps down to the road near Uzzicar and is prevented from burying it in debris only by a retaining parapet with a cleared space behind to accommodate major falls. The spoil is a sandy gravel constantly in slight motion, and the rustle of movement on the slope (no more than a whisper) can be heard on the road below. Note also an air shaft in the small field south of Uzzicar.

Barrow 3

Barrow Gill

looking up
the gill to
Barrow Door
and
Causey Pike

looking down
the gill to
Braithwaite

MAP

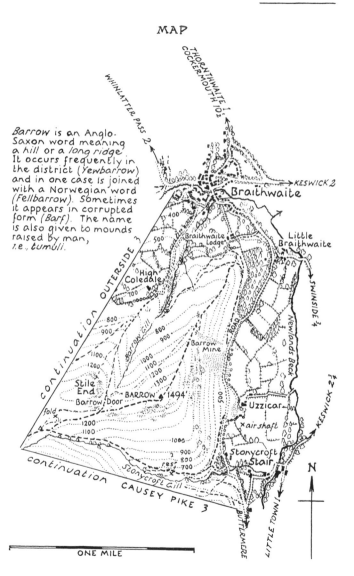

Barrow is an Anglo-Saxon word meaning a *hill* or a *long ridge*. It occurs frequently in the district (*Yewbarrow*) and in one case is joined with a Norwegian word (*Fellbarrow*). Sometimes it appears in corrupted form (*Barf*). The name is also given to mounds raised by man, *i.e.*, *tumuli*.

ONE MILE

N

ASCENT FROM BRAITHWAITE
1250 feet of ascent : 1½ miles

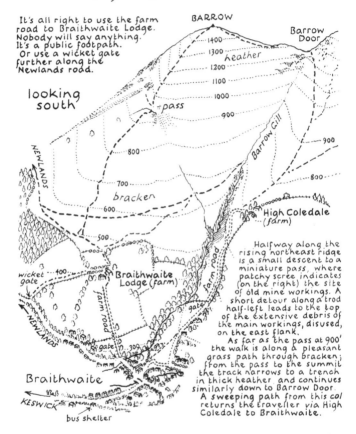

It's all right to use the farm road to Braithwaite Lodge. Nobody will say anything. It's a public footpath. Or use a wicket gate further along the Newlands road.

looking south

BARROW

Barrow Door

1400
1300
1200
1100
1000
900

heather

Barrow Gill

pass

900

NEWLANDS

800

800

700

bracken

600

High Coledale (farm)

500

Halfway along the rising northeast ridge is a small descent to a miniature pass, where patchy scree indicates (on the right) the site of old mine workings. A short detour along a trod half-left leads to the top of the extensive debris of the main workings, disused, on the east flank.
As far as the pass at 900' the walk is along a pleasant grass path through bracken; from the pass to the summit the track narrows to a trench in thick heather and continues similarly down to Barrow Door.
A sweeping path from this col returns the traveller via High Coledale to Braithwaite.

wicket gate

400

Braithwaite Lodge (farm)

farm road

NEWLANDS

gate

300

gate

Braithwaite

KESWICK

bus shelter

The ascent of Barrow from Braithwaite by its facing ridge is a favourite Sunday afternoon ramble, in the category of Latrigg and Catbells and Loughrigg Fell, and every step of the way is a joy. The walk can be extended, as indicated, to make a round journey of about two hours.

ASCENT FROM STAIR
1200 feet of ascent : 2¼ miles

looking north·west

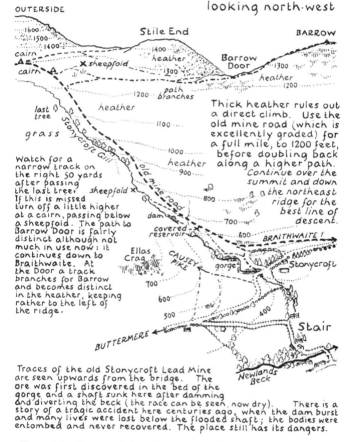

OUTERSIDE

Stile End

BARROW

1600
1500
1400
cairn
A
cairn A
X sheepfold

1400
heather
1300

Barrow
Door

1300
heather
1200

path
branches

1200

heather

1100

last
tree

grass

Stonycroft Gill

1000

heather

900

800

mine road

sheepfold X

dam

covered
reservoir

700

600

BRAITHWAITE !

gorge

Stonycroft

Ellas
Crag

CAUSEY
PIKE

700

600

500

400

Stair

BUTTERMERE

Newlands
Beck

Thick heather rules out
a direct climb. Use the
old mine road (which is
excellently graded) for
a full mile, to 1200 feet,
before doubling back
along a higher path.
Continue over the
summit and down
the northeast
ridge for the
best line of
descent.

Watch for a
narrow track on
the right 50 yards
after passing
the last tree.
If this is missed
turn off a little higher
at a cairn, passing below
a sheepfold. The path to
Barrow Door is fairly
distinct although not
much in use now: it
continues down to
Braithwaite. At
the Door a track
branches for Barrow
and becomes distinct
in the heather, keeping
rather to the left of
the ridge.

Traces of the old Stonycroft Lead Mine
are seen upwards from the bridge. The
ore was first discovered in the bed of the
gorge and a shaft sunk here after damming
and diverting the beck (the race can be seen, now dry). There is a
story of a tragic accident here centuries ago, when the dam burst
and many lives were lost below the flooded shaft; the bodies were
entombed and never recovered. The place still has its dangers.

The old mine road has become a first-class walkers way
into the hills, progress being fast and easy, and it lends
itself well, coupled with a linking path from Braithwaite,
to an ascent of Barrow, while giving an introduction to
the quiet upper reaches of Stonycroft Gill. Causey Pike
on the left of the valley dominates the walk throughout.

THE SUMMIT

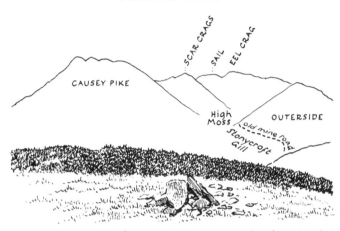

A small cairn occupies a patch of grass on the highest point with heather all around. On the right sort of day this is a grand place for settling down and getting the old pipe out for an hour's quiet meditation.

DESCENTS : Use only the track along the ridge, either way. In particular do not attempt a direct route for Newlands.

RIDGE ROUTE

To OUTERSIDE, 1863': 1¼ miles : WSW, then NW and SW
Depressions at 1270' and 1380'
800 feet of ascent
Rough walking in heather

Go down to Barrow Door and up a facing track onto Stile End, where turn right for the top and then left down to Low Moss, across which a charming track mounts through the heather to the top of Outerside.

Not recommended beyond Barrow Door in mist.

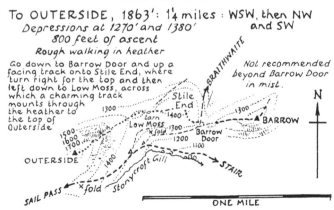

ONE MILE

THE VIEW

This is a splendid panorama, too good really for the small effort involved in earning it.

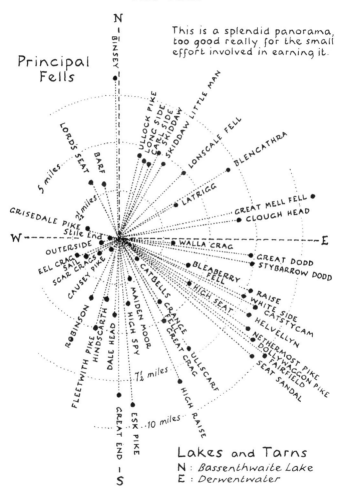

Principal Fells

Lakes and Tarns
N : Bassenthwaite Lake
E : Derwentwater

There is a remarkable contrast between the smiling Vale of Keswick, where Derwentwater is excellently displayed, and the sombre ring of fells crowded nearby in the west. Away over the head of Newlands is Esk Hause with Esk Pike soaring magnificently to the left of it and looking every inch a mountain

Broom Fell

1670'

Cockermouth

Wythop
Mill

▲ SALE FELL

LING FELL ▲

BROOM
FELL

GRAYSTONES ▲

▲ LORDS
SEAT

Low
Lorton

High
Lorton

Whinlatter Pass

MILES

0   1   2   3   4

from
Aiken Plantation

NATURAL FEATURES

Broom Fell is the geographical centre of the upland mass rising between Bassenthwaite Lake in the north and Whinlatter Pass in the south, but acknowledges the superiority of a near and higher neighbour, Lord's Seat, to which it is connected by a high ridge. There is little of interest on this rounded grassy hill, and nothing to justify a special visit to the summit; its flanking valleys, however, are sharply contrasted, each having distinguishing features worthy of note. North is the open valley of Wythop, a place of farms and green pastures, but before the descending slopes reach cultivable levels they are halted at a morass, the remarkable mile-wide Wythop Moss — a hopeless, lifeless swamp that can be traversed conveniently only at the one place where a causeway of firmer ground has been laid out and ditched to facilitate a crossing. South is the narrow side valley of Aiken Beck, with the rare distinction of being enclosed on all four sides: a hidden valley, uninhabited, and frequented only for purposes of forestry, most of it being under timber.

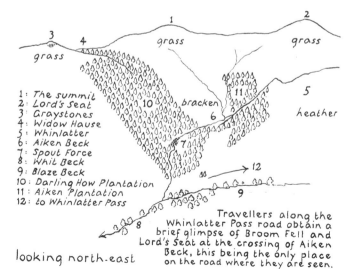

1: The summit
2: Lord's Seat
3: Graystones
4: Widow Hause
5: Whinlatter
6: Aiken Beck
7: Spout Force
8: Whit Beck
9: Blaze Beck
10: Darling How Plantation
11: Aiken Plantation
12: to Whinlatter Pass

looking north-east

Travellers along the Whinlatter Pass road obtain a brief glimpse of Broom Fell and Lord's Seat at the crossing of Aiken Beck, this being the only place on the road where they are seen.

MAP

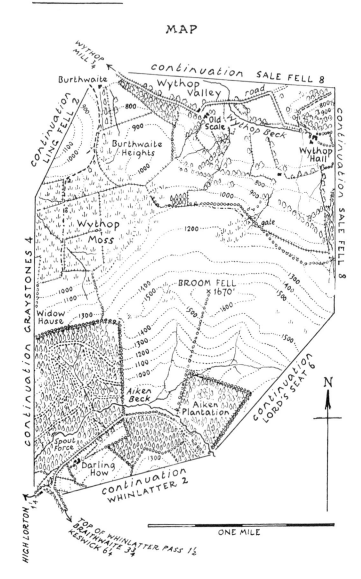

ASCENT FROM WYTHOP MILL
1450 feet of ascent · 4 miles

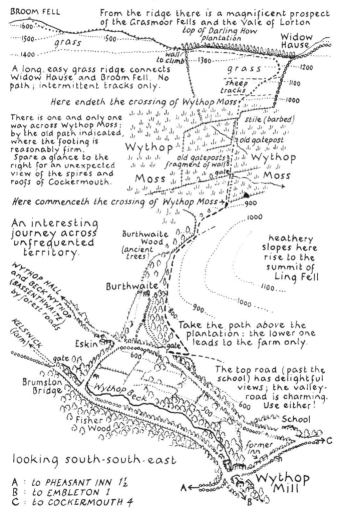

BROOM FELL

From the ridge there is a magnificent prospect of the Grasmoor Fells and the Vale of Lorton

---- 1600 ----
---- 1500 ---- grass ---- 500 ----
---- 1400 ----

top of Darling How plantation

Widow Hause

wall to climb

1300

1200

A long, easy grass ridge connects Widow Hause and Broom Fell. No path; intermittent tracks only.

grass

sheep tracks

1100

1000

Here endeth the crossing of Wythop Moss

There is one and only one way across Wythop Moss; by the old path indicated, where the footing is reasonably firm.
Spare a glance to the right for an unexpected view of the spires and roofs of Cockermouth.

stile (barbed)

old gatepost

Wythop

old gateposts
fragment of wall

Wythop

Moss

gate

Moss

Here commenceth the crossing of Wythop Moss →

900

An interesting journey across unfrequented territory.

1000

Burthwaite Wood (ancient trees)

heathery slopes here rise to the summit of Ling Fell

1100

WYTHOP HALL and BECK WYTHOP (BASSENTHWAITE) by forest roads

Burthwaite

900

1000

KESWICK (farm)

Eskin

gate

Take the path above the plantation: the lower one leads to the farm only.

gate

600

The top road (past the school) has delightful views; the valley road is charming. Use either!

Brumston Bridge

Wythop Beck

600

School

Fisher Wood

former inn

C

looking south-south-east

Wythop Mill

A : to PHEASANT INN 1½
B : to EMBLETON 1
C : to COCKERMOUTH 4

A

B

ASCENT FROM HIGH LORTON
1400 feet of ascent : 3 miles

looking east·north·east

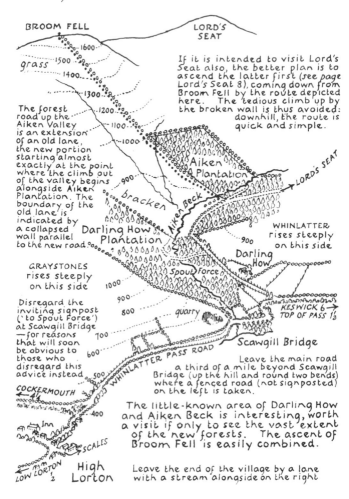

BROOM FELL

LORD'S SEAT

grass
1600
1500
1400
1300
1200
1100
1000
900

If it is intended to visit Lord's Seat also, the better plan is to ascend the latter first (see page Lord's Seat 8), coming down from Broom Fell by the route depicted here. The tedious climb up by the broken wall is thus avoided: downhill, the route is quick and simple.

The forest road up the Aiken Valley is an extension of an old lane, the new portion starting almost exactly at the point where the climb out of the valley begins alongside Aiken Plantation. The boundary of the old lane is indicated by a collapsed wall parallel to the new road.

bracken

Aiken Plantation

LORD'S SEAT

Aiken Beck

Darling How Plantation

WHINLATTER rises steeply on this side

900

Darling How

GRAYSTONES rises steeply on this side

1000

900

800

Spout Force

700

quarry

KESWICK 6 →
TOP OF PASS 1½

Disregard the inviting signpost ('to Spout Force') at Scawgill Bridge — for reasons that will soon be obvious to those who disregard this advice instead.

Scawgill Bridge

600

500

WHINLATTER PASS ROAD

Leave the main road a third of a mile beyond Scawgill Bridge (up the hill and round two bends) where a fenced road (not signposted) on the left is taken.

COCKERMOUTH 4↑

400

Inn

SCALES

The little-known area of Darling How and Aiken Beck is interesting, worth a visit if only to see the vast extent of the new forests. The ascent of Broom Fell is easily combined.

FROM LOW LORTON ½

High Lorton

Leave the end of the village by a lane with a stream alongside on the right

THE SUMMIT

looking southeast

GREAT DODD
LORD'S SEAT
HELVELLYN
NETHERMOST PIKE
DOLLYWAGGON PIKE
FAIRFIELD

The grassy top of the fell is featureless except for an oddity in the shape of a wall that comes up the fellside from Aiken Beck to end precisely at the highest point — the odd thing being that it is a perfectly straight wall throughout its length, enclosing nothing, defending nothing, sheltering nothing, marking nothing and obviously of little value because it has fallen into disrepair.

DESCENTS : All slopes are easy, the western going down to Wythop Moss, where the old path must be used to cross the morass. In mist, let the wall serve as a guide downhill for Lorton.

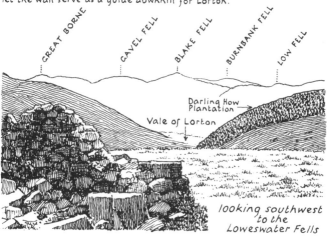

GREAT BORNE
GAVEL FELL
BLAKE FELL
BURNBANK FELL
LOW FELL

Darling How Plantation

Vale of Lorton

looking southwest to the Loweswater Fells

THE VIEW

The gem of the view is the Vale of Lorton backed by the fells around Loweswater — a lovely scene. The Grasmoor group is massed impressively across the gulf of Whinlatter Pass. Beyond Bassenthwaite Lake Skiddaw rises grandly.
Northwest is a wide sweep of the Solway Firth and the Scottish hills, with Criffell prominent.

Principal Fells

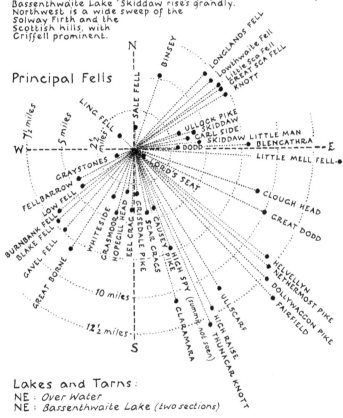

Lakes and Tarns:
NE : *Over Water*
NE : *Bassenthwaite Lake (two sections)*

The skyline to the south

RIDGE ROUTES

To LORD'S SEAT, 1811' : ⅞ mile : SE
Depression at 1586': 260 feet of ascent
An easy ridge, with nothing of special interest.

The ridge is wide, marshy in places, and carries no path; it has many small undulations, and the actual lowest point, at 1586', just before the ground steepens into the final rise of Lord's Seat, cannot be identified with certainty; not that it matters. This is the slope of Lord's Seat on which the 'seat' is supposed to be found, but its exact location is also in doubt. This doesn't matter either, the author having personally installed himself in every rock-recess hereabouts (anxious as always for the comfort of his readers) and found the process merely painful.

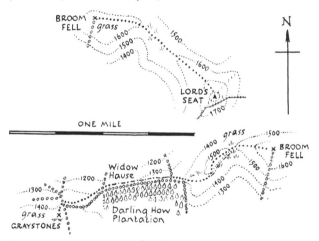

To GRAYSTONES, 1476' : 1¼ miles : WSW
Depression at 1240' (Widow Hause) : 260 feet of ascent
Interest is sustained on this easy walk by the variety of scenery

Starting due west, follow the height of land across a moist depression to firmer ground beyond, which trends south to the corner of Darling How Plantation. (Or use a narrow track that keeps just left of the 1500' contour) Here the crumbling wall that formerly ran solitary along the descending ridge to Widow Hause is now accompanied by a tight forest fence, the plantings here having been carried the full height of the fellside from the valley of Aiken Beck below. The fence continues on to Graystones, enclosing an area not yet planted, and the crossing of three walls is involved in keeping outside it. When it finally turns south the summit of Graystones is only two minutes away.

Castle Crag

985'
approx.

Grange
●

CASTLE
▲ CRAG

Rosthwaite
●

ONE MILE

from the south

NATURAL FEATURES

Perhaps, to be strictly correct, Castle Crag should be regarded not as a separate fell but as a protuberance on the rough breast of Low Scawdel, occurring almost at the foot of the slope and remote from the ultimate summit of High Spy far above and out of sight. Castle Crag has no major geographical function — it is not a watershed, does not persuade the streams of Scawdel from their predestined purpose of joining the Derwent and interrupts only slightly the natural fall of the fell to Borrowdale: on the general scale of the surrounding heights it is of little significance.

Yet Castle Crag is so magnificently independent, so ruggedly individual, so aggressively unashamed of its lack of inches, that less than justice would be done by relegating it to a paragraph in the High Spy chapter. If its top is below 1000 feet, which is doubtful (no 'official' height having been determined), it is the only fell below 1000 feet in this series of books that is awarded the full treatment; a distinction well earned.

Castle Crag conforms to no pattern. It is an obstruction in the throat of Borrowdale, confining passage therein to the width of a river and a road, hiding what lies beyond, defying cultivation. Its abrupt pyramid, richly wooded from base almost to summit but bare at the top, is a wild tangle of rough steep ground, a place of crags and scree and tumbled boulders, of quarry holes and spoil dumps, of confusion and disorder. But such is the artistry of nature, such is the mellowing influence of the passing years, that the scars of disarray and decay have been transformed in a romantic harmony, cloaked by a canopy of trees and a carpet of leaves. There are lovely copses of silver birch by the crystal-clear river, magnificent specimens of Scots pine higher up. Naked of trees, Castle Crag would be ugly; with them, it has a sylvan beauty unsurpassed, unique.

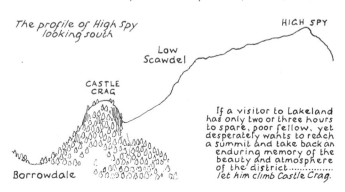

The profile of High Spy looking south

HIGH SPY

Low Scawdel

CASTLE CRAG

Borrowdale

If a visitor to Lakeland has only two or three hours to spare, poor fellow, yet desperately wants to reach a summit and take back an enduring memory of the beauty and atmosphere of the district............ let him climb Castle Crag.

Castle Crag 3

The summit-quarry

The pedestrian path to the
top goes up the grass
on the right

summit

Quarries and caves of Castle Crag

In addition to the summit-quarry, which is open to the sky
and obvious to all who climb the fell, the steep flank above the
Derwent is pitted with cuttings and caverns and levels, every
hole having its tell-tale spoilheap, but the scars of this former
industrial activity are largely concealed by a screen of trees
and not generally noticed. Much of this flank is precipitous,
the ground everywhere is very rough, and the vertically-hewn
walls of naked stone are dangerous traps for novice explorers.

Of these quarries the best known
is High Hows, the debris of which is
passed on the riverside walk from
Grange to Rosthwaite. A detour up
the quarry road leads to a series of
caverns, which for older walkers
have a nostalgic interest: here
in one of them Millican Dalton,
a mountaineering adventurer
and a familiar character in the
district between the wars (died
1947, aged 80) furnished a home
for his summer residence, using
an adjacent cave, at a higher
level (the 'Attic') as sleeping
quarters. Note here his lettering
cut in the rock at the entrance —
'Don't !! Waste words, jump to conclusions'

The Attic

Millican's Cave

MAP

The thick line forming a square has a special significance. It encloses one mile of country containing no high mountain, no lake, no famous crag, no tarn.

But, in the author's humble submission, it encloses the loveliest square mile in Lakeland — the Jaws of Borrowdale.

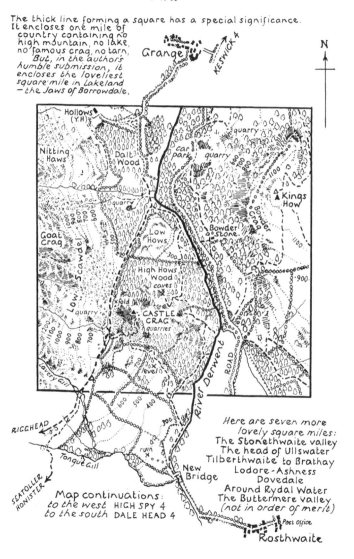

Here are seven more lovely square miles:
The Stonethwaite valley
The head of Ullswater
Tilberthwaite to Brathay
Lodore-Ashness
Dovedale
Around Rydal Water
The Buttermere valley
(not in order of merit)

Map continuations:
to the west HIGH SPY 4
to the south DALE HEAD 4

ASCENT FROM GRANGE

700 feet of ascent
1½ miles

CASTLE CRAG

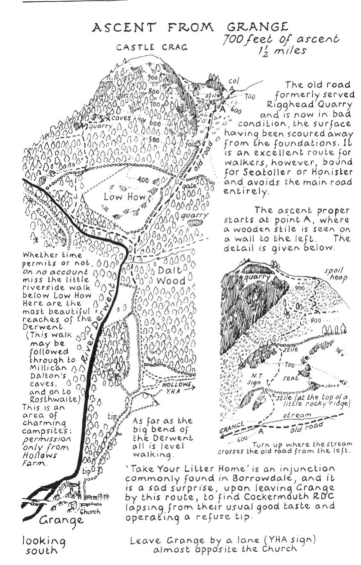

The old road formerly served Rigghead Quarry and is now in bad condition, the surface having been scoured away from the foundations. It is an excellent route for walkers, however, bound for Seatoller or Honister and avoids the main road entirely.

The ascent proper starts at point A, where a wooden stile is seen on a wall to the left. The detail is given below.

Whether time permits or not, on no account miss the little riverside walk below Low How. Here are the most beautiful reaches of the Derwent. (This walk may be followed through to Millican Dalton's caves, and on to Rosthwaite) This is an area of charming campsites: permission only from Hollows Farm.

As far as the big bend of the Derwent all is level walking.

Turn up where the stream crosses the old road from the left.

'Take Your Litter Home' is an injunction commonly found in Borrowdale, and it is a sad surprise, upon leaving Grange by this route, to find Cockermouth RDC lapsing from their usual good taste and operating a refuse tip.

looking south

Leave Grange by a lane (YHA sign) almost opposite the Church

ASCENT FROM ROSTHWAITE

700 feet of ascent
1½ miles

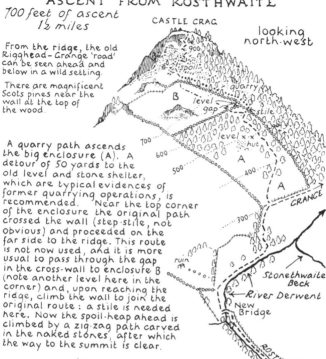

CASTLE CRAG

looking
north-west

B   level
gap

quarry

stile

level x·x
hut

700

600

500

400

300

A

A

GRANGE

ruin

Stonethwaite
Beck

River Derwent

New
Bridge

ROSTHWAITE ¼
lane

spoil

900

From the ridge, the old Rigghead–Grange 'road' can be seen ahead and below in a wild setting.

There are magnificent Scots pines near the wall at the top of the wood.

A quarry path ascends the big enclosure (A). A detour of 50 yards to the old level and stone shelter, which are typical evidences of former quarrying operations, is recommended.   Near the top corner of the enclosure the original path crossed the wall (step-stile, not obvious) and proceeded on the far side to the ridge. This route is not now used, and it is more usual to pass through the gap in the cross-wall to enclosure B (note another level here in the corner) and, upon reaching the ridge, climb the wall to join the original route: a stile is needed here. Now the spoil-heap ahead is climbed by a zig-zag path carved in the naked stones, after which the way to the summit is clear.

Leave Rosthwaite by the lane opposite the post office, bearing right at the farm buildings.

An old level

Old quarry workings, Castle Crag

A typical
stone store
or shelter
hut
(only 3
to 4 feet
high)

THE SUMMIT

The summit is circular in plan, about 60 yards in diameter, and a perfect natural stronghold. Even today, one man in possession, armed with a stick, could prevent its occupation by others whatever their number, there being one strategic point (the place of access to the top) where passage upward is restricted to single-file traffic. Authorities agree that there was once a fort here, probably early British, but it needs a trained eye to trace any earthworks—which, in any case, must have been severely disturbed by an old quarry that has cut a big slice out of the summit and, be it noted, constitutes an unprotected danger. Photographers (who have a habit of taking backward steps when composing their pictures) should take care lest they suddenly vanish.

The highest point is a boss of rock, and this is crowned by a professionally-made round flat-topped cairn, below which, set in the rock, is a commemorative tablet: a war memorial to the men of Borrowdale, effective and imaginative. A stunted larch grows alongside, clinging for dear life to the rim of a crag, and better specimens surround the perimeter.

DESCENTS: For the ordinary walker there is only one way on and off, and this is on the south side, by a clump of larch, where a clear track descends between the edge of the quarry (right) and a cutting (left) to the flat top of the spoil-heap, at the end of which a ramp on the right inclines in zigzags to the grass below. Here, if bound for Rosthwaite, climb the wall on the left; for Grange the way continues down, crossing two walls by stiles, to the old Rigghead road.

ENVIRONS OF THE SUMMIT

THE SUMMIT

The altitude of the summit has not been determined by the men of the Ordnance Survey. It is often quoted as 900 feet, but is in excess of this figure.

From High Doat (927'; 1 mile south) the summit appears to be above the horizontal plane of Latrigg (1203'; 6½ miles), giving a height of not less than 970', and probably 980' or 990'.

Look at High Doat from Castle Crag : it is obviously lower.

THE VIEW

The view is circumscribed but is open to the north, where Derwentwater, backed by Skiddaw, makes a fine scene. The steep fall from the summit on all sides provides an aerial study of the beautiful detail of mid-Borrowdale.

Principal Fells

Lakes and Tarns
N-NNE : Derwentwater

Catbells

1481′

Cat Bells
(two words)
on Ordnance maps

from Derwentwater

- Portinscale
  - Keswick

- Stair

▲ CATBELLS
- Little Town
▲ MAIDEN MOOR
  - Grange

MILES

0   1   2   3   4

from the Portinscale path

NATURAL FEATURES

Catbells is one of the great favourites, a family fell where grandmothers and infants can climb the heights together, a place beloved. Its popularity is well deserved: its shapely topknot attracts the eye, offering a steep but obviously simple scramble to the small summit; its slopes are smooth, sunny and sleek; its position overlooking Derwentwater is superb. Moreover, for stronger walkers it is the first step on a glorious ridge that bounds Borrowdale on the west throughout its length with Newlands down on the other side. There is beauty everywhere — and nothing but beauty. Its ascent from Keswick may conveniently, in the holiday season, be coupled with a sail on the lake, making the expedition rewarding out of all proportion to the small effort needed. Even the name has a magic challenge.

Yet this fell is not quite so innocuous as is usually thought, and grandmothers and infants should have a care as they romp around. There are some natural hazards in the form of a line of crags that starts at the summit and slants down to Newlands, and steep outcrops elsewhere. More dangerous are the levels and open shafts that pierce the fell on both flanks: the once-prosperous Yewthwaite Mine despoils a wide area in the combe above Little Town in Newlands, to the east the debris of the ill-starred Brandley Mine is lapped by the water of the lake, and the workings of the Old Brandley Mine, high on the side of the fell at Skelgill Bank, are in view on the ascent of the ridge from the north. A tragic death in one of the open Yewthwaite shafts in 1962 serves as a warning.

Words cannot adequately describe the rare charm of Catbells, nor its ravishing view. But no publicity is necessary: its mere presence in the Derwentwater scene is enough. It has a bold 'come hither' look that compels one's steps, and no suitor ever returns disappointed, but only looking back often. It has only to be seen from Friar's Crag — and a spell is cast. No Keswick holiday is consummated without a visit to Catbells.

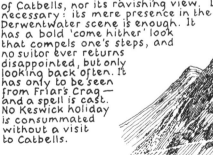

from Yewthwaite Combe

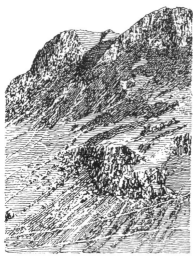

Crags and Caverns of Catbells

left: The crags of Mart Bield, below the summit on the Newlands side of the fell

right: A dangerous hole at Yewthwaite Mine.
At the end of a rock cutting the adit suggests a level (horizontal tunnel) but in fact is the opening of a vertical shaft.

below: Workings at the Old Brandley Mine.
A shaft with twin entrances, overhung by a tree, *left*, and a nearby level, *right*.

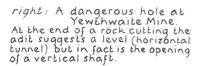

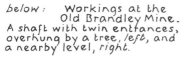

MAP

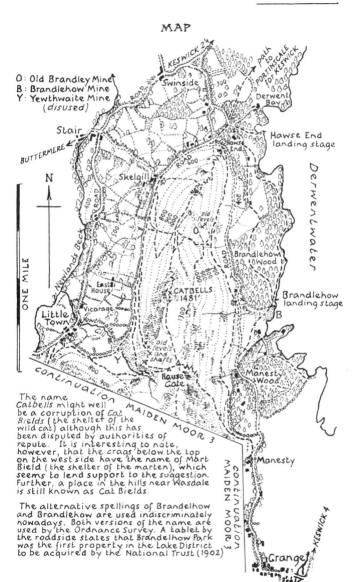

O: Old Brandley Mine
B: Brandlehow Mine
Y: Yewthwaite Mine
(disused)

KESWICK 2½

path to PORTINSCALE for KESWICK

Swinside

Derwent Bay

ROAD

Stair

BUTTERMERE

Hawse End landing stage

Hawse End

N

ROAD

Skelgill

Derwentwater

ONE MILE

old levels

O

Brandlehow Wood

East House

CATBELLS 1481

Brandlehow landing stage

Vicarage

B

Little Town

Yewthwaite

Gill

old levels and shafts

Y

continuation MAIDEN MOOR 3

Hause Gate

Manesty Wood

The name *Catbells* might well be a corruption of *Cat Bields* (the shelter of the wild cat) although this has been disputed by authorities of repute. It is interesting to note, however, that the crags below the top on the west side have the name of *Mart Bield* (the shelter of the marten), which seems to lend support to the suggestion. Further, a place in the hills near Wasdale is still known as *Cat Bields*.

The alternative spellings of *Brandelhow* and *Brandlehow* are used indiscriminately nowadays. Both versions of the name are used by the Ordnance Survey. A tablet by the roadside states that Brandelhow Park was the first property in the Lake District to be acquired by the National Trust (1902)

Manesty

continuation MAIDEN MOOR 3

KESWICK 4

Grange

ASCENT FROM HAWSE END
1250 feet of ascent : 1½ miles

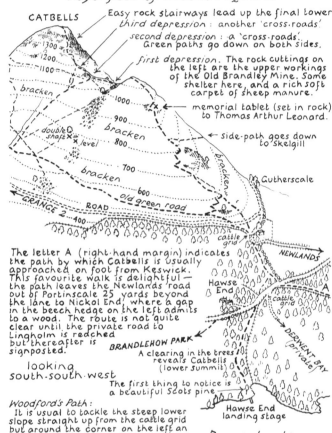

CATBELLS

Easy rock stairways lead up the final tower
third depression : another 'cross-roads'

second depression : a 'cross-roads'.
Green paths go down on both sides.

first depression. The rock cuttings on
the left are the upper workings
of the Old Brandley Mine. Some
shelter here, and a rich soft
carpet of sheep manure.

— memorial tablet (set in rock)
to Thomas Arthur Leonard.

← side-path goes down
to Skelgill

1300
1200
1100
1000
900
800
700
600
400

bracken
double shaft
level
bracken
bracken
old green road
ROAD
GRANGE 2

Gutherscale

cattle grid

NEWLANDS

Hawse End

cattle grid

DERWENT BAY (private)

BRANDLEHOW PARK

The letter A (right-hand margin) indicates
the path by which Catbells is usually
approached on foot from Keswick.
This favourite walk is delightful —
the path leaves the Newlands road
out of Portinscale 25 yards beyond
the lane to Nickol End, where a gap
in the beech hedge on the left admits
to a wood. The route is not quite
clear until the private road to
Lingholm is reached but thereafter is
signposted.

looking
south-south-west

A clearing in the trees
reveals Catbells
(lower summit)

The first thing to notice is
a beautiful Scots pine

Woodford's Path:
It is usual to tackle the steep lower
slope straight up from the cattle grid
but around the corner on the left an
exquisite series of zigzags provides a
more enjoyable start to the ascent.
These zigzags leave the old green road
80 yards along it : watch for the first.
The direct route joins in at the top of
the series ; another series is then
soon reached. This path was engineered
by a Sir John Woodford, who lived near,
and his name deserves to be remembered
by those who use his enchanting stairway.

Hawse End
landing stage

Derwentwater

Hawse End is served
by motor-launch from
Keswick (summer only)

One of the very best
of the shorter climbs.
A truly lovely walk.

ASCENT FROM GRANGE
1250 feet of ascent : 2 miles

Of course there is no gate at Hause Gate, just as there is no door at Mickledoor. 'Gate' and 'door' are local geographical terms for a way or opening through the hills or across a ridge. 'Hause' is another good Lakeland name for a pass. 'Hause Gate' is therefore really a tautological name. 'Hawse End' (with a 'w') is not a mis-spelling, 'hause' being inappropriate to the place.

Except for the zigzags below Hause Gate, the whole climb is set at an easy gradient, making it ideal for a gentle stroll on a fine evening after a big meal. The view opens beautifully as height is gained on a wide grass path, the start of which, near Manesty Farm, is the old road to Hawse End, now signposted as a footpath to Newlands.

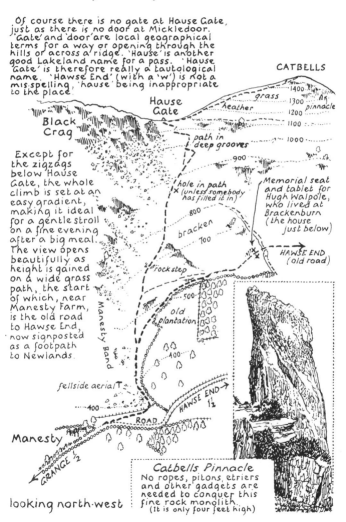

CATBELLS

Hause Gate

Black Crag

grass
heather
pinnacle
1400
1300
1200
1100
1000

path in deep grooves

900

hole in path ✕ (unless somebody has filled it in)

Memorial seat and tablet for Hugh Walpole, who lived at Brackenburn (the house just below)

800

bracken

700

HAWSE END (old road)

rock step

Manesty Band

500

old plantation

400

fellside aerial

HAWSE END 1½

400

ROAD

Manesty

GRANGE ½

looking north-west

Catbells Pinnacle
No ropes, pitons, etriers and other gadgets are needed to conquer this fine rock monolith. (It is only four feet high)

ASCENT FROM NEWLANDS

via SKELGILL
1200 feet of ascent : 1½ miles from Stair

via LITTLE TOWN
950 feet of ascent : 1½ miles from Little Town

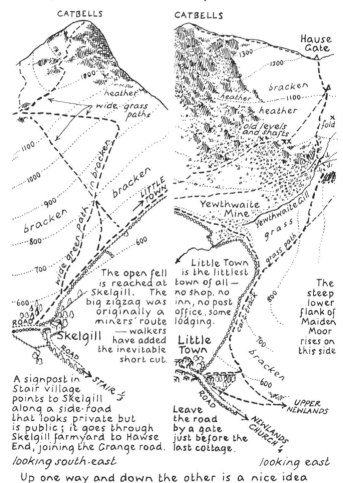

The open fell is reached at Skelgill. The big zigzag was originally a miners' route — walkers have added the inevitable short cut.

A signpost in Stair village points to Skelgill along a side-road that looks private but is public; it goes through Skelgill farmyard to Hawse End, joining the Grange road.

looking south-east

Little Town is the littlest town of all — no shop, no inn, no post office, some lodging.

The steep lower flank of Maiden Moor rises on this side

Leave the road by a gate just before the last cottage.

looking east

Up one way and down the other is a nice idea

THE SUMMIT

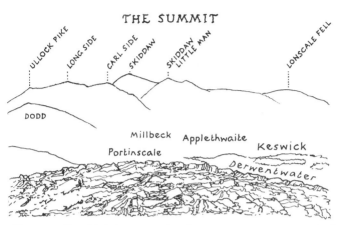

The summit, which has no cairn, is a small platform of naked rock, light brown in colour and seamed and pitted with many tiny hollows and crevices that collect and hold rainwater — so that, long after the skies have cleared, glittering diamonds adorn the crown. Almost all the native vegetation has been scoured away by the varied footgear of countless visitors; so popular is this fine viewpoint that often it is difficult to find a vacant perch. In summer this is not a place to seek quietness. DESCENTS: Leave the top only by the ridge; lower down there is a wealth of choice. Keep clear of the craggy Newlands face.

RIDGE ROUTE

To MAIDEN MOOR, 1887'

1½ miles : S. then SW
Depression (Hause Gate) at 1180'
720 feet of ascent

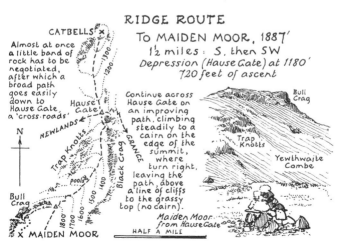

Almost at once a little band of rock has to be negotiated, after which a broad path goes easily down to Hause Gate, a 'cross-roads'.

Continue across Hause Gate on an improving path, climbing steadily to a cairn on the edge of the summit, where turn right, leaving the path, above a line of cliffs to the grassy top (no cairn).

Maiden Moor from Hause Gate

HALF A MILE

THE VIEW

Scenes of great beauty unfold on all sides, and they are scenes in depth to a degree not usual, the narrow summit permitting downward views of Borrowdale and Newlands within a few paces. Nearby valley and lake attract the eye more than the distant mountain surround, although Hindscarth and Robinson are particularly prominent at the head of Newlands and Causey Pike towers up almost grotesquely directly opposite. On this side the hamlet of Little Town is well seen down below, a charming picture, but it is to Derwentwater and mid-Borrowdale that the captivated gaze returns again and again.

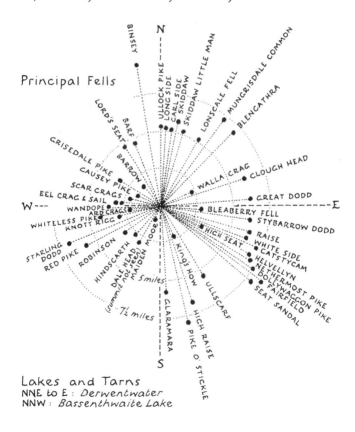

Principal Fells

Lakes and Tarns
NNE to E : Derwentwater
NNW : Bassenthwaite Lake

Hindscarth and Robinson from Catbells

Causey Pike

2035'
approx

Braithwaite
•

▲ GRISEDALE PIKE

EEL
CRAG ▲   ▲ CAUSEY PIKE

• Stair

MILES
0   1   2   3

from Swinside

NATURAL FEATURES

Most fells conform to a general pattern, but some have an unorthodoxy of shape, a peculiarity of outline, that identifies them on sight from wherever they may be seen. These not only help to fix a bearing in moments of doubt but serve also as pointers to neighbouring fells not favoured with distinctive features.

A landmark of this kind is Causey Pike, dominant in the Newlands and Derwentwater scene. The knob of the summit would itself be enough for identification in most views; repeated four times in lesser undulations as it is, like the legendary sea-serpent, the top is quite unmistakable. Even when the lesser ups and downs are concealed from sight, as when the fell is seen end on, the pyramid of the main summit is no less impressive because then it gains in slimness and elegance.

Causey Pike rises very sharply from Newlands but the steepness abates on Rowling End at 1400', whence a half-mile ridge continues easily to Sleet Hause, just below the final tower, where the steepness recurs on a narrowing crest. Rock is in evidence here, and must be handled to attain the summit. Thereafter the top of the fell is a succession of gentle undulations leading on to Scar Crags and the fine ridge that climbs up to Eel Crag and descends beyond to Crummock Water.

Bracken clothes the lower slopes and heather the higher. The confining streams are Stonycroft Beck and Rigg Beck, both feeders of Newlands Beck.

from Whiteless Breast

from Little Town

looking up the valley of
Sail Beck, with Eel Crag
and Sail on the left and
Ard Crags on the right

Causey Pike belongs wholly and exclusively to Newlands but peeps over the watershed of the Cocker, southwest, at several points.

MAP

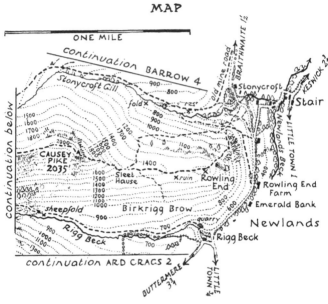

The map is extended to the west, beyond the boundaries of Causey Pike, to illustrate how the summit may be reached from the 'back' by way of Sail Pass (at the same altitude), gaining the pass by using either the Stonycroft mine road or the Rigg Beck path. The Stonycroft route is excellently graded and a very quick way of getting up to 2000' from Newlands; using this route, if Causey Pike is the sole objective, the 'road' can be left on High Moss and a beeline made for the depression between Scar Crags and the Pike. The Rigg Beck route is less satisfactory.

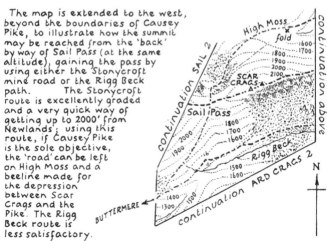

ASCENT FROM STAIR
1750 feet of ascent : 1½ miles

From Sleet House to the summit the way lies up the sharp east-south-east ridge: a delightful climb. The final rocktower requires the use of hands: it is easy, but no place for fooling about.

The direct route gains the ridge at Sleet Hause and a splendid view suddenly unfolds to the south.

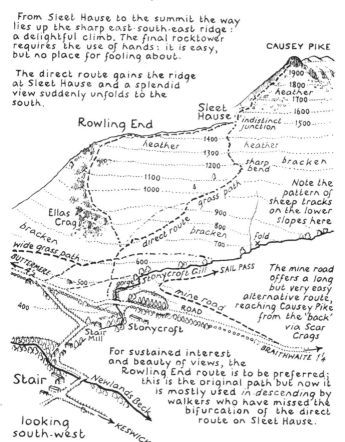

Note the pattern of sheep tracks on the lower slopes here

The mine road offers a long but very easy alternative route, reaching Causey Pike from the 'back' via Scar Crags

For sustained interest and beauty of views, the Rowling End route is to be preferred; this is the original path but now it is mostly used in descending by walkers who have missed the bifurcation of the direct route on Sleet Hause.

Deservedly this is a popular climb, with a heavy summer traffic, the route being quite charming, the views superlative, the finish a bit of real mountaineering, and the summit a place of distinctive character.

ASCENT FROM BRAITHWAITE
2150 feet of ascent : 4½ miles (via Sail Pass)

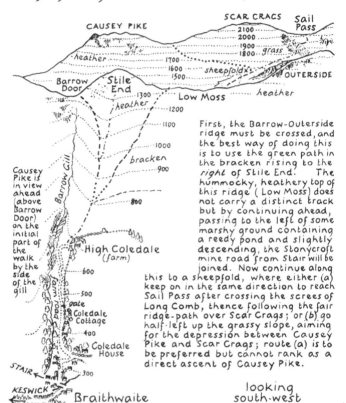

SCAR CRAGS   Sail Pass

CAUSEY PIKE
2100
2000
1900
1800 grass
heather
1700
1600 sheepfolds
1500
Barrow   Stile   OUTERSIDE
Door   End   1300   Low Moss   heather
heather   1200

Causey Pike is in view ahead (above Barrow Door) on the initial part of the walk by the side of the gill

Barrow Gill

1100
1000
bracken
900
800

High Coledale (farm)

600
500 gate
Coledale Cottage
400
Coledale House

STAIR   300
KESWICK   Braithwaite
bus shelter

First, the Barrow-Outside ridge must be crossed, and the best way of doing this is to use the green path in the bracken rising to the *right* of Stile End. The hummocky, heathery top of this ridge (Low Moss) does not carry a distinct track but by continuing ahead, passing to the left of some marshy ground containing a reedy pond and slightly descending, the Stonycroft mine road from Stair will be joined. Now continue along this to a sheepfold, where either (a) keep on in the same direction to reach Sail Pass after crossing the screes of Long Comb, thence following the fair ridge-path over Scar Crags; or (b) go half-left up the grassy slope, aiming for the depression between Causey Pike and Scar Crags; route (a) is to be preferred but cannot rank as a direct ascent of Causey Pike.

looking
south-west

Causey Pike is clearly in view from Braithwaite, and its quaint and challenging outline makes it an obvious objective for a day's walk. The route, however, is somewhat 'artificial', as an intervening ridge must first be crossed, and a better plan is to ascend direct from Stair, using the above route for the return journey.

THE SUMMIT

Coledale Hause — WHITESIDE — Sand Hill — HOPEGILL HEAD — south-west ridge of GRISEDALE PIKE

This delightful 'top' is quite unlike any other, its narrow crest undulating over five distinct bumps (meticulous visitors will count seven), the most prominent being the one terminating so abruptly the eastern end of the crest: this is the rocky knob that identifies Causey Pike unmistakably in distant views of the fell. There is no official height, which is surprising because the summit of this prominent knob seems a ready-made survey station — generally it is quoted as 2000', an approximation, but the 2½" Ordnance maps show three contour rings at 2025'. The eastern knob appears to have a slight advantage in altitude, a matter of a few feet or even inches only, over the third bump — the second bump is clearly lower yet bears the one respectable cairn. Heather covers the sides of the crest, but pedestrians are catered for by a well-worn strip of grass along the top.

DESCENTS: Leave the top by the path down the east-south-east ridge from the eastern knob; this is rocky at first, needing care in bad conditions, and is not pleasant to descend.   At the foot of the steep section, on Sleet Hause, the direct route to Stair goes off to the left at once and the original path over Rowling End continues ahead, the bifurcation (on grass) being indistinct. It is advisable to use the direct route: the way off Rowling End is on a plain but abominably rough path with no alternative possible. A little-used track also goes off to the right from Sleet Hause for Rigg Beck but after clearly threading a way through thick heather it unaccountably comes to a sudden end halfway down the slope.

THE VIEW

In all directions the scenery is of the highest order. Predominantly the view is of mountains, but the severity and starkness of their outlines is softened by the verdant loveliness of the Vales of Keswick and Newlands. Nothing is better than the challenging ridge continuing to Eel Crag. The head of Newlands, displaying the great humps of Dale Head, Hindscarth and Robinson — a magnificent grouping — is exceptionally well seen. The several Pikes of Scafell appear from this viewpoint as separate mountains.

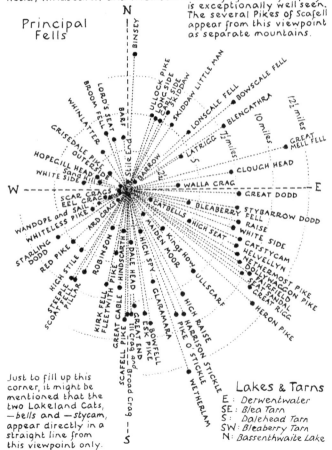

Principal Fells

Just to fill up this corner, it might be mentioned that the two Lakeland Cats, —bells and —stycam, appear directly in a straight line from this viewpoint only.

Lakes & Tarns
E : Derwentwater
SE : Blea Tarn
S : Dalehead Tarn
SW : Bleaberry Tarn
N : Bassenthwaite Lake

RIDGE ROUTE

To SCAR CRAGS, 2205': ¾ mile : WNW, then W.
Depression at 1915' : 320 feet of ascent

Traverse all the bumps and descend a wide grass path to the depression beyond. The ragged edge of Scar Crags now rears imposingly ahead, but the rising track alongside has no difficulties and the flat top is reached after a simple climb, during which striking downward views are available on the left.

HALF A MILE

looking back to Causey Pike from the depression

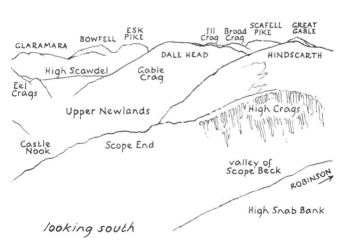

GLARAMARA
BOWFELL
ESK PIKE
ILL Crag
Broad Crag
SCAFELL PIKE
GREAT GABLE
High Scawdel
DALE HEAD
HINDSCARTH
Gable Crag
Eel Crags
Upper Newlands
High Crags
Castle Nook
Scope End
valley of Scope Beck
ROBINSON
High Snab Bank

looking south

The valley of Rigg Beck, from Causey Pike

The ridge west from Causey Pike

Key to drawings

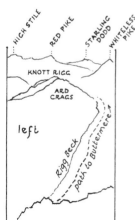

HIGH STILE
RED PIKE
STARLING DODD
WHITELESS PIKE
KNOTT RIGG
ARD CRAGS

left

Rigg Beck

path to Buttermere

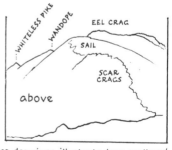

WHITELESS PIKE
WANDOPE
EEL CRAG
SAIL
SCAR CRAGS

above

These drawings illustrate two walkers' ways from Newlands to Buttermere. That *via* Rigg Beck is suitable for a wet day, but the route *par excellence* in clear weather is the ridge from Causey Pike to Whiteless Pike — a magnificent walk.

Dale Head

2473'

Little Town ●

HINDSCARTH
▲
DALE HEAD ▲   ▲ HIGH SPY
Gatesgarth ●   Rosthwaite ●
Honister ═   ●
Pass   Seatoller

MILES
0   1   2   3   4

from Castle Nook

NATURAL FEATURES

Dale Head has much in common with Eel Crag in the Grasmoor group. Their summits are focal points of high country, the meeting-place of ascending ridges. Both have craggy northern fronts, darkly shadowed, and easy southern approaches. Both enjoy extensive views of great merit, particularly northwards to Skiddaw. Taking everything into account, these two may be considered the most satisfying summits in the north western area.

Dale Head was named from Newlands, of which valley it commands a remarkable full-length view, and it is in this direction that the best, but not the best-known, items of interest are to be found. There are no walkers' tracks on the rocky northern breast of the fell, but a zigzag path to its copper veins was engineered by miners five or six centuries ago and can still be traced, while recently its steep buttresses have become a climbing-ground. The miners have long departed, but on the opposite flank of the fell, overlooking Honister Pass, quarrymen are still winning a beautiful stone from the Yew Crag workings.

For the walker, the finest attraction is the north-west ridge leading to Hindscarth, which is excellent. The easy southern slope, rising from the top of Honister Pass, lacks interest. The sharp descent to the east from the summit is soon halted by the extensive plateau of High Scawdel before continuing roughly down to the lovely foothills and woods of Borrowdale.

Dale Head has interest for the geologist, for beneath the carpet of grass there is a fusion of the Skiddaw slates and the volcanic rock of central Lakeland, some evidences of the joint being seen on the actual summit. But perhaps Dale Head's greatest triumph over its north western fellows is that it holds in its lap the only tarns of any size between Bassenthwaite and Honister, a further manifestation of the change in the underlying rock. Streams flow to all directions except west, yet it is in the west their ultimate destiny lies, the fell being wholly within the catchment of the Derwent.

Dalehead Tarn
from
High Scawdel

MAP

Honister Pass is the one (and only) place where the North Western Fells link up with another group (the Western), being otherwise isolated by valleys. Honister Pass is a watershed between the gathering grounds of the Cocker and the Derwent, which form the outer boundary of these fells.

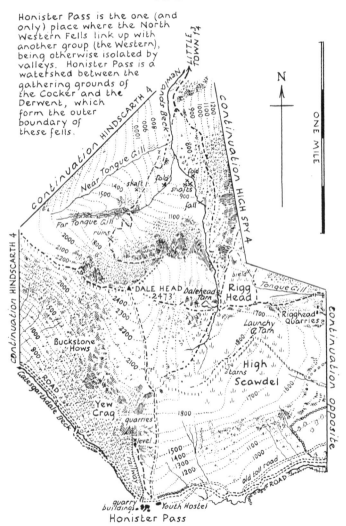

ONE MILE

N

Honister Pass

MAP

Honister Pass can only be reached on foot from Gatesgarthdale by walking along the motor road, but from Seatoller a good alternative is provided by the former toll road, which, being unfit for vehicles, has become a first-class walkers' way, in fact, a pedestrian by-pass. The surface is rough and rutted, but no fellwalker will object to this. It is the smooth hard surfaces of modern roads that tire the legs and feet, the monotony of repeating ad nauseum the same stride exactly. On rough ground no two movements are quite the same.

A good fellwalker never tramps a road that has a bus service.

A level, Rigghead Quarry

Launchy Tarn

The first big loop of the toll road can be avoided by use of a path in the next field.

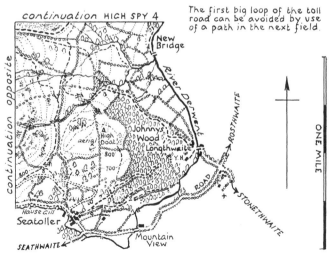

continuation HIGH SPY 4

continuation opposite

New Bridge

River Derwent

ROSTHWAITE

ONE MILE

Johnny's Wood

A High Doat 800

aerial

Longthwaite
Y.H.

700

800

ROAD

STONETHWAITE

Hause Gill

Seatoller

Mountain View

SEATHWAITE

below: Mine cuttings near the foot of Far Tongue Gill adopted for use with a sheepfold.

Copper Mines and Crags of Dale Head

left: Two mine cuttings near the sheepfold on Newlands Beck at 800'; the lower one is flooded, forming a rocky-sided pool.

below: Dale Head Pillar, Gable Crag, from the ruined mine buildings.

ASCENT FROM LITTLE TOWN

2000 feet of ascent
4 miles via Dalehead Tarn
3½ miles via the copper mine

looking south

DALE HEAD

2400
2300
2200
2100

awkward scree slope

← narrow track on bilberry shelf

1800

grass

Rigg Head

Dalehead Tarn

Cable Crag

Dale Head Mine × ruins

1600

1600

Considering that this path was made many centuries ago it is remarkably good

1500
1400

groove

An amazing ravine

1300

1500

1400

1300

shelter

1200

At the ruined buildings of Dale Head Mine are small heaps of spoil. Note the bright green veins in many stones here: this is copper malachite

Newlands Beck

× shaft

1200

waterfall

1000

father and mother of all boulders

Far Tongue Gill

1100

screes of Eel Crags

1100

larch

mine cuttings
××× and
× shafts

cuttings
sheepfold

grassy shelf

Near Tongue Gill

All mines shown on this page are disused.

fold

800

1000

700

After crossing the beck the path is indefinite but it can be clearly seen rising across the fellside ahead.

1000

old ford (now unrecognisable)

Castle Nook is the very prominent 'headland' abutting into the mid-valley two miles above Little Town

Newlands Beck

water cut

old shaft ×

Castlenook Mine

900

fold

The usual route of ascent is that on the left of the diagram, via Dalehead Tarn, a tedious way to the top. That on the right, via the old copper-mine, although little known, is much to be preferred in clear weather, being interesting throughout its more direct course, giving smoother walking amid fine rock-scenery and providing an ingenious avoidance of steep craggy places. This is a mountaineering 'must'!

The mine road leaves Little Town at a gate beyond the last cottage and gives a splendid walking surface as far as Castlenook Mine. No height is gained in these two miles.

mine road

LITTLE TOWN

ASCENT FROM HONISTER PASS
1300 feet of ascent : 1¼ miles

The first lesson that every fellwalker learns, and learns afresh every time he goes on the hills, is that summits are almost invariably more distant, a good deal higher, and require greater effort, than expected. Fellwalking and wishful thinking have nothing in common.

Here is an exception. This ascent may well be longer than expected, but the climbing is so very simple and the gradients so very easy that the top cairn is reached, unbelievably, before one has started to feel that enough has been done to earn it.

DALE HEAD

2400

2300 — grass

2200

2100

grass

Apparently for no reason at all the path switches from one side of the fence-posts to the other. A likely explanation is that there would be a gate at this point when the fence was in its heyday.

← This line of fence-posts leads to High Scawdel and Launchy Tarn

looking north-north-east

old level ×
stone hut ▣
old quarries

At this point a quarry hole encroaches almost to the fence. Its dangers are obvious when ascending, but could be realised too late in a running descent in mist.

1800

Yew Crag

quarry level

1700

1600

The fence wires have gone completely but the iron posts are still in place (with a few exceptions) and make a perfect guide-line to the top.

1500

Quarry road

× × sheepfolds

railway

1300

1200

1100

1000

BUTTERMERE 4   ROAD

SEATOLLER 1½

Youth Hostel
cutting sheds

Honister Pass
1190'

No other summit of like altitude is reached so quickly and easily from a motor road. Indeed, if a car be used to the top of the pass, a man of conscience must feel he is cheating the mountain.

Old level, indicated on diagram. The hut nearby provides shelter.

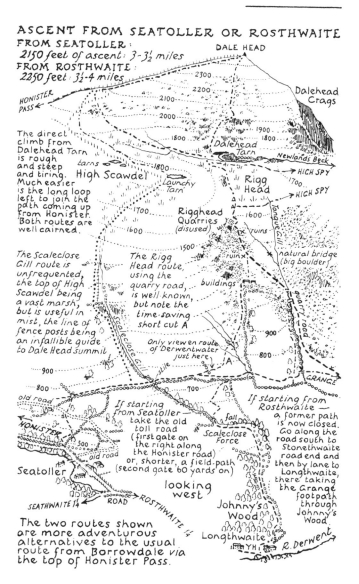

ASCENT FROM SEATOLLER OR ROSTHWAITE

FROM SEATOLLER:
2150 feet of ascent: 3-3½ miles
FROM ROSTHWAITE:
2250 feet 3½-4 miles

DALE HEAD

Dalehead Crags

HONISTER PASS ←

2300
2200
2100
2000
1900
1800

Dalehead Tarn

Newlands Beck

→ HIGH SPY
1700
→ HIGH SPY

The direct climb from Dalehead Tarn is rough and steep and tiring. Much easier is the long loop left to join the path coming up from Honister. Both routes are well cairned.

tarns

High Scawdel

Launchy Tarn

Rigg Head

1800
1700
1600

Rigghead Quarries (disused)

ruins

1500

ruins

natural bridge (big boulders)

The Scaleclose Gill route is unfrequented, the top of High Scawdel being a vast marsh, but is useful in mist, the line of fence posts being an infallible guide to Dale Head summit.

The Rigg Head route, using the quarry road, is well-known, but note the time-saving short cut A.

buildings

900

Only view en route of Derwentwater just here

A

800

GRANGE

900
800
700

old road

If starting from Seatoller — take the old toll road (first gate on the right along the Honister road) or, shorter, a field-path (second gate 60 yards on)

HONISTER

500

old road

Seatoller

SEATHWAITE 1¼

ROAD

ROSTHWAITE 1¼

looking west

fall

Scaleclose Force

If starting from Rosthwaite — a former path is now closed. Go along the road south to Stonethwaite road end and then by lane to Longthwaite, there taking the Grange footpath through Johnny's Wood.

Johnny's Wood

Longthwaite

YH

R. Derwent

The two routes shown are more adventurous alternatives to the usual route from Borrowdale via the top of Honister Pass.

THE SUMMIT

SKIDDAW

Newlands

There are hundreds of unnecessary cairns on the fells, and no great loss would be suffered if they were scattered, but those on the summits of the mountains have a special significance: they are old friends and should be left inviolate in their lonely stations to greet their visitors. This was how it used to be, and they were treated with respect. Fellwalkers knew them well.

But not now. Lunatics are loose on the hills; not many, just a few idiots whose limit of bravery is to destroy what others have created. The fine columns on Pike o' Blisco and Lingmell have both been wrecked in recent years (and rebuilt by walkers who felt bereaved by their absence, and to whom thanks are due). Dale Head's original cairn has fallen to the destroyers, too; but here has arisen an even nobler edifice. An expert working party has been on the job, and the stones appear to have come from Yew Crag quarry. This new cairn is unusual in shape being wider at mid-height than at the base, but it is a very solid and sound effort. Long may it reign over Dale Head.

Its situation is dramatic, immediately on the brink of the great northern downfall, but there is an easy parade on both sides. It is along here that the Skiddaw slates and the Borrowdale volcanic rocks converge, but a knowledge of geology is needed to find evidence of this.

DESCENTS: The way down to Honister Pass, with fenceposts as infallible guides, is foolproof, fast and easy. Do not stray from the fence in mist (quarry holes).

For Dalehead Tarn and Borrowdale or Newlands, aim east and find a line of cairns and then a track.

For Newlands direct, via the copper mine, clear weather is essential unless the way is already known. The place to leave the north-east ridge is a pale outcrop with steep ground obviously beyond: here turn very sharp left to find a thin track to easy ground.

RIDGE ROUTES

To HINDSCARTH, 2385': 1¼ miles: WNW, then NNE
Depression at 2156': 250 feet of ascent
An easy walk, with excellent views.

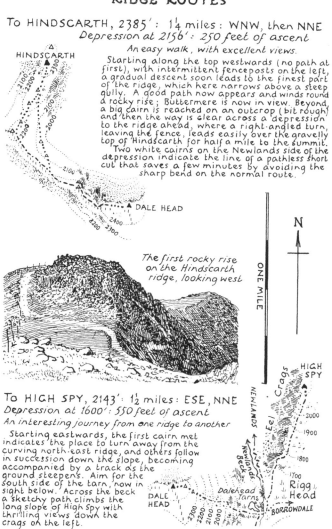

Starting along the top westwards (no path at first), with intermittent fenceposts on the left, a gradual descent soon leads to the finest part of the ridge, which here narrows above a steep gully. A good path now appears and winds round a rocky rise; Buttermere is now in view. Beyond, a big cairn is reached on an outcrop (bit rough) and then the way is clear across a depression to the ridge ahead, where a right-angled turn, leaving the fence, leads easily over the gravelly top of Hindscarth for half a mile to the summit.

Two white cairns on the Newlands side of the depression indicate the line of a pathless short cut that saves a few minutes by avoiding the sharp bend on the normal route.

The first rocky rise on the Hindscarth ridge, looking west

To HIGH SPY, 2143': 1½ miles: ESE, NNE
Depression at 1600': 550 feet of ascent
An interesting journey from one ridge to another

Starting eastwards, the first cairn met indicates the place to turn away from the curving north-east ridge, and others follow in succession down the slope, becoming accompanied by a track as the ground steepens. Aim for the south side of the tarn, now in sight below. Across the beck a sketchy path climbs the long slope of High Spy with thrilling views down the crags on the left.

THE VIEW

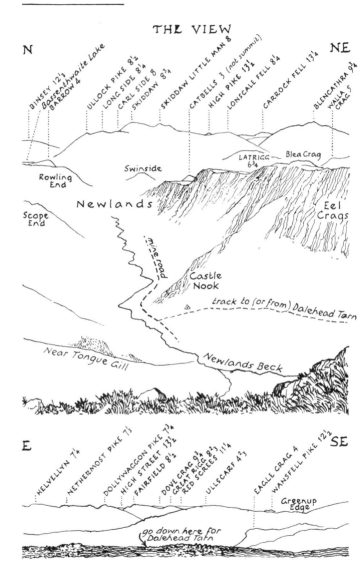

N

NE

BINSEY 12½
Bassenthwaite Lake
BARROW 4
ULLOCK PIKE 8½
LONG SIDE 8¼
CARL SIDE 8
SKIDDAW 8¾
SKIDDAW LITTLE MAN 8
CATBELLS 3 (not summit)
HIGH PIKE 13½
LONSCALE FELL 8¼
CARROCK FELL 13¼
BLENCATHRA 9¾
WALLA CRAG 5

Rowling End

Swinside

LATRIGG 6¾

Blea Crag

Newlands

Scope End

Eel Crags

mine road

Castle Nook

track to (or from) Dalehead Tarn

Near Tongue Gill

Newlands Beck

E

SE

HELVELLYN 7¼
NETHERMOST PIKE 7⅓
DOLLYWAGGON PIKE 7¼
HIGH STREET 13½
FAIRFIELD 8½
DOVE CRAG 9¼
GREAT RIGG 8⅓
RED SCREES 11¼
ULLSCARF 4⅓
EAGLE CRAG 4
WANSFELL PIKE 12½

Greenup Edge

go down here for Dalehead Tarn

THE VIEW

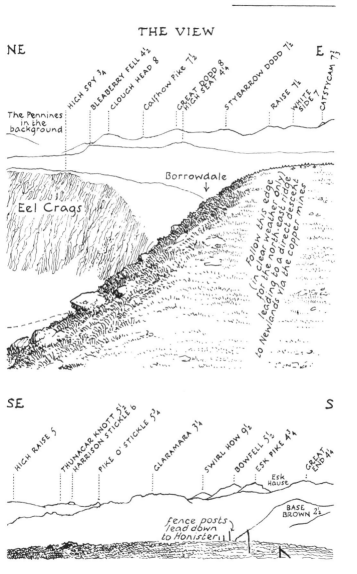

NE

The Pennines in the background

HIGH SPY 3¼
BLEABERRY FELL 4½
CLOUGH HEAD 8
CALFHOW PIKE 7½
GREAT DODD 8
HIGH SEAT 4¼
STYBARROW DODD 7½
RAISE 7¼
WHITE SIDE 7
CATSTYCAM 7¾

E

Borrowdale

Eel Crags

Follow this edge (in clear weather only) for the north-east ridge leading to a direct descent to Newlands via the copper mines

SE

HIGH RAISE 5
THUNACAR KNOTT 5½
HARRISON STICKLE 6
PIKE O' STICKLE 5¾
GLARAMARA 3¾
SWIRL HOW 9½
BOWFELL 5½
ESK PIKE 4¾
GREAT END 4¼

Esk Hause

BASE BROWN 2½

S

fence posts lead down to Honister

THE VIEW

S   SW

Broad Crag 4¾   SCAFELL PIKE 5   SCAFELL 5½   GREEN GABLE 2¾   GREAT GABLE 3   KIRK FELL 3½   Stirrup Crag (YEWBARROW) 3¾   MIDDLE FELL 6¼

BRANDRETH 2   Beck Head

GREY KNOTTS   Black Sail
Gillercombe   1½ 1¾   Pass
Buttress

Honister   path   to Great   Gable   HAYSTACKS

W   NW

RED PIKE 4¾   STARLING DODD 5   GREAT BORNE 6   GAVEL FELL 7   BLAKE FELL 7½   ROBINSON 1¾

Buttermere
↓

fence

fence

easy route of descent into Newlands

*Follow this edge,
with a ruined fence
on the left, for
Hindscarth and
Robinson.*

*(If followed to its termination
the fence will lead to the plantation
on the fellside above Hassness, Buttermere)*

The figures accompanying the names
of fells indicate distances in miles

THE VIEW

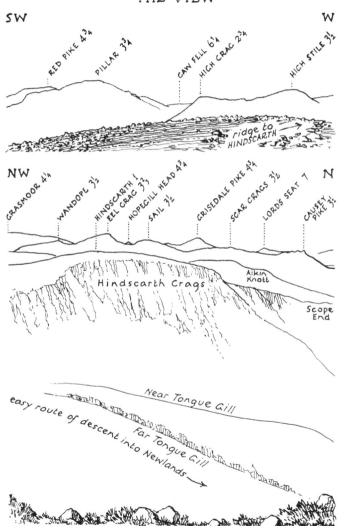

SW
W

RED PIKE 4¼   PILLAR 3¾   CAW FELL 6¼   HIGH CRAG 2¾   HIGH STILE 3½

ridge to HINDSCARTH →

NW   N

GRASMOOR 4¼   WANDOPE 3½   HINDSCARTH ¾   EEL CRAG 3¾   HOPEGILL HEAD 4¾   SAIL 3½   GRISEDALE PIKE 4¾   SCAR CRAGS 3½   LORDS SEAT 7   CAUSEY PIKE 3½

Hindscarth Crags

Aikin Knott

Scope End

Near Tongue Gill

Far Tongue Gill

easy route of descent into Newlands →

Eel Crag

2749'

Crag Hill
on Ordnance
Survey maps

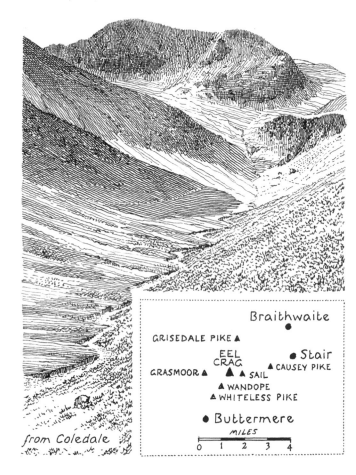

GRISEDALE PIKE ▲

EEL
CRAG

● Braithwaite

● Stair

GRASMOOR ▲ ▲ ▲ SAIL ▲ CAUSEY PIKE

▲ WANDOPE

▲ WHITELESS PIKE

● Buttermere

MILES

0   1   2   3   4

from Coledale

NATURAL FEATURES

Although of rather lower elevation than the neighbouring Grasmoor, Eel Crag is more truly the focal point of the concentration of fells rising between the valleys of Newlands and Lorton. Unlike Grasmoor, Eel Crag is supported by ridges. Unlike Grasmoor, it stands in the midst of a group of satellites. Unlike Grasmoor, it commands an excellent all-round view. It is in the centre of things. It is an obvious objective. Tracks lead up to its stony top naturally and inevitably. It is a traffic junction, while Grasmoor is a cul-de-sac.

The shadowed north-east face of the fell, towering high above the head of Coledale, is a fine sight. Even steeper, but less familiar, is the craggy southern slope, seamed with gullies, overlooking Sail Beck: this is a no-man's-land. Walkers prefer the exciting ridges, of which a narrowing crest coming up from the east gives the best approach; another, shorter, traverses the summit from Coledale Hause, and a third curves south-west to a grassy depression from which three spurs lead separately to Wandope, Whiteless Pike and the great bulk of Grasmoor. Streams from the fell flow to two main rivers, from Grasmoor to one, and this is the great test of superiority. Eel Crag is a watershed but Grasmoor is not.

The east ridge

The name of the fell is unfortunate and inaccurate. Eel Crag is properly the rocky buttress above Coledale Hause, but for a century or more the whole fell has been popularly known by this name. The Ordnance maps, in all series, use *Crag Hill*, and, if adopted generally, this name would avoid the confusion that has arisen due to the recent development of Eel Crags in nearby Newlands as a climbing ground. But walkers are conservative folk: they do not like change in old favourites, and Eel Crag it will remain.

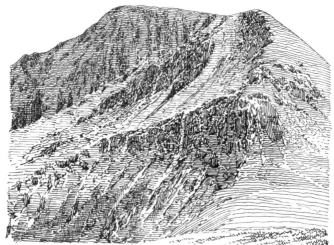

The north-east face, from the lower slopes of Sand Hill

The south face,
with Sail beyond,
from Wandope

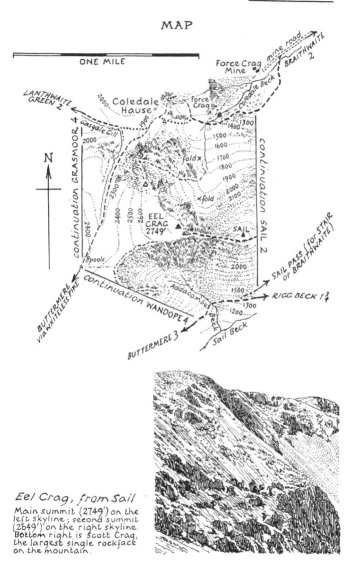

MAP

ONE MILE

Eel Crag, from Sail
Main summit (2749') on the
left skyline; second summit
(2649') on the right skyline.
Bottom right is Scott Crag,
the largest single rockface
on the mountain.

ASCENT FROM RANNERDALE
2400 feet of ascent : 2½ miles

looking northeast

Although Eel Crag has a profound influence in the geography of the Buttermere-Crummock area it hides from view behind lower but nearer fells and has no footing in the valley. There is only one route of direct ascent, avoiding other fells, and that is by way of the ravine of Rannerdale, following the gill to its head, when the mountain is a short distance ahead and easily reached.

Rannerdale itself has much antiquarian interest in its pleasant lower reaches but above the stone wall its character is entirely different. Deeply enclosed between steep fellsides of tumbled scree, the stream forms four pronounced bends in a desolate and arid cutting, a wilderness of stones. This upper valley (High Rannerdale) emerges from the hills at an angle to the parent valley and is not seen or suspected until entered at the sheepfold.

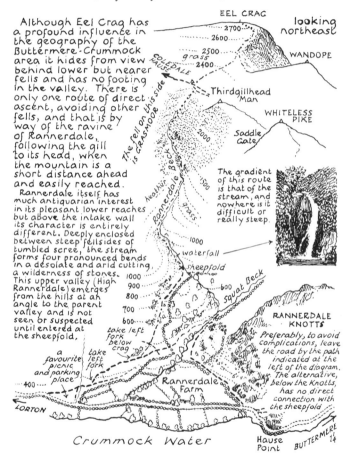

EEL CRAG

2700
2600
2500 grass
2400
COLEDALE HAUSE

WANDOPE

Thirdgillhead Man

The fell on this side is Grasmoor

2000

WHITELESS PIKE

Saddle Gate

The gradient of this route is that of the stream, and nowhere is it difficult or really steep.

1500

Rannerdale Beck

heathery

grass

1000

waterfall

sheepfold

1000
900
800
700
600

600

Squat Beck

take left fork below crag

RANNERDALE KNOTTS

Preferably, to avoid complications, leave the road by the path indicated at the left of the diagram. The alternative, below the Knotts, has no direct connection with the sheepfold.

a favourite picnic and parking place

take left fork

400

Rannerdale Farm

LORTON

Crummock Water

Hause Point

BUTTERMERE

14

Every direct route has something to commend it, if only its directness. Rannerdale additionally is sheltered, has water at hand, and is absolutely unloseable in mist. BUT its charms are few, and, in the upper reaches, the view is limited to the immediate unattractive surroundings.

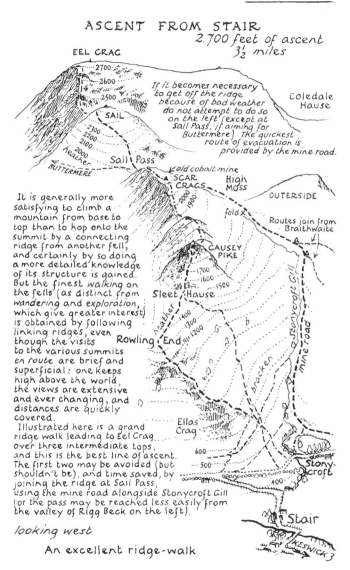

ASCENT FROM STAIR
2,700 feet of ascent
3½ miles

EEL CRAG

2700
2600
2500

SAIL

2300
2200
2100
2000 heather
BUTTERMERE
Sail Pass

If it becomes necessary to get off the ridge because of bad weather do not attempt to do so on the left (except at Sail Pass, if aiming for Buttermere). The quickest route of evacuation is provided by the mine road.

Coledale Hause

old cobalt mine
SCAR CRAGS
High Moss

2000
1900

fold ×

OUTERSIDE

Routes join from Braithwaite

CAUSEY PIKE

1700
1600
1500

Sleet Hause

Rowling End

heather
1400
1300
1200

Stonycroft Gill

mine road

bracken

Ellas Crag

600
500

Stonycroft

400

It is generally more satisfying to climb a mountain from base to top than to hop onto the summit by a connecting ridge from another fell; and certainly by so doing a more detailed knowledge of its structure is gained. But the finest walking on the fells (as distinct from wandering and exploration, which give greater interest) is obtained by following linking ridges, even though the visits to the various summits en route are brief and superficial: one keeps high above the world, the views are extensive and ever changing, and distances are quickly covered.

Illustrated here is a grand ridge walk leading to Eel Crag over three intermediate tops, and this is the best line of ascent. The first two may be avoided (but shouldn't be), and time saved, by joining the ridge at Sail Pass, using the mine road alongside Stonycroft Gill (or the pass may be reached less easily from the valley of Rigg Beck on the left).

Stair
KESWICK 3

looking west

An excellent ridge-walk

Eel Crag 7

ASCENT FROM BRAITHWAITE
(DIRECT) 2500 feet of ascent
3¼ miles (A); 4 miles (B).

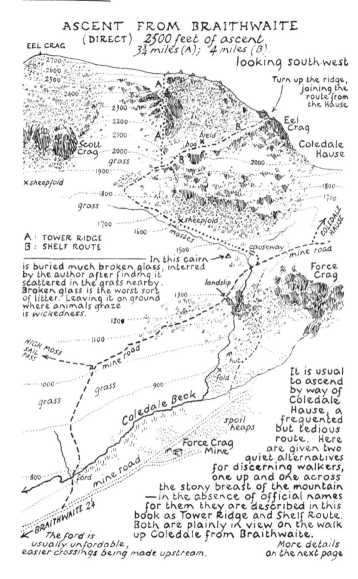

looking south-west

EEL CRAG

2700
2600
2500
2400
2300
2200
2100
2000
1900
1800
1700
1600
1500

A
A
field
dog
B
B
2000

Turn up the ridge, joining the route from the Hause

Eel Crag
Coledale Hause

Scott Crag

grass

× sheepfold

grass

× sheepfold

masses

causeway

mine road

COLEDALE HAUSE

A : TOWER RIDGE
B : SHELF ROUTE

In this cairn, interred
by the author after finding it
scattered in the grass nearby.
Broken glass is the worst sort
of litter. Leaving it on ground
where animals graze
is wickedness.

Force Crag

landslip

1300

1200

1100

HIGH MOSS
SAIL PASS

mine road

grass

1000

grass

900

hut.
× fold

800   ford

mine road

Coledale Beck

spoil heaps

Force Crag Mine

BRAITHWAITE 2¼

The ford is
usually unfordable,
easier crossings being made upstream.

It is usual
to ascend
by way of
Coledale
Hause, a
frequented
but tedious
route. Here
are given two
quiet alternatives
for discerning walkers,
one up and one across
the stony breast of the mountain
—in the absence of official names
for them they are described in this
book as Tower Ridge and Shelf Route.
Both are plainly in view on the walk
up Coledale from Braithwaite.

More details
on the next page

The Shelf Route and Tower Ridge

On the ordinary route from Braithwaite, via Coledale Hause, it is usual to tackle the slope of scree 'around the corner' from the Hause (although this can be avoided by continuing forward to the headwaters of Gasgale Gill). This scree is extensive; it is tiresome to ascend and unpleasant to descend.

A way of cutting out this abomination is provided by the Shelf Route, which, rarely used, adds a little thrill of exploration and more interest to the climb. The Shelf, once reached, is obvious ahead: a rising green strip of bilberry and mosses between the screes from the summit-rim and the broken line of crags facing the head of Coledale. It joins the usual route on the ridge at a point just above the steeper rocks overlooking the Hause.

2749'   2649'

Coledale Hause

north slope of Sail

usual route

The approach from Braithwaite.

Force Crag

In spring and autumn the Shelf and Tower Ridge are the last two places on the face to be illumined by morning sunlight, the rest then being in dark shadow.

A very thin track runs along the shelf. Cairns are absent, but a few small ones would be a help in navigation. A guide-cairn never needs to consist of more than two or three stones, placed one on top of another. Siting is more important. From one cairn the next should be visible, preferably on a skyline.

The end of the shelf

Turn up the ridge behind the rocks on the left

Tower Ridge :

Just before reaching the start of the shelf (at a green bog behind a prominent rocky tor) walkers who like a scramble may make their way up the bouldery ridge on the left, which is broad but soon narrows to a well-defined rocky tower, with a secondary buttress alongside on the right. The steeper rises on the ridge can be avoided on the left until the final pyramid, of short vertical steps, is reached. A ledge of scree rising 20 yards to the right is now followed and then a grass terrace rising to the left for the same distance, a high stride in a corner here gaining the easy ground at the top of the tower. A simple grassy neck then connects with the summit of the mountain just south of the big cairn on the lower top at 2649'. This variation is direct and cuts out the scree slope altogether. It is necessary in a few places to handle rocks but there is nothing to cause fear or panic, although ladies in ankle-length skirts may find odd places a little troublesome.

Tower Ridge from the end of the shelf

ASCENT FROM COLEDALE HAUSE
850 feet of ascent : 1 mile

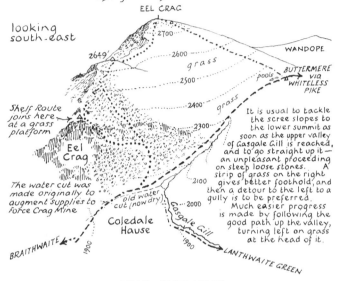

EEL CRAG

looking
south-east

2700

2649'

2600

WANDOPE

grass

2500

BUTTERMERE
via
WHITELESS
PIKE

pools

2400

grass

2300

Shelf Route
joins here
at a grass
platform

Eel
Crag

2100

It is usual to tackle
the scree slopes to
the lower summit as
soon as the upper valley
of Gasgale Gill is reached,
and to go straight up it —
an unpleasant proceeding
on steep loose stones.   A
strip of grass on the right
gives better foothold, and
then a detour to the left to a
gully is to be preferred.
Much easier progress
is made by following the
good path up the valley,
turning left on grass
at the head of it.

The water cut was
made originally to
augment supplies to
Force Crag Mine

Old water
cut (now dry)

2000

Coledale
Hause

BRAITHWAITE

1900

Gasgale Gill

1900

LANTHWAITE GREEN

THE SUMMIT

The top is flat and
stony, being littered
with slate fragments
easy to walk upon, so
that no paths have
been formed in the
vicinity of the survey
column marking the
highest point (S.5993)

DESCENTS:
All routes of ascent may be
reversed, but the bad scree
above Coledale Hause ought
to be avoided in favour of
a direct descent on grass,
west, to the headwaters
of Gasgale Gill. This is
the best line off the top
in mist for Braithwaite
(path right), Buttermere
(path left), or Lanthwaite
Green (follow stream).

The route to Stair over Causey Pike (or turning off left at Sail Pass) is
picked up at the corner of the summit formed by the north-east and
south slopes of the fell, 100 yards south-east of the column; in mist
it is quite safe, but under snow or ice care is needed on the rocksteps.

RIDGE ROUTES

To SAIL, 2530': ⅖ mile : E
Depression at 2430'
100 feet of ascent
The best way off Eel Crag

No definite path leaves the survey column, but one starts at a cairn in the 'corner' of the summit 100 yds south-east and is thereafter clear, there being no possibility of going astray on the narrow falling ridge. Timid walkers will be aware of their disability at two places where rock must be descended, but may safely venture. Across the depression (not to be mistaken for Sail Pass) a good path climbs up to Sail summit, the small cairn here being half-hidden by vegetation some 25 yards to the left of the path and often passed unnoticed.

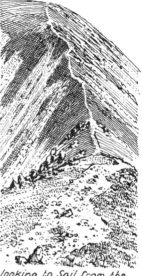

looking to Sail from the top of the east ridge.

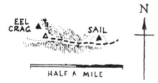

To GRASMOOR, 2791': 1¼ miles : generally W.
Depression at 2350' : 450 feet of ascent
A long moorland tramp, not recommended in mist

Go down the easy slope west to cross the Coledale Hause-Whiteless Pike path near two small pools. Beyond, follow a rising line of cairns up the grassy breast to the vast, gently rising top of Grasmoor, the main cairn of which is still a further half-mile distant.

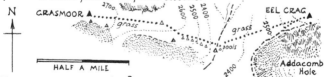

To WANDOPE, 2533': ¾ mile : SW, then S ▲ WANDOPE
Depression at 2420' : 120 feet of ascent
A bird's-eye view of Addacomb Hole

A beeline may be made, soon joining a track skirting the edge of the steep south face overlooking the hanging valley of Addacomb Hole. A simple final slope, all grass, curves round to the top of Wandope.

THE VIEW

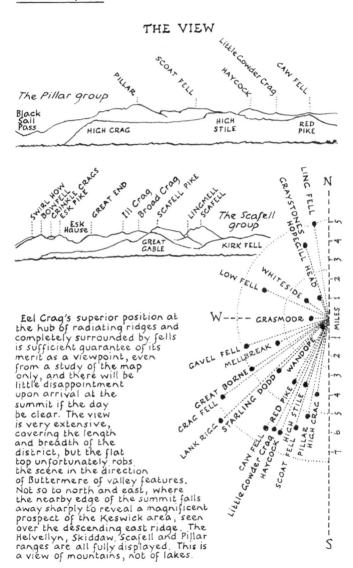

The Pillar group

Black Sail Pass

PILLAR — SCOAT FELL — Little Gowder Crag — HAYCOCK — CAW FELL

HIGH CRAG — HIGH STILE — RED PIKE

SWIRL HOW — BOWFELL — CRINKLE CRAGS — ESK PIKE — GREAT END — Ill Crag — Broad Crag — SCAFELL PIKE — LINGMELL — SCAFELL

Esk Hause

GREAT GABLE — KIRK FELL

The Scafell group

LINC FELL — GRAYSTONES — HOPEGILL HEAD — N — 5 — 4 — 3 — 2 — 1

WHITESIDE — LOW FELL

W — — — GRASMOOR — MILES

GAVEL FELL — MELLBREAK — WANDOPE

GREAT BORNE — STARLING DODD — RED PIKE — HIGH STILE — HIGH CRAG

CRAG FELL — LANK RIGG — CAW FELL — Little Gowder Crag — HAYCOCK — SCOAT FELL — PILLAR

S

Eel Crag's superior position at the hub of radiating ridges and completely surrounded by fells is sufficient guarantee of its merit as a viewpoint, even from a study of the map only, and there will be little disappointment upon arrival at the summit if the day be clear. The view is very extensive, covering the length and breadth of the district, but the flat top unfortunately robs the scene in the direction of Buttermere of valley features. Not so to north and east, where the nearby edge of the summit falls away sharply to reveal a magnificent prospect of the Keswick area, seen over the descending east ridge. The Helvellyn, Skiddaw, Scafell and Pillar ranges are all fully displayed. This is a view of mountains, not of lakes.

THE VIEW

Principal Fells

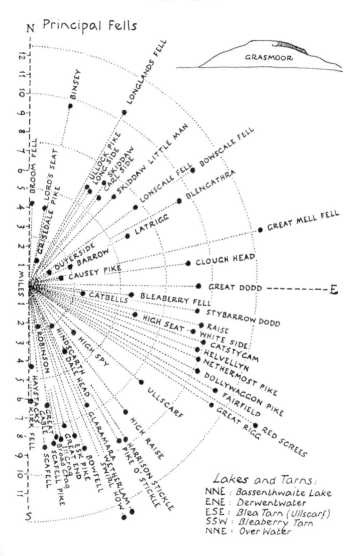

GRASMOOR

Lakes and Tarns:
NNE : Bassenthwaite Lake
ENE : Derwentwater
ESE : Blea Tarn (Ullscarf)
SSW : Bleaberry Tarn
NNE : Over Water

Grasmoor

2791'

from Lanthwaite Hill

NATURAL FEATURES

The culminating point of the North Western Fells occurs overlooking Crummock Water, where the massive bulk of Grasmoor towers above the threshold of the Buttermere valley, showing its full height to great advantage from the shores of the lake.   As Nature has arranged matters this particular aspect of the fell, facing west, is also the finest : a steep pyramid of rocky ribs and broken crags suspended far above the road along its base, the road that carries travellers to Buttermere — and few go this way who do not look upwards rather fearfully to the cliffs poised overhead, seeming to threaten safe passage. Yet familiarity with this monstrous monolith dispels fear and the brackeny hollows below, adjoining the unfenced road, harbour summer migrants in the shape of campers, motorists and caravanners: it is a favourite picnic and recreation ground for discerning West Cumbrians. Apart from the two dark clefts on this face, there are no continuous courses to attract rockclimbers; the only crags of any size circle an upland combe on the north flank and rim the edge of the summit. On the south side are the most extensive scree-slopes in the district: a colourful but arid desert of stones.   Eastwards there is a high link with Eel Crag and a fine ridge descending into Newlands.   But probably most visitors to Grasmoor will remember the fell for a summit-plateau remarkable both for its extent and its luxurious carpet of mossy turf, close-cropped by the resident sheep who range these broad acres. In structure the fell assumes a simple form, the only unorthodoxy being a ramp down the middle of the south slope curving round into the heathery spur of Lad House, now known as Lad Hows. The streams bounding Grasmoor occupy the stony side-valleys of Gasgale Gill and Rannerdale Beck. It has no tarns.

The name of the fell is commonly mis-spelt as Grassmoor, even in print, by writers who would never dream of mis-spelling Grasmere Grassmere.   There is only one 's'. The gras derives from grise — wild boar — as in so many Lakeland names e.g. Grisedale.

MAP

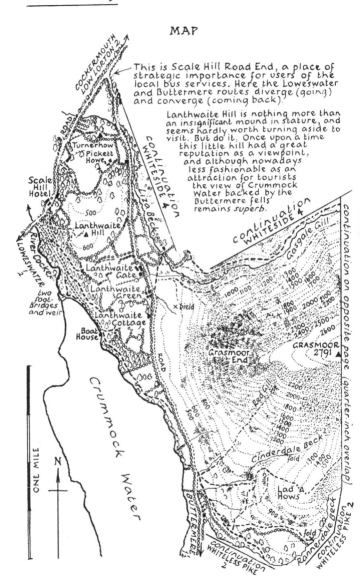

This is Scale Hill Road End, a place of strategic importance for users of the local bus services. Here the Loweswater and Buttermere routes diverge (going) and converge (coming back).

Lanthwaite Hill is nothing more than an insignificant mound in stature, and seems hardly worth turning aside to visit. But do it. Once upon a time this little hill had a great reputation as a viewpoint, and although nowadays less fashionable as an attraction for tourists the view of Crummock Water backed by the Buttermere fells remains superb.

MAP

The natural boundaries of mountains tend to be obscured by man's lines of communications. It is not the valley roads that define the limits of a mountain but the main watercourses. Here is a case in point (opposite page). The road along the bases of Whiteside and Grasmoor appears to terminate their slopes, but these fells are divided by Liza Beck (Gasgale Gill higher up), which, instead of completing the severance neatly by a direct cut into Crummock Water, turns north to join the River Cocker beyond the outflow of the lake and thereby claims for Grasmoor a wedge of low country that, to a casual observer, would seem to belong to Whiteside. Thus Lanthwaite Hill is Grasmoor's cub although it sits at the feet of Whiteside.

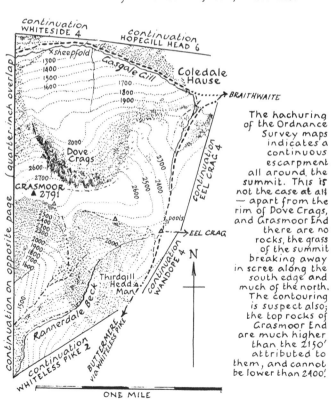

The hachuring of the Ordnance Survey maps indicates a continuous escarpment all around the summit. This is not the case at all — apart from the rim of Dove Crags, and Grasmoor End there are no rocks, the grass of the summit breaking away in scree along the south edge and much of the north. The contouring is suspect also; the top rocks of Grasmoor End are much higher than the 2150' attributed to them, and cannot be lower than 2400!

ASCENT FROM LANTHWAITE GREEN
VIA DOVE CRAGS
2300 feet of ascent : 2 miles

GRASMOOR

2700

2600 grass

Dove Crags

2500

2400 grass

Grasmoor End

2300

-2200

rock slab

2100

-2000

grassy basin at 1900'

grassy arete

1800

1700

1600

1500

1400

1300

1200

-1100

heather

One of the natural wonders of Grasmoor is the profound hollow scooped out of its north flank and encircled by Dove Crags. The floor of this amphitheatre is a grassy basin, surrounded on all sides by higher ground. It seems an obvious site for a tarn, yet is dry, although clearly all the drainage from the crags must be received there. Because of the raised edge of the hollow there is no issuing stream, nor indeed are there any watercourses within it. All this is very odd. What happens to all the water falling within the area of the combe? The explanation can only be that the screes below the crags act as soakaways and absorb all moisture from above as it falls, releasing it to the basin so slowly that evaporation and not accumulation takes place.

Many sheep tracks are crossed during the early stages of the climb from the valley. One of these (at about 1500') is a particularly clear trail (it is used by shepherds also): it traverses the fellside and links with the terrace on the direct route.

×field

1000

Gasgale Gill

This old walkers' path on the Grasmoor side of the gill now serves only for sheep. It is rough, but still fairly clear

900

2 larches

usual path to Coledale Hause

DIRECT ROUTE

Gasgale Gill is a narrow V-shaped cutting, no wider than the bed of the stream. On the north side Whiteside rises even more steeply than Grasmoor on the south side.

800

Nature never uses straight lines in her designs, but has come remarkably close to doing so in fashioning this arete and the approach to it from the gill along the edge of the scree. A plumb-line dropped from the summit to the valley would lie over the route almost exactly. This is very noticeable from the top of Whiteside.

bracken

falls

bracken

700

water cut

There are no difficulties in this ascent. The rock slab is set at an easy gradient but is greasy and needs care. The views down the crags from the arete are tremendous.

600

600

grassy

weir

The route can be identified from the road. Looking up the valley of Gasgale Gill, it is the skyline ridge rising smoothly to the right, the one roughness on it being the rock slab.

cattle grid

ROAD

Lanthwaite Green

LORTON 3½

Lanthwaite Gate

looking south·south·east

ASCENT FROM LANTHWAITE GREEN
DIRECT
2300 feet of ascent
1½ miles

GRASMOOR

grass and mosses

2500

Grasmoor End 2400'

Upon reaching the Pinnacle (a fine vantage point) jaws drop with dismay at the sight of Grasmoor End, still distant and considerably higher. The ground between is very rough, but a curving ridge (not at first obvious) leads up to it.

2300
2200
2100

Pinnacle 2000'

The Pinnacle dominates this section of the route, forming a fine rock pyramid high above the terrace. Take to a rocky arête on the left from the terrace by way of a splintered crag (a Fat Man's Agony) and gain height by scrambling over or around a series of little cliffs.

arête

Fat Man's Agony
— terrace (1800')
rake (1500'-1600')

Immediately above the rock gateway turn up a green rake on the right (this reminds one of Lord's Rake — on a smaller and gentler scale). The rake leads to a terrace carrying (unexpectedly) a clear track, but this runs horizontally both ways and is no help in the ascent.

rock gateway 1500'

rock gateway now seen directly ahead

a detached block below the first crag

The tortuous crawl up the 40° slope provides opportunity for observing the flora at very close range. There are various berried shrublets, and, on the higher rocks, excellent specimens of prostrate juniper.

big gully

1300
1200
1100

heather

Take direction from this conspicuous tongue of light-coloured scree (it is plainly in view from the road).

Go straight up (a rough, steep pull up heather and stones)

Grasmoor is a very formidable object above Lanthwaite, its tiered crags seeming almost impregnable. The direct climb, up the angle between the north and west faces, is a continuously steep and rough scramble and a severe test in route selection.
On the whole, however, the climb is probably less difficult than the North Wall of the Eiger.

heather

800

falls

A fair path through the bracken comes to an end when the first stones are reached

700

bracken

climbers' track to Grasmoor gullies

bield

600

Liza Beck

water cut

weir

Pick up a thin track on the south side of the water cut (a line of rushes)

500

BUTTERMERE

BB

grass

cattle grid

Lanthwaite Green

ROAD

Lanthwaite Gate

LORTON 3½

looking southeast

ASCENT FROM RANNERDALE
2430 feet of ascent : 1¼ miles

GRASMOOR

via RED GILL

Grasmoor End

top of
south
spur

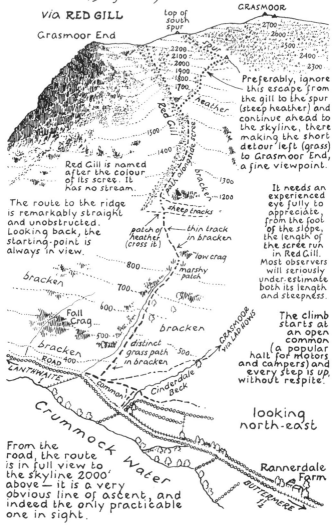

2700
2600
2500
2400
2300

2200
2100
2000
1900
1800
1700

spur

heather

Red Gill

1500

1400

walk alongside scree

bracken

1300

1200

sheep tracks

patch of
heather
(cross it)

thin track
in bracken

low crag

marshy
patch

800

700

600

500

400

bracken

bracken

distinct
grass path
in bracken

500

GRASMOOR
via LAD HOWS

ROAD

LANTHWAITE

Fall
Crag

Common

Cinderdale
Beck

Crummock Water

Rannerdale
Farm

BUTTERMERE
1½

Red Gill is named
after the colour
of its scree. It
has no stream.

The route to the ridge
is remarkably straight
and unobstructed.
Looking back, the
starting-point is
always in view.

Preferably, ignore
this escape from
the gill to the spur
(steep heather) and
continue ahead to
the skyline, there
making the short
detour left (grass)
to Grasmoor End,
a fine viewpoint.

It needs an
experienced
eye fully to
appreciate,
from the foot
of the slope,
the length of
the scree run
in Red Gill.
Most observers
will seriously
under-estimate
both its length
and steepness.

The climb
starts at
an open
common
(a popular
halt for motors
and campers) and
every step is up,
without respite.

looking
north-east

From the
road, the route
is in full view to
the skyline 2000'
above — it is a very
obvious line of ascent, and
indeed the only practicable
one in sight.

ASCENT FROM RANNERDALE
2450 feet of ascent : 1¼ miles
VIA LAD HOWS

looking east-north-east

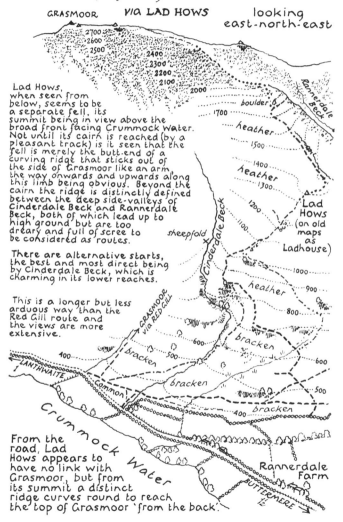

GRASMOOR

2700
2600
2500
2400
2300
2200
2100
2000
1700

boulder

heather

1500

1400
heather
1300

1200

Lad Hows (on old maps as Ladhouse)

1100

sheepfold ×

1000

900

heather

800

GRASMOOR VIA RED GILL

600

700

bracken

600

400

bracken

600

bracken

500

400

LANTHWAITE

Common

Crummock Water

Rannerdale Beck

Cinderdale Beck

Rannerdale Farm

BUTTERMERE 12

Lad Hows, when seen from below, seems to be a separate fell, its summit being in view above the broad front facing Crummock Water. Not until its cairn is reached (by a pleasant track) is it seen that the fell is merely the butt-end of a curving ridge that sticks out of the side of Grasmoor like an arm the way onwards and upwards along this limb being obvious. Beyond the cairn the ridge is distinctly defined between the deep side-valleys of Cinderdale Beck and Rannerdale Beck, both of which lead up to high ground but are too dreary and full of scree to be considered as routes.

There are alternative starts, the best and most direct being by Cinderdale Beck, which is charming in its lower reaches.

This is a longer but less arduous way than the Red Gill route and the views are more extensive.

From the road, Lad Hows appears to have no link with Grasmoor, but from its summit a distinct ridge curves round to reach the top of Grasmoor 'from the back'.

The Scafell group

from Grasmoor

ASCENT FROM COLEDALE HAUSE
850 feet of ascent
1¼ miles

looking southeast

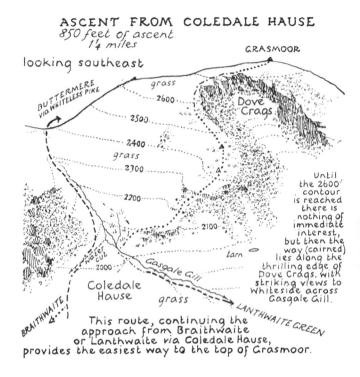

Until the 2600' contour is reached there is nothing of immediate interest, but then the way (cairned) lies along the thrilling edge of Dove Crags, with striking views to Whiteside across Gasgale Gill.

This route, continuing the approach from Braithwaite or Lanthwaite *via* Coledale Hause, provides the easiest way to the top of Grasmoor.

RIDGE ROUTE

TO EEL CRAG, 2749': 1¼ miles: generally E
Depression at 2350': 400 feet of ascent
A long moorland tramp, excellent underfoot

The first half-mile is the easiest walking to be found anywhere; keep left for a sight of Dove Crags. After crossing the depression, bear right for a look down into Addacomb Hole. These are the only excitements.

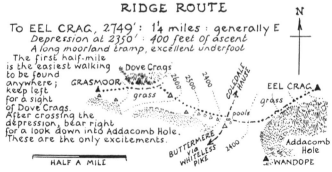

HALF A MILE

THE SUMMIT

There are many cairns at various stations on the broad top, but no mistaking the highest of all, which is a huge heap of stones divided into shelter compartments, open to the sky, designed to give protection from wind (but not wet) coming from any direction. Some skill and much labour has gone into its construction (where did the stones come from?) and visitors should feel a sense of responsibility for keeping it in repair. It stands a score of yards only from the edge of the south face, and a smaller wind-shelter perched here on the brink marks a better viewpoint. The summit has a covering of shale hereabouts, but elsewhere a soft mossy turf is a pleasure to walk upon.

The top of the fell is a long plateau coming up from the east and is generally broad but midway it narrows to a waist a hundred yards wide, the north side of this section being rimmed by the top rocks of Dove Crags. This scene, and the exciting scaffold of Grasmoor End (which should be visited if time permits) are the finest topographical features of an otherwise rather dull summit.

DESCENTS: Generally, ways off lie along the plateau eastwards whatever the destination, but Red Gill is a quick and safe way down to Crummock Water for Buttermere, and the left edge of Dove Crags is a practicable route down to Gasgale for Lanthwaite and Loweswater. Grasmoor End leads only to trouble. *In mist,* go east for half a mile, descending very little, to the good path through the grassy hollow between Grasmoor and Eel Crag, and here turn left for Coledale Hause, right for Buttermere.

PLAN OF SUMMIT

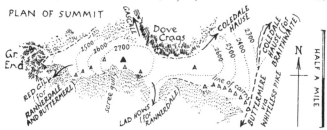

THE VIEW

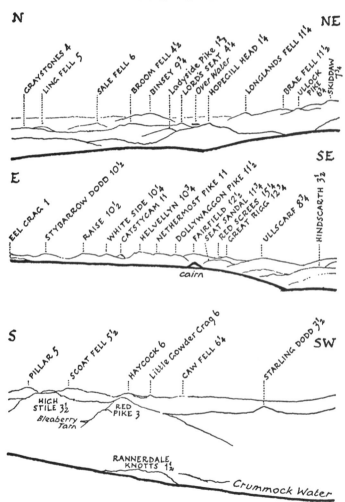

The thick line marks the visible boundaries
of the summit from the cairn

THE VIEW

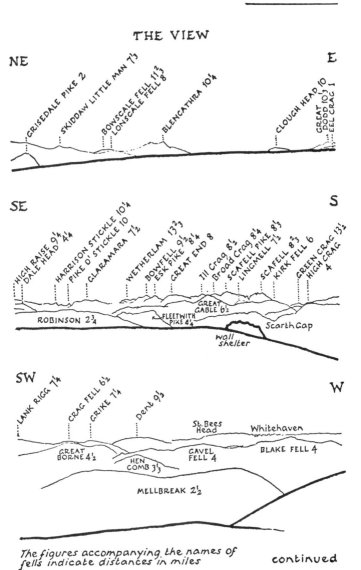

NE

GRISEDALE PIKE 2
SKIDDAW LITTLE MAN 7½
BOWSCALE FELL 11¾
LONSCALE FELL 8¾
BLENCATHRA 10¼
CLOUGH HEAD 10
GREAT DODD 10½
EEL CRAG 1

E

SE

HIGH RAISE 9¼ 4¼
DALE HEAD
HARRISON STICKLE 10¼
PIKE O' STICKLE 10
GLARAMARA 7½
WETHERLAM 13⅔
BOWFELL 9½
ESK PIKE 8¼
GREAT END 8
ILL CRAG 8½
BROAD CRAG 8¼
SCAFELL PIKE 8⅓
LINGMELL 7½
SCAFELL 8⅔
KIRK FELL 6
GREEN CRAG 13½
HIGH CRAG 4

ROBINSON 2¾
GREAT GABLE 6½
FLEETWITH PIKE 4¼
Scarth Gap
wall shelter

S

SW

LANK RIGG 7¼
CRAG FELL 6½
GRIKE 7¼
DENT 9½
St. Bees Head
Whitehaven
GREAT BORNE 4½
HEN COMB 3⅓
GAVEL FELL 4
BLAKE FELL 4
MELLBREAK 2½

W

*The figures accompanying the names of
fells indicate distances in miles*

continued

THE VIEW
continued

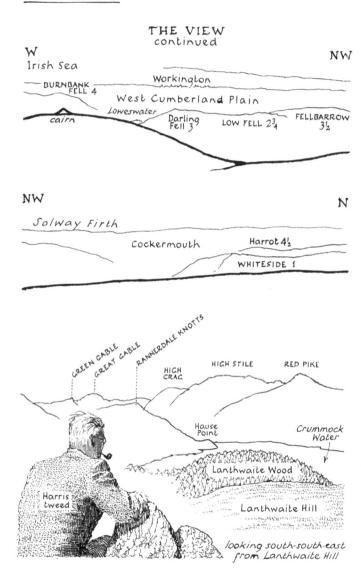

W   NW

Irish Sea

Workington

BURNBANK FELL 4

West Cumberland Plain

Loweswater

cairn   Darling Fell 3   LOW FELL 2¾   FELLBARROW 3½

NW   N

Solway Firth

Cockermouth   Harrot 4½

WHITESIDE 1

GREEN GABLE   GREAT GABLE   RANNERDALE KNOTTS

HIGH CRAG   HIGH STILE   RED PIKE

Hause Point

Crummock Water

Lanthwaite Wood

Harris tweed

Lanthwaite Hill

looking south-south-east from Lanthwaite Hill

Cinderdale Beck : a favourite stream, well known (but not by name) to the many motorists and campers who enjoy the freedom of the open fell alongside the road to Buttermere at the base of Grasmoor.

Dove Crags

Grasmoor End from Crummock Water

Graystones

1476'

Cockermouth

Wythop Mill

LING FELL ▲

GRAYSTONES ▲

BROOM FELL ▲

Low
Lorton ●

▲ LORD'S
SEAT

● High
Lorton

Whinlatter Pass ●

MILES

0   1   2   3   4

from
Aiken Plantation

NATURAL FEATURES

Graystones is the name of a summit only. The fell of which it is the highest point is Kirk Fell, rising above the western end of the motor road through the pass of Whinlatter at the head of the Vale of Lorton. This aspect of the fell is its most impressive, the declivity here being rough and steep, but northwards, facing Wythop, the slopes fall away more easily to merge in upland and undulating pastures before declining finally to the wide Embleton valley.   The western flanks too descend in simple stages to the flat land of the River Cocker, although interrupted, midway, by the small eminence of Harrot, which has a lovely view to the south. These smooth upper expanses are of grass, but the sharper eastern slope, overlooking the side valley of Aiken Beck where the long climb to Whinlatter Pass starts in earnest, is now almost completely patterned by the young evergreens and forest roads of Darling How Plantation.   At the foot of this slope, hidden in a jungle of new conifers, is a fine waterfall, Spout Force, where Aiken Beck plunges into a deep chasm before joining Whit Beck, a principal tributary of the Cocker.

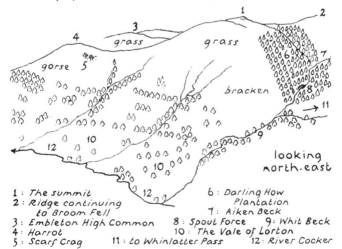

looking north-east

1 : The summit
2 : Ridge continuing
    to Broom Fell
3 : Embleton High Common
4 : Harrot
5 : Scarf Crag
6 : Darling How
    Plantation
7 : Aiken Beck
8 : Spout Force   9 : Whit Beck
10 : The Vale of Lorton
11 : to Whinlatter Pass   12 : River Cocker

MAP

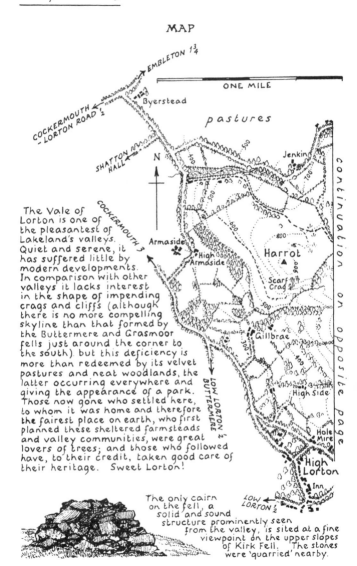

EMBLETON 1¾

ONE MILE

COCKERMOUTH
— LORTON ROAD ½

Byerstead

pastures

SHATTON
HALL

N

Jenkin

COCKERMOUTH 3

Armaside

High
Armaside

Harrot

Scarf
Crag

Gillbrae

continuation on opposite page

The Vale of
Lorton is one of
the pleasantest of
Lakeland's valleys.
Quiet and serene, it
has suffered little by
modern developments.
In comparison with other
valleys it lacks interest
in the shape of impending
crags and cliffs (although
there is no more compelling
skyline than that formed by
the Buttermere and Grasmoor
fells just around the corner to
the south). but this deficiency is
more than redeemed by its velvet
pastures and neat woodlands, the
latter occurring everywhere and
giving the appearance of a park.
Those now gone who settled here,
to whom it was home and therefore
the fairest place on earth, who first
planned these sheltered farmsteads
and valley communities, were great
lovers of trees; and those who followed
have, to their credit, taken good care of
their heritage. Sweet Lorton!

LOW LORTON ½
BUTTERMERE

High Side

Hole
Mire

High
Lorton

Inn

LOW
LORTON ½

The only cairn
on the fell, a
solid and sound
structure prominently seen
from the valley, is sited at a fine
viewpoint on the upper slopes
of Kirk Fell.   The stones
were 'quarried' nearby.

MAP

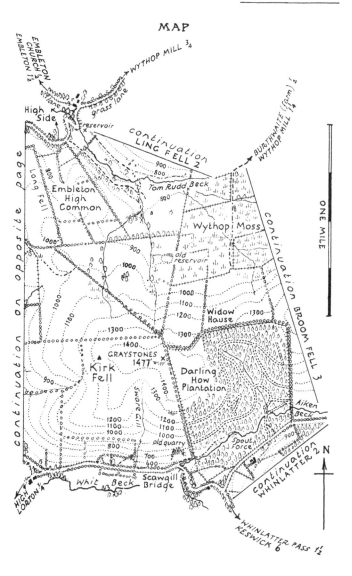

EMBLETON CHURCH 2 : EMBLETON 1½

WYTHOP MILL ¾

BURTHWAITE (farm) ½ : WYTHOP MILL 1¼

continuation LING FELL 2

continuation on opposite page

continuation BROOM FELL 3

continuation WHINLATTER 2

WHINLATTER PASS 1½ : KESWICK 6

HIGH LORTON ¼

High Side

reservoir

Long Fell

Embleton High Common

Tom Rudd Beck

Wythop Moss

old reservoir

Widow House

GRAYSTONES 1477'

Kirk Fell

Darling How Plantation

Aiken Beck

Swore Gill

old quarry

Spout Force

Whit Beck

Scawgill Bridge

900 800 1000 900 1000 1100 1200 1300 1300 1300 1400 900 1400 1300 1200 1100 1000 800 700 600 900 800

grass lane

lane

ONE MILE

N

ASCENT FROM EMBLETON CHURCH
1200 feet of ascent: 2½ miles

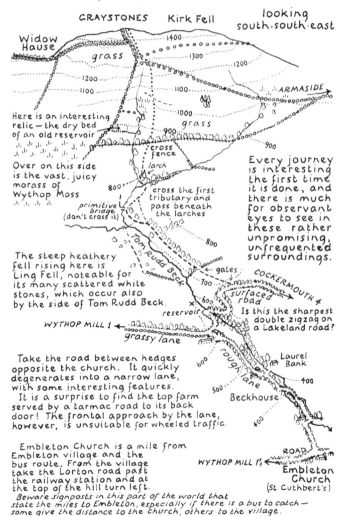

GRAYSTONES   Kirk Fell   looking south-south-east

Widow Hause

grass

1400
1300
1200

ARMASIDE

1200
1100

1000
grass
900

Here is an interesting relic — the dry bed of an old reservoir

900

cross fence

larch

Over on this side is the vast, juicy morass of Wythop Moss

Every journey is interesting the first time it is done, and there is much for observant eyes to see in these rather unpromising, unfrequented surroundings.

800

cross the first tributary and pass beneath the larches

primitive bridge (don't cross it)

Tom Rudd Beck

800

The steep heathery fell rising here is Ling Fell, noteable for its many scattered white stones, which occur also by the side of Tom Rudd Beck

gates

COCKERMOUTH

700

surfaced rbad

reservoir

600

WYTHOP MILL 1

grassy lane

Is this the sharpest double zigzag on a Lakeland road?

Laurel Bank

Take the road between hedges opposite the church. It quickly degenerates into a narrow lane, with some interesting features.
It is a surprise to find the top farm served by a tarmac road to its back door! The frontal approach by the lane, however, is unsuitable for wheeled traffic.

rough lane

600

500

400

Beckhouse

400

Embleton Church is a mile from Embleton village and the bus route. From the village take the Lorton road past the railway station and at the top of the hill turn left.

ROAD

WYTHOP MILL 1¼

Embleton Church (St. Cuthbert's)

Beware signposts in this part of the world that state the miles to Embleton, especially if there is a bus to catch — some give the distance to the church, others to the village.

ASCENT FROM ARMASIDE
1200 feet of ascent : 2¼ miles

looking south-east

The long drag up by the wall
on the last mile to the summit
is the least interesting part of
the ascent. It can be varied
by climbing the easy slopes
directly ahead beyond the
old plantation to the grass
plateau of Kirk Fell, where
there is a fine cairn.
By this alternative
a view southwards
over Lorton can be
maintained to the
top of Graystones.

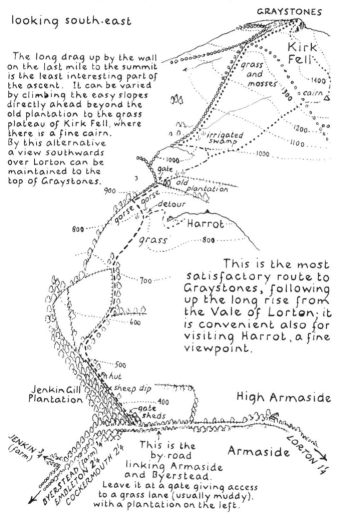

GRAYSTONES

Kirk Fell

grass
and
mosses

1400
cairn
1300
1200
1100
1000

irrigated
swamp

gate
old
plantation

3
900

gorse gorse
detour
Harrot

grass   800

800

700

600

500
hut
sheep dip
400

Jenkin Gill
Plantation

High Armaside

gate
sheds

JENKIN 3
(farm)

BYERSTEAD 1¼
EMBLETON 2¼
COCKERMOUTH 2¼

Armaside

LORTON 1¼

This is the most
satisfactory route to
Graystones, following
up the long rise from
the Vale of Lorton; it
is convenient also for
visiting Harrot, a fine
viewpoint.

This is the
by-road
linking Armaside
and Byerstead.
Leave it at a gate giving access
to a grass lane (usually muddy),
with a plantation on the left.

ASCENT FROM SCAWGILL BRIDGE
900 feet of ascent : 3/4 mile

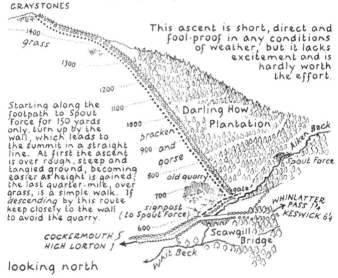

GRAYSTONES

1400
grass

1300

1200

1100

1000

900

800

700

600

This ascent is short, direct and fool-proof in any conditions of weather, but it lacks excitement and is hardly worth the effort.

Darling How Plantation

bracken and gorse

old quarry

Aiken Beck

Spout Force

Starting along the footpath to Spout Force for 150 yards only, turn up by the wall, which leads to the summit in a straight line. At first the ascent is over rough, steep and tangled ground, becoming easier as height is gained; the last quarter-mile, over grass, is a simple walk. If descending by this route keep closely to the wall to avoid the quarry.

gate

signpost
(to Spout Force)

WHINLATTER
PASS 1¼
KESWICK 6¼

COCKERMOUTH 5
HIGH LORTON 1

Scawgill Bridge

Whit Beck

looking north

A big bridge and a little one......
Scawgill Bridge on the Whinlatter road

Spout Force

A signpost at Scawgill Bridge, inviting passers-by to use a footpath "to Spout Force only", must tempt many people upstream in search of it. Only a few, grimly determined, will ever see it.

The signpost, due to the effluxion of time and in particular to the habit of young spruce to add a foot a year to their height, has become a bad joke. Originally it was provided by the Forestry Commission as a concession to the public, the waterfall in its rocky gorge being well worth seeing. Notwithstanding their signpost, the Commission then proceeded to plant the route with prickly young trees, which, with the passing years, have encroached upon the path and obliterated it.

There are evidences of violent struggles, man versus vegetation, and signs that some hardy individuals have forced a way into the jungle, emerging on an extremely dangerous slope above the gorge, but the nearest approach is gained by following the stream strictly almost to the portals of the gorge, where a water-barrier stops further progress. In neither case does one get a glimpse of the waterfall.   A few yards above the stream, after more painful gymnastics, a forlorn noticeboard is found in the forest and this announces the end of the path (joke no.2). At this point an abnormally tall person could just see the upper part of the fall up to 1963, but from 1964 onwards the growing trees will have concealed it completely.

Unless and until it occurs to the Commission to clear the path, the only place for viewing Spout Force is the old Scale Hill road, south of Scawgill Bridge, half a mile distant.

right: The gorge

below: The force
(top left corner,
as seen in 1962)

THE SUMMIT

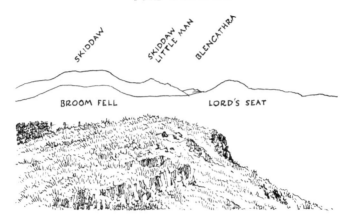

There is no cairn, but the highest point, on grass above a slight upthrust of rocky ground, is not in doubt; it occurs within a few yards of the broken wall and fence crossing the top of the fell.

DESCENTS: The most direct way off follows the wall straight down to Scawgill Bridge on the Whinlatter Pass road; simple at first, the ground steepens and becomes very rough near the bottom, but keep closely to the wall to avoid a gaping quarry at the foot of the slope. The other routes of ascent provide pleasant walking in reverse and should give no trouble even in mist, using as guides the walls indicated on the map.

RIDGE ROUTE

To BROOM FELL, 1670' : 1½ miles : N, then ENE.

Depression at 1240' (Widow Hause) : 450 feet of ascent

A pleasant walk on grass, interest being added by the plantation.

Keep outside the forest fence by starting north, then east down to Widow Hause and so along above the plantation, crossing three walls en route. Bear left when the open fell is reached.

ONE MILE

THE VIEW

A dreary foreground detracts from the view, which reveals a fine sweep of the Scottish coast with Criffell prominent, the Skiddaw group, a good section of the Helvellyn skyline and the towering Grasmoor mass across Whinlatter Pass as its best features. The Vale of Lorton, backed by the Loweswater Fells, is well seen.

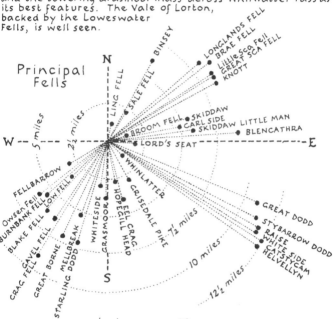

Principal Fells

Lakes and Tarns

No lakes or tarns can be seen, but Crummock Water is brought into view by walking west to the next prominence and more of it by continuing to the subsidiary summit of Harrot, where too the Vale of Lorton appears at its best.

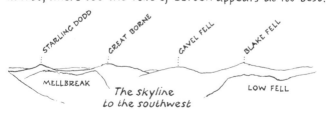

The skyline to the southwest

Grisedale Pike   2593'

from High Moss

NATURAL FEATURES

All visitors to Lakeland who come to walk on the hills turn their footsteps in due course to Grisedale Pike. It is seldom a prime objective, being a little out of the way, but the graceful peak piercing the western sky is a nagger of conscience and cannot long be ignored. Nor should it be. Conspicuously in view from the environs of Keswick, it is one of those fells that compels attention by reason of shapeliness and height.

The Pike, although of slender proportions on and towards the top, is quite broadly based, occupying the west side of Coledale through the three-mile length of the valley, from which the slopes of the fell rise steeply and unbroken for 2000 feet to a narrow crest. On this face heather and scree below the summit-rocks offer nothing to the climber but hard labour, a fact so obvious that it is virtually a no-man's-land; and the lines of approach lie along four ridges— a short one joined from Coledale Hause, and, at divergent points between north and east, three others rise from the plantations of Whinlatter, the most easterly carrying the popular route from Braithwaite. These three ridges enclose two deep valleys, partly afforested, pathless, and unfrequented, while the sombre depths of Hobcarton mark the boundary of the fell and an impressive neighbour, Hopegill Head, which are linked also at a high level, above a rim of crags, by the short ridge referred to.

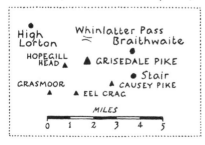

Why *Grisedale* Pike? Why not *Coledale* Pike after the valley below? Generally a mountain takes its name from a valley only if it stands *at the head*, and the rule is followed here — one of the two short valleys running north-east is named Grisedale (a fact little known), the summit of the fell being centred exactly *at the head*.

Force Crag

Coledale is straight and narrow, and without incident until, two miles up, a high barrier of rock extends across the valley like a huge dam. This is Force Crag. Over its lip pours a long cascade (Low Force) and at its foot are the buildings and the spoil-heaps of Force Crag Mine. The scene, backed by the towering skyline of Eel Crag, is magnificently wild.

Escape for the walker bound for Coledale Hause is provided by a wide path that crosses the beck and climbs round to the left of the crag. Ahead, grass slopes lead to Coledale Hause. But follow the path: it passes through a portal on the right into an amphitheatre above Force Crag, where, amazingly, the scene below is repeated. In front again now is another high wall of rock, and again a long cascade (High Force) pours over the lip. Here, too, are mine-buildings and spoil-heaps. The stream (Pudding Beck) is the same; between its two excitements it meanders quietly through this hanging valley. Force Crag is a natural formation not repeated in any other Lakeland dale and to find its unusual arrangement occurring twice, in close proximity, is remarkable.

The mine, always a rich one but not continuously worked, is again operating, after a lengthy closure, for the extraction of barytes.

High Force

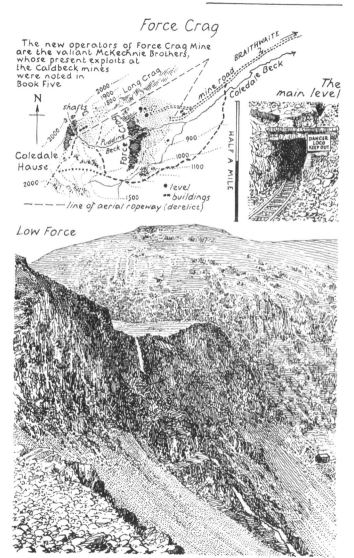

Force Crag

The new operators of Force Crag Mine are the valiant McKechnie Brothers, whose present exploits at the Caldbeck mines were noted in Book Five

BRAITHWAITE 2

N

Long Crag

mine road

Coledale Beck

shafts

Pudding Beck

Force Crag

2000
1900
1800

Coledale House

2000

level
buildings
------- line of aerial ropeway (derelict)

900

1000

1100

1500

HALF A MILE

The main level

DANGER
LOCO
KEEP OUT

Low Force

MAP

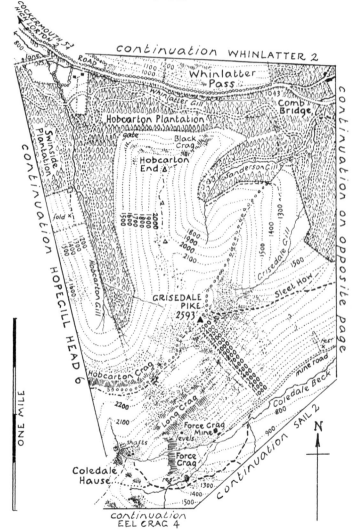

continuation WHINLATTER 2

Whinlatter Pass

Comb Bridge

Hobcarton Plantation

Swinside Plantation

gate

Black Crag

Hobcarton End △

Sanderson Gill

Grisedale Gill

continuation HOPEGILL HEAD 6

continuation on opposite page

fold

Hobcarton Gill

GRISEDALE PIKE 2593 ▲

Sleet How

ONE MILE

Hobcarton Crag

Long Crag

Force Crag Mine

shafts

levels

Force Crag

Coledale Hause

red

Coledale Beck

mine road

terr

continuation SAIL 2

N

continuation EEL CRAG 4

COCKERMOUTH ST HIGH LORTON 2

lane

ROAD

Whinlatter Gill

1043

MAP

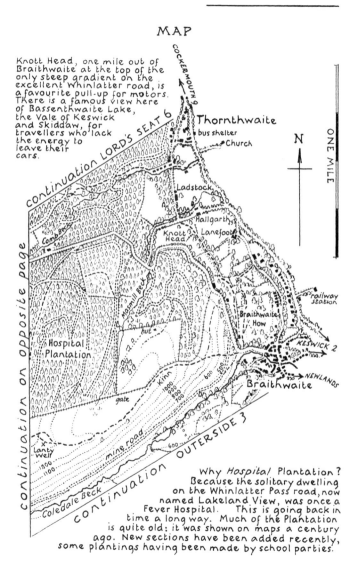

Knott Head, one mile out of Braithwaite at the top of the only steep gradient on the excellent Whinlatter road, is a favourite pull-up for motors. There is a famous view here of Bassenthwaite Lake, the Vale of Keswick and Skiddaw, for travellers who lack the energy to leave their cars.

continuation LORD'S SEAT 6

continuation on opposite page

COCKERMOUTH 9

Thornthwaite

bus shelter

Church

N

ONE MILE

Ladstock

Hallgarth

Knott Head

Lanefoot

Comb Beck

Mosmill Beck

hut

a.a.

Braithwaite How

railway station

KESWICK 2

Hospital Plantation

Kinn

gate

1000

900

800

700

600

600

NEWLANDS

Braithwaite

+ Lanty Well

1200

1100

mine road

continuation OUTERSIDE 3

Coledale Beck

Why *Hospital* Plantation? Because the solitary dwelling on the Whinlatter Pass road, now named Lakeland View, was once a Fever Hospital. This is going back in time a long way. Much of the Plantation is quite old: it was shown on maps a century ago. New sections have been added recently, some plantings having been made by school parties.

Three
Ridges

the east ridge — *the final section, from Sleet How*

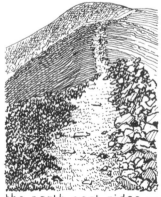

the north-east ridge —
the path by the broken wall

the north ridge —
looking from Hobcarton End

ASCENT FROM BRAITHWAITE
2400 feet of ascent : 3 miles

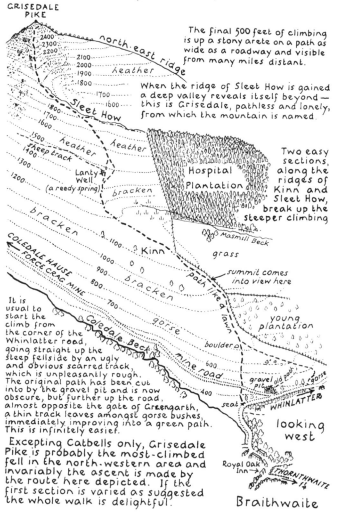

GRISEDALE PIKE

2400
2300
2200
2100
2000
1900
1800
1700
1600

north-east ridge

heather

Sleet How

1800
1700
1600
1500
1400

sheep track

heather   heather

1300
1200

Lanty Well
(a reedy spring)   bracken

bracken

1100   Kinn

1000
900
800
700

COLEDALE HAUSE
FORCE CRAG MINE

Coledale Beck

bracken

gorse

mine road

Coledale Hause

The final 500 feet of climbing is up a stony arete on a path as wide as a roadway and visible from many miles distant.

When the ridge of Sleet How is gained a deep valley reveals itself beyond — this is Grisedale, pathless and lonely, from which the mountain is named.

Hospital Plantation

Two easy sections, along the ridges of Kinn and Sleet How, break up the steeper climbing

Masmill Beck

grass

path like a lawn

summit comes into view here

young plantation

boulder

gravel old path

600

seat

400

gorse

WHINLATTER

looking west

It is usual to start the climb from the corner of the Whinlatter road, going straight up the steep fellside by an ugly and obvious scarred track, which is unpleasantly rough. The original path has been cut into by the gravel pit and is now obscure, but further up the road, almost opposite the gate of Greengarth, a thin track leaves amongst gorse bushes, immediately improving into a green path. This is infinitely easier.

Royal Oak Inn

THORNTHWAITE 14

Excepting Catbells only, Grisedale Pike is probably the most-climbed fell in the north-western area and invariably the ascent is made by the route here depicted. If the first section is varied as suggested the whole walk is delightful.

Braithwaite

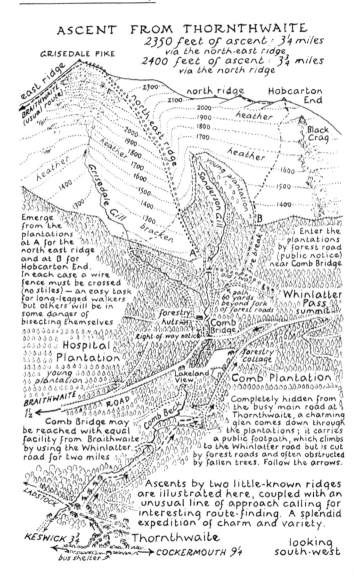

ASCENT FROM THORNTHWAITE
2350 feet of ascent : 3¼ miles
via the north-east ridge
2400 feet of ascent : 3¼ miles
via the north ridge

GRISEDALE PIKE

east ridge

BRAITHWAITE (usual route)

north ridge   Hobcarton End

Black Crag

heather

Grisedale Gill

heather

heather

Grisedale Gill

2300
2100
2000
1900
1800
1700
1600
1500
1400
1400
1300

north-east ridge

2000
1900
1800
1700
1600
1500
1400
1300

bracken

young plantation

Sanderson Gill

heather

A   B

Emerge from the plantations at A for the north east ridge and at B for Hobcarton End. In each case a wire fence must be crossed (no stiles) — an easy task for long-legged walkers but others will be in some danger of bisecting themselves

Enter the plantations by forest road (public notice) near Comb Bridge

old wall   fire break

path 60 yards beyond fork of forest roads

Whinlatter Pass summit

forestry huts

Comb Bridge

Right-of-way notice

Hospital Plantation

young plantation

forestry cottage

Comb Plantation

Lakeland View

BRAITHWAITE 1½   ROAD

Comb Beck

KESWICK 3¾

bus shelter   COCKERMOUTH 9¼

Thornthwaite

LADSTOCK

Comb Bridge may be reached with equal facility from Braithwaite by using the Whinlatter road for two miles

Completely hidden from the busy main road at Thornthwaite, a charming glen comes down through the plantations; it carries a public footpath, which climbs to the Whinlatter road but is cut by forest roads and often obstructed by fallen trees. Follow the arrows.

Ascents by two little-known ridges are illustrated here, coupled with an unusual line of approach calling for interesting route-finding. A splendid expedition of charm and variety.

looking south-west

ASCENT FROM WHINLATTER PASS
1600 feet of ascent : 2¼ miles from the road

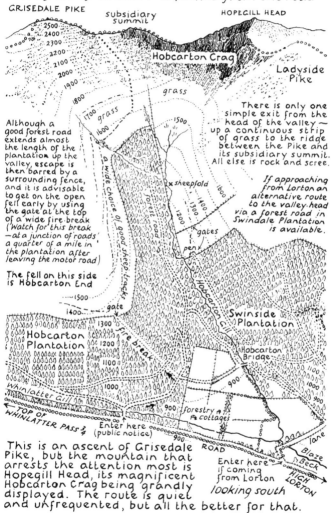

GRISEDALE PIKE

subsidiary summit

HOPEGILL HEAD

2500
2400
2300
2200
2100
2000
1900
1800

Hobcarton Crag

Ladyside Pike

grass

1700 grass

1600

1500

grass

There is only one simple exit from the head of the valley — up a continuous strip of grass to the ridge between the Pike and its subsidiary summit. All else is rock and scree.

Although a good forest road extends almost the length of the plantation up the valley, escape is then barred by a surrounding fence, and it is advisable to get on the open fell early by using the gate at the top of a wide fire-break (Watch for this break — at a junction of roads a quarter of a mile in the plantation after leaving the motor road)

a wide choice of good sheep-tracks

forest road

x sheepfold

1600

1500

1400

1300

1200

1100

gates

pen

If approaching from Lorton an alternative route to the valley head via a forest road in Swindale Plantation is available.

The fell on this side is Hobcarton End

1500
1400

gate

1300

1200

1100

1000

Hobcarton Plantation

fire break

Hobcarton Gill

Swinside Plantation

Hobcarton Bridge

1100

1000
900

Whinlatter Gill

← TOP OF WHINLATTER PASS ¾

900

1000

forestry cottages

Enter here (public notice)

900

ROAD

Enter here if coming from Lorton

lane

Blaze Beck

HIGH LORTON

looking south

This is an ascent of Grisedale Pike, but the mountain that arrests the attention most is Hopegill Head, its magnificent Hobcarton Crag being grandly displayed. The route is quiet and unfrequented, but all the better for that.

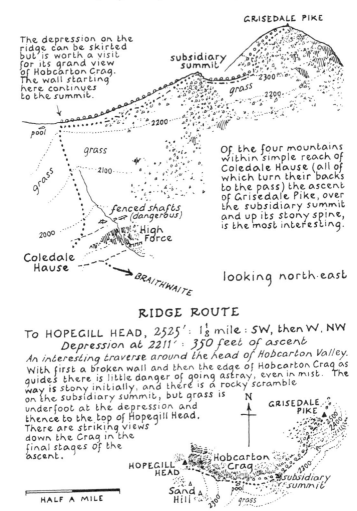

ASCENT FROM COLEDALE HAUSE
700 feet of ascent : 1¼ miles

GRISEDALE PIKE

The depression on the ridge can be skirted but is worth a visit for its grand view of Hobcarton Crag. The wall starting here continues to the summit.

subsidiary summit

2300

grass

2200

pool

grass

2200

grass

2100

Of the four mountains within simple reach of Coledale Hause (all of which turn their backs to the pass) the ascent of Grisedale Pike, over the subsidiary summit and up its stony spine, is the most interesting.

fenced shafts
(dangerous)

2000

High Force

Coledale Hause

BRAITHWAITE

looking north·east

RIDGE ROUTE

To HOPEGILL HEAD, 2525′ : 1⅛ mile : SW, then W, NW
Depression at 2211′ : 350 feet of ascent

An interesting traverse around the head of Hobcarton Valley. With first a broken wall and then the edge of Hobcarton Crag as guides there is little danger of going astray, even in mist. The way is stony initially, and there is a rocky scramble on the subsidiary summit, but grass is underfoot at the depression and thence to the top of Hopegill Head. There are striking views down the Crag in the final stages of the ascent.

N

GRISEDALE PIKE

2500

2400

2300

Hobcarton Crag

HOPEGILL HEAD

subsidiary summit

2300

Sand Hill

pool

2300

grass

HALF A MILE

THE SUMMIT

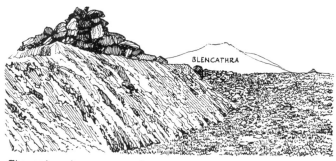

BLENCATHRA

The cairn sits upon a plinth of slate, fragments of which litter the summit thickly and add a musical tinkling to the march of boots. Much of this debris originated as a wall, now unrecognisable as such. The ridge is narrow at this point, only a few paces wide, and provides little shelter against the strong winds to which it is exposed.

DESCENTS : There may be initial difficulty in locating the start of the path down to Braithwaite, which is over-run by scree, but it soon becomes obvious, taking a line down the distinct ridge from the eastern corner of the summit; in mist, turn right where the wall turns left. A smoother alternative is provided by the north-east ridge, keeping alongside the wall down to the plantations. For Coledale Hause follow the wall west to its sudden end over and beyond the subsidiary top and then turn left, bearing right when fenced shafts appear ahead.

PLAN OF SUMMIT

N

NORTH-EAST RIDGE

2400
2500

PATH TO BRAITHWAITE

2400

COLEDALE HAUSE

100 YARDS

The main summit (left) from the subsidiary summit (right)

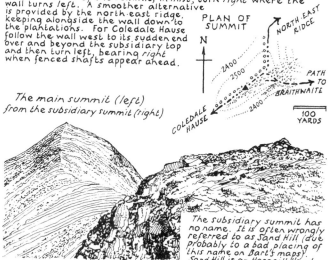

The subsidiary summit has no name. It is often wrongly referred to as Sand Hill (due probably to a bad placing of this name on Bart's maps). Sand Hill is on Hopegill Head.

THE VIEW

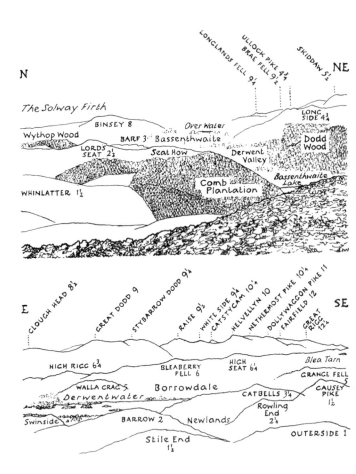

NE

N

LONGLANDS FELL 9¼

ULLOCK PIKE 4¾
BRAE FELL 9½

SKIDDAW 5½

The Solway Firth

LONG SIDE 4¾

BINSEY 8

Over Water

Wythop Wood

BARF 3 Bassenthwaite

Dodd Wood

LORDS SEAT 2½

Seat How

Derwent Valley

WHINLATTER 1½

Comb Plantation

Bassenthwaite Lake

E

SE

CLOUGH HEAD 8½

GREAT DODD 9

STYBARROW DODD 9¼

RAISE 9½

WHITE SIDE 9¼

CATSTYCAM 10¼

HELVELLYN 10

NETHERMOST PIKE 10¼

DOLLYWAGGON PIKE 11

FAIRFIELD 12

GREAT RIGG 12¼

HIGH RIGG 6¾

BLEABERRY FELL 6

HIGH SEAT 6¼

Blea Tarn

WALLA CRAG 5

Borrowdale

GRANGE FELL

Derwentwater

CATBELLS 3¼

CAUSEY PIKE 1½

Swinside

BARROW 2

Newlands

Rowling End 2¼

Stile End 1½

OUTERSIDE 1

From E to S, Coledale occupies the bottom of the view

THE VIEW

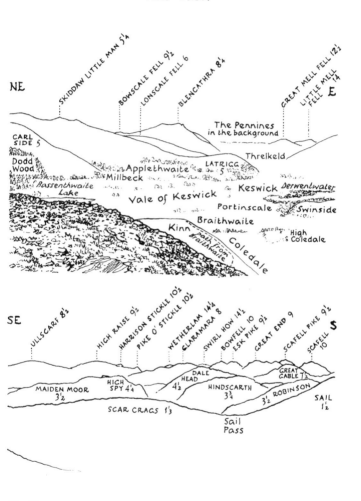

NE

SKIDDAW LITTLE MAN 5¼
BOWSCALE FELL 9½
LONSCALE FELL 6
BLENCATHRA 8¼
GREAT MELL FELL 12½
LITTLE MELL FELL 14
E

The Pennines
in the background

CARL
SIDE 5

Threlkeld

Dodd
Wood

LATRIGG
5

Applethwaite

Millbeck

Keswick   Derwentwater

Bassenthwaite
Lake

Vale of Keswick

Portinscale   Swinside

Braithwaite

Kinn

path from Braithwaite

Coledale

High
Coledale

SE

ULLSCARF 8½
HIGH RAISE 9½
HARRISON STICKLE 10½
PIKE O' STICKLE 10½
WETHERLAM 14¼
GLARAMARA 8
SWIRL HOW 14½
BOWFELL 10
ESK PIKE 9½
GREAT END 9
SCAFELL PIKE 9½
SCAFELL 10
S

DALE
HEAD
4½

GREAT
GABLE 7½

MAIDEN MOOR
3½

HIGH
SPY 4¼

HINDSCARTH
3¾

ROBINSON 3½

SAIL
1½

SCAR CRAGS 1⅓

Sail
Pass

*The figures accompanying the names of fells
indicate distances in miles*

continued

THE VIEW

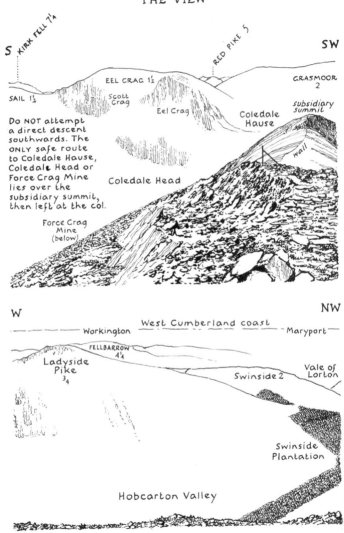

S

Kirk Fell 7½

SW

Sail 1½

Scott Crag

EEL CRAG 1½

Red Pike 5

Eel Crag

GRASMOOR 2

subsidiary summit

Coledale Hause

wall

Do NOT attempt a direct descent southwards. The ONLY safe route to Coledale Hause, Coledale Head or Force Crag Mine lies over the subsidiary summit, then left at the col.

Coledale Head

Force Crag Mine (below)

W

NW

West Cumberland coast

Workington

Maryport

FELLBARROW 4¼

Ladyside Pike 3 4

Swinside 2

Vale of Lorton

Swinside Plantation

Hobcarton Valley

THE VIEW

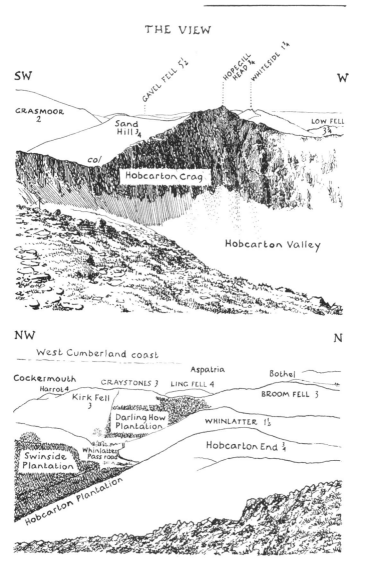

SW

GRASMOOR 2

GAVEL FELL 5½

Sand Hill ¾

col

Hobcarton Crag

HOPEGILL HEAD ¾

WHITESIDE 1¼

W

LOW FELL 3½

Hobcarton Valley

NW

N

West Cumberland coast

Cockermouth

Harrot 4

Kirk Fell 3

CRAYSTONES 3

LING FELL 4

Aspatria

Darling How Plantation

WHINLATTER 1½

Bothel

BROOM FELL 3

Hobcarton End ¾

Swinside Plantation

Whinlatter Pass road

Hobcarton Plantation

High Spy

2143'

also variously known as
Eel Crags, Lobstone Band
and Scawdel Fell

from
Dalehead Tarn

Little Town
●
  ▲ MAIDEN
  ▲ MOOR
Grange ●
  ▲ HIGH SPY
DALE
HEAD ▲
  Rosthwaite ●
Honister   ●
Pass ≈   Seatoller

MILES

0   1   2   3

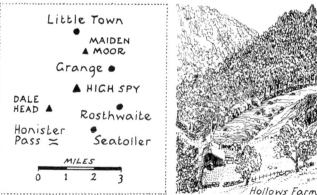

Hollows Farm

NATURAL FEATURES

The middle reaches of Borrowdale are bounded on the west by high fellsides, colourful and attractive side-curtains that contribute much to the beauty of the valley, yet which have never really been fully accepted by visitors as part of the lovely setting of the natural stage they come to admire. This lack of popular appeal, which is relative only to the quite unsurpassed scenery all around, is mainly because, when viewed from the valley, the rough slopes offer no obvious routes for walkers and the flat skyline promises no interesting summits above. In fact, between Catbells and Honister there is only a single breach in the four-mile wall carrying a beaten path (and *that* was beaten by quarrymen, not fellwalkers) and consequently the scenic beauties of Borrowdale are more often sought on the eastern slopes, where good paths abound.

High country can rarely be appraised properly from valley-level, however. The long skyline visible from below is not the ridge of the fell, as it appears to be, but the edge of a wide plateau where the steep rise of the slopes eases to a gentler gradient, the true spine lying well back, and it is here, along a crest, that one really enters upon fellwalkers' territory, a splendid elevated track traversing the whole length of the fell. Interest is sustained by the succession of cliffs and aretes falling away abruptly from the crest to the desolate upper Newlands valley, for on this western flank there is no wide plateau, but, in contrast, the appalling mile-long precipice known to the rock-climbing fraternity as Eel Crags. This, and the great bastion of Goat Crag above Borrowdale, are distinctive features.

The culminating point on a top of fairly uniform height is High Spy. To the south there is an easy decline to the marshy depression of Rigg Head, where many routes converge; north, the long crest descends to the level summit of Maiden Moor and continues to Catbells.

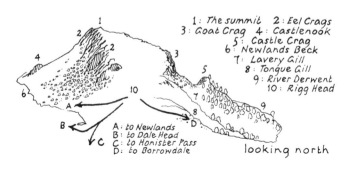

1 : The summit   2 : Eel Crags
3 : Goat Crag   4 : Castlenook
          5 : Castle Crag
6 : Newlands Beck
       7 : Lavery Gill
          8 : Tongue Gill
              9 : River Derwent
10 : Rigg Head

A : to Newlands
B : to Dale Head
C : to Honister Pass
D : to Borrowdale

looking north

Eel Crags

looking south from Castlenook

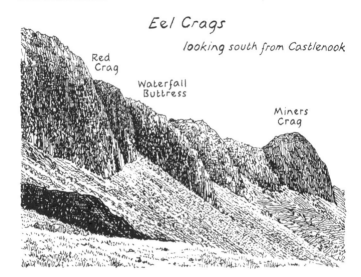

Red Crag

Waterfall Buttress

Miners Crag

looking north from the foot of Miner's Crag

MAP

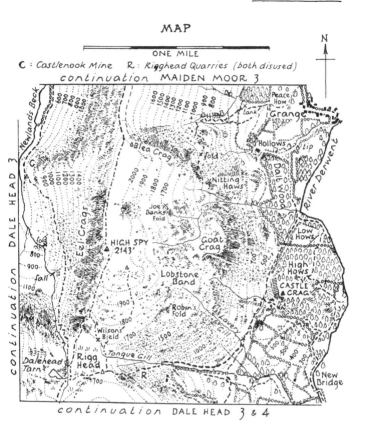

ONE MILE

C : Castlenook Mine   R : Rigghead Quarries (both disused)

continuation MAIDEN MOOR 3

continuation DALE HEAD 3

continuation DALE HEAD 3 & 4

For the place-names on their maps, the Ordnance Survey rely on the information gathered over the years in their files, supplied or verified by church records, title deeds, estate books and other written sources, and often on the statements of local residents. On the Lakeland map, much reliance has been placed on spoken information volunteered locally (and in a few instances it would seem that the dialect has not been interpreted quite correctly).

The Ordnance map of the High Spy area is interesting because of the naming of the sheepfolds. This occurs elsewhere in the district, but infrequently. All sheepfolds, of course, have identifying names known to farmers and shepherds, but not normally made public. It would appear, however, that the tenant of the grazing on Scawdel has been unusually communicative. Thus the Ordnance map names Joe Bank's (? Banks') Fold, Robin's Fold and Wilson's Bield on 2½" and 6" editions, yet these are unremarkable structures bettered by many others elsewhere not distinguished by 'official' names.

The hinterland of Goat Crag

Joe Banks' Fold

The only frequented walkers' route on the higher parts of the fell runs along the crest of the ridge; the wide upland east of the summit, ending in a two-mile escarpment above Borrowdale, is rarely visited. This escarpment is almost continuous from Blea Crag to and beyond Goat Crag, being breached only by High White Rake and Low White Rake, both very steep passages. The upland, however, although broken by many outcrops, is good grazing ground. Getting the sheep down through the escarpment to the valley, as is necessary on occasion, is a problem that has been solved by slanting a drove-way between the top of Low White Rake and the foot of High White Rake, and this is the only route by which sheep may safely be brought down from the tops.

Immediately behind the rocky turrets of Nitting Haws and Goat Crag there is a spacious hollow, an amphitheatre, before the slope resumes its climb over the upland to the summit of High Spy, and in this hollow, where the sheep are gathered, a meandering stream finds a way down a stony ravine to the valley.

This hollow is a surprising place: it is unsuspected from the valley and is unseen from the summit-ridge. Although poised close above the busy holiday traffic of Borrowdale, it lies lonely and silent in a circle of craggy outcrops. Vegetation is lush: bracken, heather and mosses form a rich carpet of colourful pattern. Here the staghorn moss occurs profusely, covering large areas in dense mats resembling crowded nests of little green snakes, which writhe and squirm realistically under the tread of a boot.

Cockley
de How
×fold

Blea Crag

H
drove way
L

A: Amphitheatre
H: High White Rake
L: Low White Rake

Nitting Haws

Eel Crags

summit ridge

2000
1900
1800
1700

Joe Banks
Fold ×

A

Minum
Crag

N

Goat
Crag

QUARTER MILE

Staghorn moss
(Common Club-moss)

ASCENT FROM GRANGE
1950 feet of ascent : 2 miles via High White Rake
2½ miles via Narrow Moor

looking west

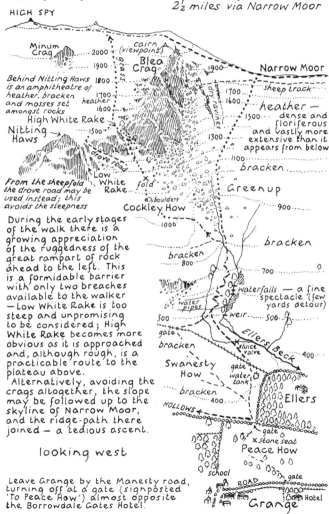

HIGH SPY

Minum Crag — 2000 — cairn (viewpoint)

1900 — Blea Crag

Behind Nitting Haws is an amphitheatre of heather, bracken and mosses set amongst rocks

1800
1700 heather
1600

High White Rake — 1500

Narrow Moor

1900

sheep track

1700
1600

1500

heather — dense and floriferous and vastly more extensive than it appears from below

Nitting Haws

drove road

1300

1100

bracken

From the sheepfold the drove road may be used instead; this avoids the steepness

Low White Rake
fold — boulders

Greenup

Cockley How — 1000

900

During the early stages of the walk there is a growing appreciation of the ruggedness of the great rampart of rock ahead to the left. This is a formidable barrier with only two breaches available to the walker — Low White Rake is too steep and unpromising to be considered; High White Rake becomes more obvious as it is approached and, although rough, is a practicable route to the plateau above.
Alternatively, avoiding the crags altogether, the slope may be followed up to the skyline of Narrow Moor, and the ridge-path there joined — a tedious ascent.

bracken
800

bracken

700

waterfalls — a fine spectacle (few yards detour)

water pipes

weir

500

500

gate

bracken

Ellers Beck

sluice valve

400

Swanesty How

gate
water tank

bracken — 400

HOLLOWS

Ellers

gate

stone seat

Peace How

school

ROAD

gate

Leave Grange by the Manesty road, turning off at a gate (signposted 'To Peace How') almost opposite the Borrowdale Gates Hotel.

Hotel

Grange

ASCENT FROM SEATOLLER OR ROSTHWAITE
FROM SEATOLLER: *1800 feet of ascent : 2½ miles*
FROM ROSTHWAITE: *1900 feet; 2½ miles*

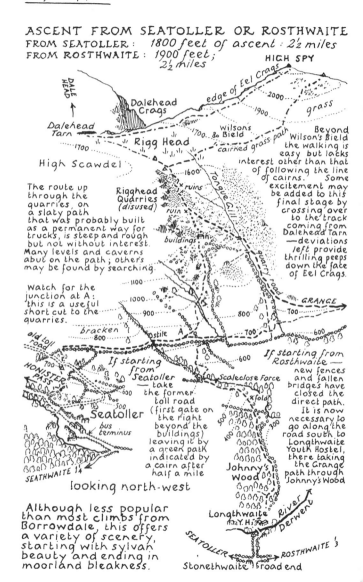

DALE HEAD

HIGH SPY

Dalehead Crags

edge of Eel Crags

2000

1900

grass

Dalehead Tarn

1700

Rigg Head

Wilsons Bield

cairned grass path

High Scawdel

1700

1600

Beyond Wilson's Bield the walking is easy but lacks interest other than that of following the line of cairns. Some excitement may be added to this final stage by crossing over to the track coming from Dalehead Tarn —deviations left provide thrilling peeps down the face of Eel Crags.

The route up through the quarries, on a slaty path that was probably built as a permanent way for trucks, is steep and rough but not without interest. Many levels and caverns abut on the path; others may be found by searching.

Rigghead Quarries (disused)

× ruins

Tongue Gill

ruin

buildings

quarry road

Watch for the junction at A: this is a useful short cut to the quarries.

1100

1000

900

GRANGE

700

800

700

old toll road

bracken 800

stile A

600

600

700

HONISTER PASS

700

600

500

If starting from Seatoller —take the former toll road (first gate on the right beyond the buildings) leaving it by a green path indicated by a cairn after half a mile

Scaleclose Force

× fold

If starting from Rosthwaite —new fences and fallen bridges have closed the direct path. It is now necessary to go along the road south to Longthwaite Youth Hostel, there taking the Grange path through Johnny's Wood.

Seatoller

bus terminus

SEATHWAITE 1¼

looking north-west

Johnny's Wood

Longthwaite Y.H.

River Derwent

SEATOLLER

ROSTHWAITE ¾

Stonethwaite road end

Although less popular than most climbs from Borrowdale, this offers a variety of scenery, starting with sylvan beauty and ending in moorland bleakness.

ASCENT FROM LITTLE TOWN
1650 feet of ascent : 4 miles

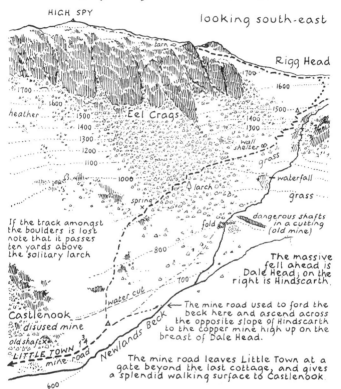

HIGH SPY

looking south-east

HIGH SPY

tarn

Rigg Head

1700

1600

1700

1600

heather

1500

Eel Crags

1500

1400

1400

1300

1300

wall shelter

1200

grass

1100

waterfall

1000

larch

grass

spring

fold

dangerous shafts
in a cutting
(old mine)

If the track amongst
the boulders is lost
note that it passes
ten yards above
the solitary larch

800

The massive
fell ahead is
Dale Head; on the
right is Hindscarth.

700

water cut

Castlenook
disused mine
old shaft

← The mine road used to ford the
beck here and ascend across
the opposite slope of Hindscarth
to the copper mine high up on the
breast of Dale Head.

LITTLE TOWN 1½
mine road

Newlands Beck

The mine road leaves Little Town at a
gate beyond the last cottage, and gives
a splendid walking surface to Castlenook.

600

The first thing to note about this route (which may also be used
for crossing from Newlands to Borrowdale or Honister) is that the
path as delineated on Ordnance and other maps, closely following
the side of the beck, has largely gone to seed. Instead, a popular
track now turns off the mine road just around the corner from the
old workings at Castlenook, a cairn marking the junction, and at
once starts climbing to swing round across the screes of Eel Crags,
finally joining the original zig-zags.

The upper reaches of the Newlands valley are wild and
secluded, with many evidences of man's searches for
its precious minerals, and this route gives an excellent
opportunity of seeing its features at close quarters.

THE SUMMIT

Bassenthwaite Lake

SKIDDAW

SKIDDAW LITTLE MAN

The top of the fell undulates without much variation in height over a considerable distance, and although the ultimate point is not in doubt the rough ground above Blea Crag, half a mile from the summit-cairn, is little inferior in elevation. Between the two is a simple promenade, easy walking among many small outcrops, but sustained excitement may be added to the journey by keeping to the fringe of the precipice of Eel Crags, which extends unbroken along the Newlands edge in a bewildering array of aretes, gullies and cliffs. The summit cairn is a solid, well-built structure, the result of diligent toil: a memorial to its unknown builders.

DESCENTS: Leave the fell by the ridge, either south to Rigg Head or north to Hause Gate before turning off. The easy slope down towards Borrowdale is tempting, but ends in crags; and a direct descent unscathed into Newlands is palpably impossible.

The summit, looking south

GREAT END

SCAFELL PIKE

SCAFELL

GREAT GABLE

DALE HEAD

Dalehead Tarn

THE VIEW

The view is extensive and generally good, the main interest being centred in the south, where the Scafell group captures attention and Great Gable is especially prominent. The long ten-mile wall of the Helvellyn range forms the limit of view eastwards, and Skiddaw and Blencathra stand up well in the north. As a viewpoint, the cairn is a little too far from the edge of the precipice to add drama to the scene, but there are several places nearby where profound glimpses down into the wild recesses of upper Newlands may be obtained.

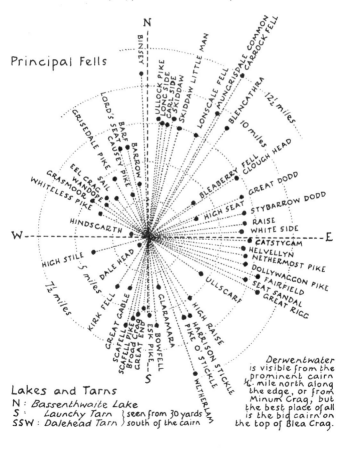

Principal Fells

Lakes and Tarns

N : Bassenthwaite Lake
S : Launchy Tarn } seen from 30 yards
SSW : Dalehead Tarn } south of the cairn

Derwentwater is visible from the prominent cairn ¼ mile north along the edge, or from Minum Crag, but the best place of all is the big cairn on the top of Blea Crag.

RIDGE ROUTES

To MAIDEN MOOR, 1887' : 1½ miles : N
Depression at 1860' : 100 feet of ascent
Half-an-hour's pleasant, straightforward walking.
Easy walking on a sketchy track along the undulating top leads to a long incline down to Narrow Moor, the path hereabouts being excellent. Continue with a steep fall on the left to the indefinite top of Maiden Moor. A detour to the Blea Crag cairn is recommended.

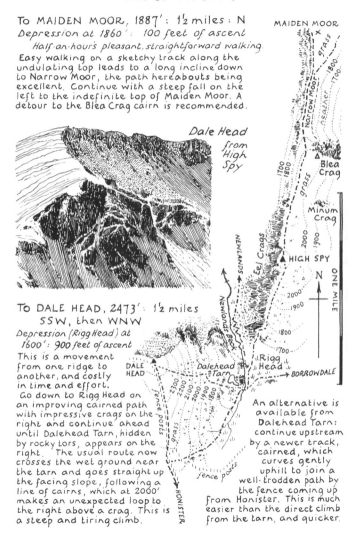

Dale Head from High Spy

To DALE HEAD, 2473' : 1½ miles
SSW, then WNW
Depression (Rigg Head) at 1600' : 900 feet of ascent
This is a movement from one ridge to another, and costly in time and effort.
Go down to Rigg Head on an improving cairned path with impressive crags on the right and continue ahead until Dalehead Tarn, hidden by rocky tors, appears on the right. The usual route now crosses the wet ground near the tarn and goes straight up the facing slope, following a line of cairns, which at 2000' makes an unexpected loop to the right above a crag. This is a steep and tiring climb.

An alternative is available from Dalehead Tarn : continue upstream by a newer track, cairned, which curves gently uphill to join a well-trodden path by the fence coming up from Honister. This is much easier than the direct climb from the tarn, and quicker.

Goat (or Gate) Crag
from Castle Crag

Hindscarth

2385'

from High Snab Bank

Little Town ●

⌒ Newlands Hause
ROBINSON ▲
● ▲ HINDSCARTH
Buttermere
DALE HEAD ▲
Seatoller ●

Honister Pass ⌒
MILES
0   1   2   3   4

NATURAL FEATURES

Only a minority of the walkers who traverse the fine ridge between Dale Head and Robinson turn aside for a visit to the intermediate summit of Hindscarth, this lying half a mile off the direct course across a simple but uninteresting plateau. Comparatively few, too, climb the fell for its own sake; those who do invariably ascend from Newlands along the only natural line of approach, the ridge of Scope End. Steep-sided and narrow-crested, and richly carpeted in heather, this ridge is a beauty.

Hindscarth is a twin to Robinson. Both were created in the same upheaval and sculptured in the same mould. They turn broad backs to the Buttermere valley and go hand-in-hand together down to Newlands, their ridges reaching the valley at the beautiful watersmeet near the little church. Between them is the upland hollow of Little Dale, much of it a bog, but having an interesting feature in a rocky gorge where waterfalls leap to lower levels beneath the near-vertical acclivity of Scope End; further down an old reservoir has served its purpose and become a charming pool. Mining operations have left a few scars on Scope End, and some open shafts, levels and fractures that invite attention. Gold has been won here, giving Hindscarth its greatest distinction — but walkers who halt in their travels to search the spoilheaps for discarded nuggets will be wasting their time, the area having already been thoroughly combed by the author — also without success. Those who carry their search into the long-abandoned workings are unlikely to return.

The eastern flank of Hindscarth falls very roughly and steeply into the upper Newlands valley, draining to the fell's main watercourse, Newlands Beck, which goes on to join the Derwent. A few feeble streams flow south to Gatesgarthdale and unexpectedly become subterranean at the 500' contour.

1 : The summit
2 : Ridge continuing to Robinson
3 : High Crags
4 : Scope End

grass

grass

waterfalls

reservoir

5 : Little Dale
6 : Scope Beck
7 : Newlands Beck
8 : Step Gill

pastures

looking south

Newlands is exceptionally
well-favoured by its circle
of exciting mountain peaks
and wide choice of ascents,
and is an ideal centre for
fellwalking. Among many
striking outlines, Scope End
in particular arrests one's
attention, assuming, when
seen from Little Town, the
shape of a narrow-crested
ridge with three turrets —
an aspect illustrated above.
In this view Hindscarth (on
the left) appears to be quite
detached from Scope End,
but they are connected
by a simple rising ridge.

Newlands Church

MAP

The summit contours on the Ordnance Survey 2½" map are misleading. They indicate a sharp fall of nearly 200 feet from the summit cairn to the big cairn on the edge of the plateau to the north, but actually the gradient is gentle and the difference in height only 50 feet.

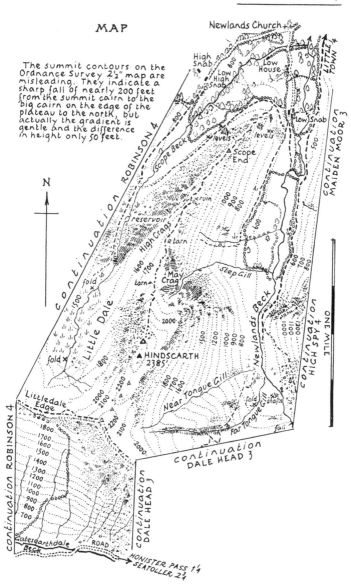

Goldscope Mine

Goldscope Mine was abandoned a hundred years ago after intermittent operation over a period of six centuries. One of the oldest mines in the district, it was also the most important in output, having rich veins of lead and copper. Silver and gold, too, have been extracted. Its early development, on a large scale, was undertaken by Germans, and its long history has been marked by many adventures and much litigation.

Upper Pan Holes

External evidence of the mine is indicated mainly by spoil-heaps on the Newlands Beck side of Scope End: immediately above is the main adit of Lower Pan Holes (from which a stream issues) with a second opening a few yards higher, under a tree. Further up the fellside is a curious slanting gash in a rockface — the Upper Pan Holes. On the other (Scope Beck) flank of the ridge are several levels.

Scope End is therefore pierced from both sides and the main level runs into the fell for such a considerable distance (over 300 yards) before becoming impassable, due to roof-falls, that it is reasonable to suppose that in the later years of operation it would be possible to walk right through the heart of it. In the darkness of these inner workings is a great shaft, which was sunk to such a depth ultimately that the pumping of water from it became too costly — this, not exhaustion of the minerals, was the reason for closure.

Lower Pan Holes

ASCENT FROM NEWLANDS CHURCH
2000 feet of ascent
2½ miles

HINDSCARTH

big cairn, in view during the ascent

2300

2200

2100

grass

2000

On the final pull up to the big cairn, the path (on grass) degenerates into a line of footmarks and vanishes completely upon reaching an area of loose scree just below the top.

pool

From Scope End to the little pool in the last depression the journey is sheer delight — very easy walking for a mile on a good path that winds in and out and up and down along a steepsided ridge.

May Crag

tarn

path below crest

High Crags

1500

ruin

path below crest

heather

Scope End

The valley on this side is that of Scope Beck, becoming Little Dale higher up.

The mountain opposite is Robinson, rising from High Snab

1100

1000

900

Pan Holes

Goldscope Mine

spoil heap

bracken

700

looking south-west

UPPER NEWLANDS and DALE HEAD

gate

600

500

Low Snab

Take the left fork of the road at the Church

Make a special note of the Scope End ridge: this route, on an enchanting track along the heathery crest, is really splendid. Only the final rather dull climb robs this ascent of four-star rating. In descent the route earns full marks because of the lovely views of Newlands directly ahead.

Newlands Beck

500

Church

old mine road

LITTLE TOWN

ASCENT FROM GATESGARTH

2050 feet of ascent
3 miles

looking
north east

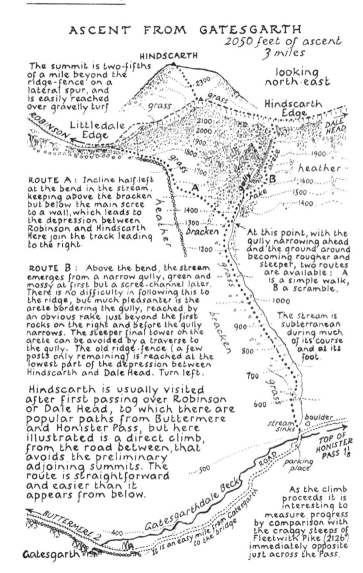

The summit is two-fifths of a mile beyond the ridge-fence on a lateral spur, and is easily reached over gravelly turf

HINDSCARTH

Hindscarth Edge

Littledale Edge

ROBINSON Edge

DALE HEAD

grass

grass

heather

bracken

rake

ROUTE A : Incline half-left at the bend in the stream, keeping above the bracken but below the main scree to a wall, which leads to the depression between Robinson and Hindscarth. Here join the track leading to the right.

At this point, with the gully narrowing ahead and the ground around becoming rougher and steeper, two routes are available : A is a simple walk, B a scramble.

ROUTE B : Above the bend, the stream emerges from a narrow gully, green and mossy at first but a scree-channel later. There is no difficulty in following this to the ridge, but much pleasanter is the arete bordering the gully, reached by an obvious rake just beyond the first rocks on the right and before the gully narrows. The steeper final tower on the arete can be avoided by a traverse to the gully. The old ridge-fence (a few posts only remaining) is reached at the lowest part of the depression between Hindscarth and Dale Head. Turn left.

The stream is subterranean during much of its course and at its foot.

Hindscarth is usually visited after first passing over Robinson or Dale Head, to which there are popular paths from Buttermere and Honister Pass, but here illustrated is a direct climb, from the road between, that avoids the preliminary adjoining summits. The route is straightforward and easier than it appears from below.

stream sinks

boulder

TOP OF HONISTER PASS 1⅛

ROAD

parking place

As the climb proceeds it is interesting to measure progress by comparison with the craggy steeps of Fleetwith Pike (212b) immediately opposite just across the Pass.

BUTTERMERE 2

Gatesgarthdale Beck

it is an easy mile from Gatesgarth to the bridge

Gatesgarth

THE SUMMIT

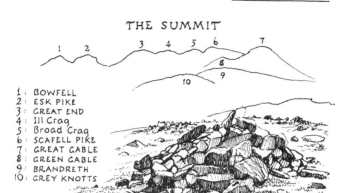

1 : BOWFELL
2 : ESK PIKE
3 : GREAT END
4 : Ill Crag
5 : Broad Crag
6 : SCAFELL PIKE
7 : GREAT GABLE
8 : GREEN GABLE
9 : BRANDRETH
10 : GREY KNOTTS

The top of Hindscarth is a full half-mile in length, the contours gently building up to the highest point, near the north-east end, where a large and untidy pile of stones stands amongst embedded rocks. Elsewhere the summit is grassy, with patches of gravel.

Continuing the line of the ridge and 200 paces away, on the edge of the north-east declivity, there is a big circular cairn of some antiquity, the Ordnance Survey maps giving it distinction by the use of the lettering reserved for objects of historic interest. This is the cairn prominently seen from Newlands, and it commands the finest view from the mountain. The interior is hollowed out to provide a wind-shelter — a function performed with increasing inefficiency as the cavity slowly fills with stones fallen from the parapet.

DESCENTS : The summit is pathless, but simple in design and uncomplicated in structure. Ways off are along the axis, which runs NNE and SSW. Both flanks are scarped.

For Newlands, go down by the big cairn, keeping the long ridge of Scope End in front and descending to it. A fair track materialises below the initial scree. *In mist, it is important (but not easy) to find it.*

Go SSW to the fence, for Buttermere or Honister. Leftwards the fence climbs over Dale Head (which can NOT be by-passed) before going down to Honister Pass. Rightwards, from the first depression a safe descent may be made down an easy slope to Gatesgarthdale.

"A .... cairn of some antiquity"

THE VIEW

There is a good all-round panorama, especially pleasing over Newlands to the Vale of Keswick and Skiddaw — the big north cairn is a better place for photographs in this direction — with, in contrast, a rugged skyline forming the southern horizon. The familiar shape of Scafell is missing from the scene, hidden behind Great Gable.

Principal Fells

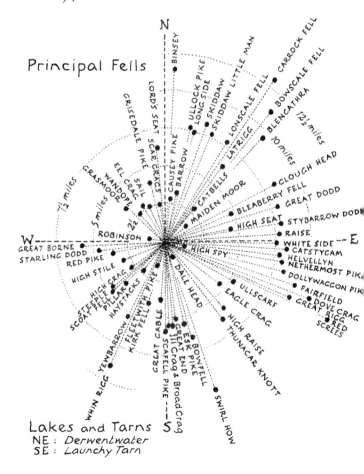

Lakes and Tarns
NE : Derwentwater
SE : Launchy Tarn

RIDGE ROUTES

To ROBINSON, 2417': 1½ miles: SSW, WNW and N.
Depression at 1880': 550 feet of ascent
A simple circuit around the head of Little Dale

Hindscarth and Robinson are lateral spurs springing from the main fenced ridge of the north wall of Gatesgarthdale. A beeline between the two summits is

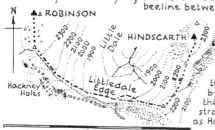

out of the question and the ridge must be used to pass from one to the other. The depression midway is considerable. An interest can be added to the climb therefrom by a short detour over the fence to look at the strange formation known as Hackney Holes.

To DALE HEAD, 2473': 1¼ miles: SSW, then ESE
Depression at 2156': 330 feet of ascent
Increasing interest and excellent views

The intervening depression is slight, and, in clear weather, a short cut to it is feasible. (In mist, continue SSW to join the fence). The main ridge from here onwards is very good, although not as exciting as it promises to be. Buttermere is in view temporarily when the ridge narrows. In mist, keep the line of fence-posts in sight.

Briefly and inadequately glimpsed from the ridge to Dale Head, down on the left, is the strange ravine of Far Tongue Gill. For half a mile this huge cut in the side of Hindscarth, a remarkable chasm out of all proportion to the stream it accommodates, is walled by great pale slabs of slate. Remote from usual walkers tracks, the best view of it from a distance is seen along the ridge of High Spy.

The ravine of Far Tongue Gill

Hopegill Head

also known as
Hobcarton Pike

2525'

from Scar Crags

NATURAL FEATURES

A high mountain ridge leaps like a rainbow from the woods and fields of Brackenthwaite and arcs through the sky for five miles to the east, where the descending curve comes down to the village of Braithwaite. This ridge has three main summits, of which the central one (and the finest, but not the highest) is known locally as Hobcarton Pike and to mapmakers as Hopegill Head. The supporting fell stretches far to the north, having roots in Whinlatter and the Vale of Lorton, whence the heathery flanks of Swinside rise to form the main ridge to the top peak, passing over the subsidiary Ladyside Pike (formerly Lady's Seat). Scarped edges join the two neighbouring fells of Grisedale Pike, east, and Whiteside, west, while a short slope, halted by the rounded hump of Sand Hill, falls easily to Coledale Hause southwards. But it is the aspect to the north that invests the mountain with its special character. Here, Swinside is bounded, on both sides, by deep valleys : sterile Hope Gill and afforested Hobcarton. The latter, now a coniferous jungle, leads up to a great semicircle of cliffs around the valley-head: this is a nature stronghold, Hobcarton Crag. The valley of Hope Gill is rarely visited and has little of interest; it seems rather surprising that this valley, and not the other, has given its name to the fell —— until one stands on the shapely summit and sees Hope Gill winding away directly below, while the valley of Hobcarton is obscured by the north ridge. Then the choice of name of the cartographers cannot be questioned. 'Hopegill Head' is right.

1: The summit
2: Ridge continuing to Grisedale Pike
3: Ridge continuing to Whiteside
4: Ladyside Pike   5: Swinside
6: Hobcarton Crag   7: Swinside Plantation
8: Hobcarton Plantation
9: Hobcarton Gill   10: Hope Gill

looking south

Hobcarton Crag

Hobcarton Crag is the property of the National Trust, and no ordinary cliff. Its size is impressive — 500 feet in height above the scree along a half-mile curve — but the rocks are broken and interspersed with lush bilberry meadows, so that the appeal of the crag is not related to climbing: indeed, the rock is unsuitable for exploration.

This is Skiddaw slate, fracturing and splintering easily, yet it has a special attraction nevertheless, obvious to all who observe as they walk: where natural weathering has taken place and erosion is absent there is a very high degree of contortion and striation, evidence of the severe pressures to which it was subjected during formation.

A greater fame, although also within a specialist field of study, is attributable to the rare species of flora in the two main gullies; in particular, here is the only known habitat in England of the red alpine catchfly (*Viscaria alpina*). The National Trust were largely influenced in their acquisition of the Crag by its great botanical interest (and partly by a desire to limit the afforestation of the valley-head below).

The Crag is a haven of quiet solitude, within sight but out of reach of a popular walking route. In summer sunlight there is pleasant colour, the bilberry — greenest of greens — making a luxuriant velvety patchwork among the grey and silver rocks. In shadow, the scene is sombre and forbidding. The silence is interrupted only by the croaking of the resident ravens and the occasional thud of a falling botanist.

This is a place to look at and leave alone.

A feature of the northern rim of Hobcarton Crag is a curious break in the curtain of rocks forming the sharp arete below the summit: here, a steep scree gully falls from a square cleft in the vertical wall of crag. A name is needed for this strange place and The Notch fits it well.

The lower picture shows the arete rising above the Notch to the summit. An arrow at the side indicates the direction of a groove or fault in the slabs, and this is advised for ascent or descent if the rocks are icy or greasy. In the foreground is a platform of rock — a perfect spot for a sunbathe but not for slumber, the unprotected edge here falling away sheer.

The Notch,
Hobcarton Crag

MAP

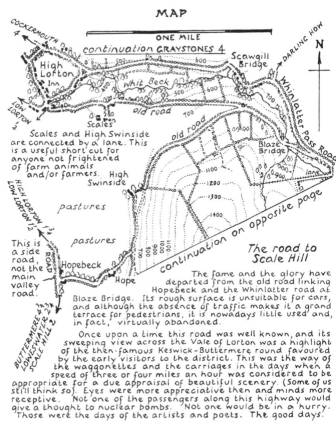

Scales and High Swinside are connected by a lane. This is a useful short cut for anyone not frightened of farm animals and/or farmers.

This is a side road, not the main valley road.

The road to Scale Hill

The fame and the glory have departed from the old road linking Hopebeck and the Whinlatter road at Blaze Bridge. Its rough surface is unsuitable for cars, and although the absence of traffic makes it a grand terrace for pedestrians, it is nowadays little used and, in fact, virtually abandoned.

Once upon a time this road was well known, and its sweeping view across the Vale of Lorton was a highlight of the then-famous Keswick-Buttermere round favoured by the early visitors to the district. This was the way of the waggonettes and the carriages in the days when a speed of three or four miles an hour was considered to be appropriate for a due appraisal of beautiful scenery. (Some of us still think so). Eyes were more appreciative then and minds more receptive. Not one of the passengers along this highway would give a thought to nuclear bombs. Not one would be in a hurry. Those were the days of the artists and poets. The good days!

The coaching-house in the valley was the Scale Hill Inn, a hostelry of renown and good reputation, the accepted centre for visitors to western Lakeland. Today the Scale Hill Inn (now Hotel) is as charming as ever, and no less favourably situated in one of the most delectable corners of a lovely landscape, but its former significance in the itinerary of tourists has gone. Langdale and Borrowdale are in current fashion. Most visitors have never heard of Scale Hill, and anyway would consider the place too remote, too quiet, off today's beaten tracks.

In these changed circumstances it gives an old-timer a certain nostalgic pleasure to note that the old signpost at the junction with the Whinlatter road still points to 'Scale Hill', a name that thrilled Victorian and Edwardian hearts but now means nothing to the neurotic Elizabethan lunatics who rattle past at 60 m.p.h. This old signpost is a lost link with the days of sanity. But few choose to follow its direction.

MAP

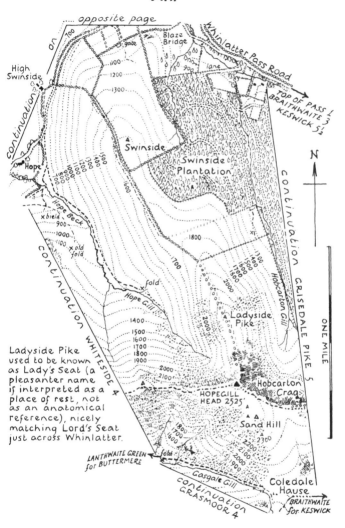

Ladyside Pike
used to be known
as Lady's Seat (a
pleasanter name
if interpreted as a
place of rest, not
as an anatomical
reference), nicely
matching Lord's Seat
just across Whinlatter.

Hobcarton

Viscaria alpina

*Hobcarton Valley and Crag —
the only English home of Viscaria alpina*

ASCENT FROM COLEDALE HAUSE
600 feet of ascent : ¾ mile

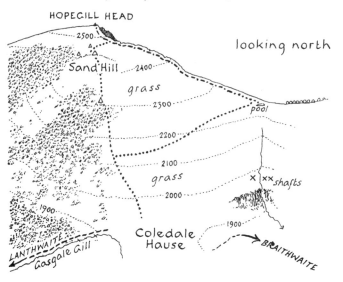

There is no path, and the summit remains concealed until the cairn on Sand Hill is reached. Go anywhere up the easy slope, keeping rather to the Gasgale side for a view to relieve the monotony of the ascent; or, more interesting, contour round to the depression on the right and then go up the edge of Hobcarton Crag.

The summit of Hopegill Head, from the cairn on Sand Hill

ASCENT FROM WHINLATTER PASS
1850 feet of ascent : 2½ miles from the road

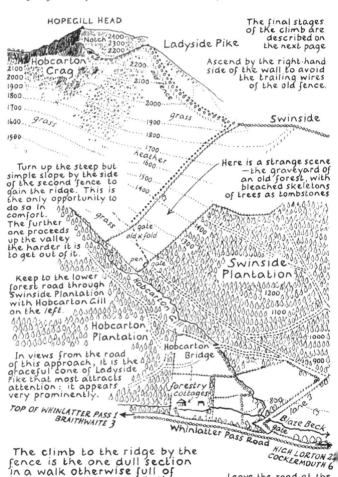

HOPEGILL HEAD

Notch 2400 2300 2200

Ladyside Pike

Hobcarton Crag

2100
2000
1900
1800
1700
1600 grass
1500

2200
2100

2000

1900 grass
1800
1700 heather
1600
1500
1400

grass

gate
old × fold

pen gate

Hobcarton Gill

1400
1300
1200

Swinside Plantation

1200
1100

1000

Hobcarton Plantation

Hobcarton Bridge

900

forestry cottages

800

Swinside

The final stages of the climb are described on the next page

Ascend by the right-hand side of the wall to avoid the trailing wires of the old fence.

Here is a strange scene — the graveyard of an old forest, with bleached skeletons of trees as tombstones

Turn up the steep but simple slope by the side of the second fence to gain the ridge. This is the only opportunity to do so in comfort. The further one proceeds up the valley the harder it is to get out of it.

Keep to the lower forest road through Swinside Plantation with Hobcarton Gill on the *left*.

In views from the road of this approach, it is the graceful cone of Ladyside Pike that most attracts attention : it appears very prominently.

TOP OF WHINLATTER PASS 1
BRAITHWAITE 3

Whinlatter Pass Road

Blaze Beck
gate

lane

HIGH LORTON 2½
COCKERMOUTH 6

The climb to the ridge by the fence is the one dull section in a walk otherwise full of interest, and, towards the end, quite exhilarating.

Leave the road at the gated lane 300 yards west of the cottages.

looking south

ASCENT FROM HIGH LORTON
2450 feet of ascent : 3¾ miles

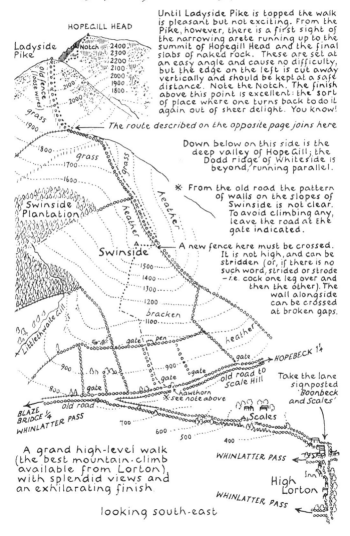

HOPEGILL HEAD

Ladyside Pike

Notch 2400
2300
2200
2100
2000
1900
1800

old fence (loose wires)

2100

2000

grass

1900

Until Ladyside Pike is topped the walk is pleasant but not exciting. From the Pike, however, there is a first sight of the narrowing arête running up to the summit of Hopegill Head and the final slabs of naked rock. These are set at an easy angle and cause no difficulty, but the edge on the left is cut away vertically and should be kept at a safe distance. Note the Notch. The finish above this point is excellent: the sort of place where one turns back to do it again out of sheer delight. You know!

The route described on the opposite page joins here

Down below on this side is the deep valley of Hope Gill; the Dodd ridge of Whiteside is beyond, running parallel.

1800 grass

1700

1600

slabs heather

heather

⁂ From the old road the pattern of walls on the slopes of Swinside is not clear. To avoid climbing any, leave the road at the gate indicated.

Swinside Plantation

heather

Swinside

1500

1400

1300

1200

bracken

1100

A new fence here must be crossed. It is not high, and can be stridden (or, if there is no such word, strided or strode – i.e. cock one leg over and then the other). The wall alongside can be crossed at broken gaps.

Littlethwaite Gill

gate pen

heather

900

gate

gate

gate

gate

old road to Scale Hill

HOPEBECK 1¼

800

gate

hawthorn ✕ see note above

Take the lane signposted 'Hopebeck and Scales'

BLAZE BRIDGE ¼
WHINLATTER PASS

old road

700

Scales

600

500

400

WHINLATTER PASS

A grand high-level walk (the best mountain-climb available from Lorton) with splendid views and an exhilarating finish.

Inn

High Lorton

WHINLATTER PASS

looking south-east

ASCENT FROM HOPEBECK
2150 feet of ascent : 2½ miles

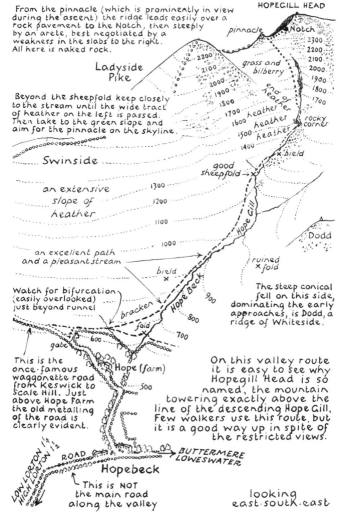

From the pinnacle (which is prominently in view during the ascent) the ridge leads easily over a rock pavement to the Notch, then steeply by an arête, best negotiated by a weakness in the slabs to the right. All here is naked rock.

HOPEGILL HEAD

pinnacle   Notch

Ladyside Pike

grass and bilberry

2300
2200
2100
2000
1900
1800
1700

Beyond the sheepfold keep closely to the stream until the wide tract of heather on the left is passed. Then take to the green slope and aim for the pinnacle on the skyline.

2200
2100
2000
1900
1800
end of heather
1700 heather
1600 heather
1500 heather
1400

rocky corner

× bield

good sheepfold →×

Swinside

an extensive slope of heather

1300
1200
1100
1000

Hope Gill

Dodd

an excellent path and a pleasant stream

bield ×

ruined × fold

The steep conical fell on this side, dominating the early approaches, is Dodd, a ridge of Whiteside.

Watch for bifurcation (easily overlooked) just beyond runnel

bracken
fold

Hope Beck

900
800
700

gate

This is the once-famous waggonette road from Keswick to Scale Hill. Just above Hope Farm the old metalling of the road is clearly evident.

Hope (farm)

600
500

On this valley route it is easy to see why Hopegill Head is so named, the mountain towering exactly above the line of the descending Hope Gill. Few walkers use this route, but it is a good way up in spite of the restricted views.

LOW LORTON
HIGH LORTON

ROAD

→ BUTTERMERE LOWESWATER

Hopebeck

This is NOT the main road along the valley

looking east-south-east

THE SUMMIT

The culmination of the rising lines of the fell occurs where the slender ridge coming up from Whiteside quite suddenly collapses in the contorted rocks of Hobcarton Crag, exactly at the point of junction of routes ascending the two flanks of the precipice to its apex. Thus, in the space of a few feet, is formed a small, neat summit, a true peak poised above a profound abyss, its delicate proportions uncharacteristic of the general expansiveness of the fell. It is a delightful top, fashioned for the accommodation of solitary walkers: large parties here are an intrusion. Slate debris litters the ground and visitors occasionally scrape a little together to make an insignificant cairn.

The summit is a favourite haunt of birds, which have quick selective eyes for good vantage points. The Hobcarton ravens make a fine sight as they soar and spiral above the gullies and rock battlements, often alighting on the narrow top to survey the domain of which they are undisputed overlords; and particular mention must be made of the regular summer visitations of swifts, which have a liking for steep cliffs and airy summits, and here dart and swoop through the air in an ecstatic and erratic highspeed flight, their whirring wings creating a commotion of vibrating sound.

This summit is a generous reward for the effort of reaching it.

DESCENTS : For High Lorton, Hopebeck or Whinlatter Pass, reverse the routes of ascent: they have a common start down the north slabs. Use a fault or groove away from the edge for safer foothold. In mist, this initial section looks intimidating, but step bravely into the void and go cautiously. Anybody who finds himself falling through space will have missed the route.

PLAN OF SUMMIT

Coledale Hause is quickly reached by following the natural slope down from the protuberance of Sand Hill, taking patches of scree in the stride. In mist, be on guard against two hazards, dangerous because unexpected: the fenced mine-shafts and the crag-edge of High Force; keep well to the right if these appear out of the gloom.

THE VIEW

The view is less comprehensive than the diagram suggests, the best part of the Lakeland skyline, to the south, being concealed by Grasmoor and Eel Crag, but in other directions, particularly west (across the Solway Firth) and east (to the Helvellyn range) the panorama is unrestricted. There is a satisfactory grouping of the Scafells just left of Wandope, however, and a quaint glimpse of Pike o' Stickle — a remarkable outline — between Sail and Eel Crag.

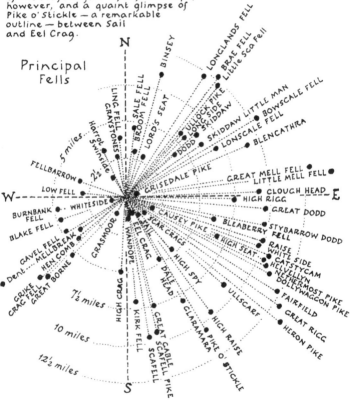

Principal Fells

Lakes and Tarns
NNE: *Over Water*
SE: *Blea Tarn (Ullscarf)*
WSW: *Crummock Water*

RIDGE ROUTES

To GRISEDALE PIKE, 2593′ : 1⅛ mile : SE, then E, NE
Depression at 2211′ : 400 feet of ascent

An interesting traverse around the head of Hobcarton Valley.
With the precipice close on the left hand, but not too close, go
down to the grassy depression south-eastwards, where a broken
wall is joined and followed upwards, first over a minor summit
and then on to the main top. The well-defined rim of crags on the
left throughout, plus the wall, makes the crossing safe in mist.

To WHITESIDE, 2317′ : 1⅛ mile : Generally W, then SW
Main depression at 2200′ : 150 feet of ascent

A splendid high-level walk with striking views of Gasgale Gill.
The way leads down the straight and narrow grassy west ridge,
becoming rough and rocky as it descends to a pronounced hollow
bridged by a heathery crest: this is the best section of the journey.
Beyond, easy rocks are climbed, or skirted on the right, and the
ridge widens although continuing sharply defined along the left
edge. In mist, the east top may be mistakened for the main top.

The ridge to Whiteside

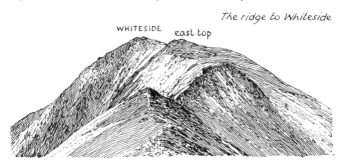

Knott Rigg

1790'
approx.

from Buttermere

Keskadale is the long arm of Newlands extending southwest and providing the only outlet for vehicles from the head of the valley. The road is accommodated for two long miles along the side of a narrow and steepsided ridge of moderate height before climbing over a pass, Newlands Hause, formed by the gentle termination of the ridge; lovely Buttermere is beyond. This ridge has two distinct summits: the higher, overlooking Newlands, is Ard Crags; the lower, overlooking Buttermere, is Knott Rigg.

Sail Beck, coming down from the Eel Crag massif, of which Knott Rigg is an offshooting spur, very sharply marks the western boundary of the fell.

EEL CRAG ▲

● Rigg Beck

▲ ARD CRAGS

● Keskadale

▲ KNOTT RIGG

≈ Newlands Hause

● Buttermere

MILES

0   1   2   3

MAP

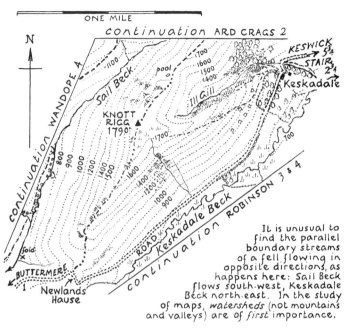

ONE MILE

continuation ARD CRAGS 2

N

continuation WANDOPE 4

1100

Sail Beck

pool

1700
1600
1500
1400

KESWICK
STAIR
Keskadale

KNOTT
RIGG
1790

Ill Gill

1700

800
900
1000
1200
1400
1500
1600

1600
1400
1200
1000
900

ROAD

100

Keskadale Beck

continuation ROBINSON 3 & 4

fold

BUTTERMERE

Newlands
Hause

It is unusual to
find the parallel
boundary streams
of a fell flowing in
opposite directions, as
happens here: Sail Beck
flows south-west, Keskadale
Beck north-east. In the study
of maps, *watersheds* (not mountains
and valleys) are of *first* importance.

looking down to
the Buttermere
valley from the
south end of the
ridge, with High
Stile and Red Pike
in the background
and the Newlands
road descending
across the side of
Robinson in the
middle distance

ASCENT FROM NEWLANDS HAUSE
720 feet of ascent : 1 mile

Upon reaching the ridge there is at once a fine view down the other side to Sail Beck and across it to the tremendous scarred wall of Wandope, Eel Crag and Sail.

Beyond the last outcrop the excellent turf of the ridge gives place to tougher grass, the summit being reached across a marshy plateau.

An advantage of solitary travel on the fells, greatly appreciated by all lone walkers, is the freedom to perform a certain function as and where one wishes, without any of the consultations and subterfuges necessitated by party travel. The narrow crest of the Knott Rigg ridge is no place for indulging the practice, however, whether alone or accompanied, walkers here being clearly outlined against the sky and in full view from two valleys. This comment is intended for males particularly. Women (according to an informant) have a different way of doing it.

Newlands Hause is commonly but wrongly referred to as Buttermere Hause

KNOTT RIGG

pools

summit now comes into view

outcrop astride ridge

grass

1500

pleasant grey rocks

1400

the ridge is reached between two small outcrops

1300

1200

grass

bracken

1100

depression

bracken

BUTTERMERE

Newlands Hause 1096'

ROAD

1000

Moss Beck

NEWLANDS KESWICK

looking north

Start anywhere across the gentle alp on the north side of the pass. From the little hollow beyond the thin track climbing up to the ridge can be seen ahead. This is one of a few paths in Lakeland owing their existence very largely to motorists exercising their legs from cars left at the Hause, where wide verges provide plenty of space for parking.

This is a simple and straightforward climb on the sunny side of the Hause, requiring an absence of one hour only from a car parked there. It affords a pleasant exercise, very suitable for persons up to 7 years of age or over 70.

ASCENT FROM KESKADALE
1000 feet of ascent : 1¼ miles

Upland *marshes* occur on almost all fells : on flat summits and plateaux, in hollows and on grassy shelves. They act as reservoirs for the streams, draining very slowly and holding back moisture to ensure continuous supplies independent of present prevailing weather. It is because of the marshes that the streams seldom lack water. They are safe to walk upon and cause little discomfort.
   Bogs are not functional. They are infrequent in Lakeland; there are no places bad enough to trap walkers, but some are a danger to sheep.

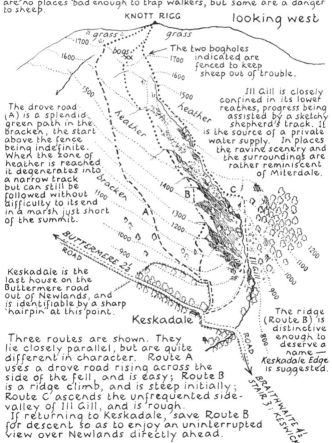

KNOTT RIGG

looking west

grass   grass

1700

1600

bogs ×× ← The two bogholes indicated are fenced to keep sheep out of trouble.

1700

1600

1500

1500

heather

heather

The drove road (A) is a splendid green path in the bracken, the start above the fence being indefinite. When the zone of heather is reached it degenerates into a narrow track but can still be followed without difficulty to its end in a marsh just short of the summit.

Ill Gill is closely confined in its lower reaches, progress being assisted by a sketchy shepherd's track. It is the source of a private water supply. In places the ravine scenery and the surroundings are rather reminiscent of Miterdale.

bracken

1100

1400   B   C

1300

1200

1000

900

A

BUTTERMERE 2½
ROAD

Keskadale is the last house on the Buttermere road out of Newlands, and is identifiable by a sharp hairpin at this point.

Keskadale

1200

1100

1000

900

ROAD

800

BRAITHWAITE 4½   KESWICK 6
STAIR 3

The ridge (Route B) is distinctive enough to deserve a name — *Keskadale Edge* is suggested.

Three routes are shown. They lie closely parallel, but are quite different in character. Route A uses a drove road rising across the side of the fell, and is easy; Route B is a ridge climb, and is steep initially; Route C ascends the unfrequented side-valley of Ill Gill, and is rough.
   If returning to Keskadale, save Route B for descent so as to enjoy an uninterrupted view over Newlands directly ahead.

THE SUMMIT

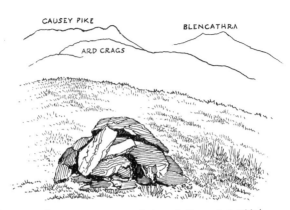

CAUSEY PIKE BLENCATHRA
ARD CRAGS

The summit, a grassy mound, is not the point 1772' as maps appear to suggest. It lies 400 yards beyond, across a marsh, and overlooking the valley of Sail Beck.

DESCENTS:

The simplest way off the fell is south to Newlands Hause, and the finest is via Keskadale Edge, but between these routes (assuming they cannot be located in mist) there should not be any trouble in going straight down to the road at the base of the fell.   Sail Beck is rougher to approach and saves nothing.

Considering that it is clearly in view to travellers along the Buttermere road and conveniently near, the side valley of Ill Gill is rarely entered. It has many charming features beyond its rather hostile portals and is worth a visit as far as a waterslide a quarter-mile in.

Keskadale Edge and Ill Gill

THE VIEW

Knott Rigg is so tightly sandwiched between the impending masses of Robinson and the Eel Crag range that an extensive view is not to be expected. The distant scene is not completely restricted, however, and eastwards there is a glorious outlook across the valley of Newlands to the lofty skyline of Helvellyn and the Dodds.

Principal Fells

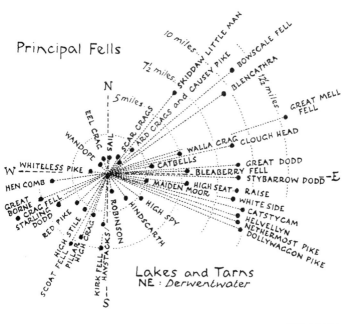

W — E

N

S

5 miles

7½ miles

10 miles

12½ miles

SKIDDAW LITTLE MAN
BOWSCALE FELL
CAUSEY PIKE
ARD CRAGS AND CAUSEY PIKE
BLENCATHRA
GREAT MELL FELL
SCAR CRAGS
SAILS
EEL CRAG
WANDOPE
WALLA CRAG
CLOUGH HEAD
WHITELESS PIKE
CATBELLS
GREAT DODD
BLEABERRY FELL
HEN COMB
STYBARROW DODD
MAIDEN MOOR
HIGH SEAT
RAISE
GREAT BORNE
CRAG FELL
WHITE SIDE
STARLING DODD
RED PIKE
HIGH SPY
CATSTYCAM
HIGH STILE
HINDSCARTH
HELVELLYN
HIGH CRAG
ROBINSON
NETHERMOST PIKE
SCOAT FELL
PILLAR
KIRK FELL
HAYSTACKS
DOLLYWAGGON PIKE

Lakes and Tarns
NE : Derwentwater

RIDGE ROUTE

TO ARD CRAGS, 1860' : 1 mile : NE
Depression at 1660'
200 feet of ascent

There is little fall in height for a furlong or so, then follows a gradual descent to a hollow occupied by a patch of gravel and a pond (sometimes dry). Thereon a better path rises through heather to Ard Crags.

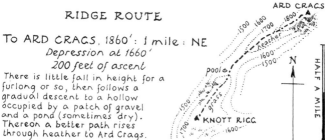

ARD CRAGS

KNOTT RIGG

N

HALF A MILE

1500 1600 1700 1800
heather
pools
grass
1700 1600 1500
1600

Ling Fell

from Sale Fell

Embleton

● Cockermouth

SALE
FELL ▲

Wythop
Mill ●

▲ LING
FELL

Shatton
Hall ●

BROOM ▲
FELL ▲

LORD'S SEAT ▲

● High
Lorton

MILES

0   1   2   3

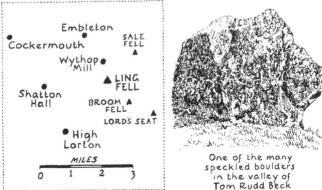

One of the many
speckled boulders
in the valley of
Tom Rudd Beck

NATURAL FEATURES

Ling Fell is an isolated rounded hill on the northwest perimeter of Lakeland, its unattractive appearance on all sides being accentuated by a dark covering of heather that makes it look gloomy and sulky even on the sunniest of days. Its lack of visual appeal, however, is somewhat misleading and belies its nature, for the easy slopes and commodious top are extremely pleasant to wander upon, heather, bracken, incipient gorse and grass alternating underfoot in colourful patches but never so densely as to impede progress.

The fell is one of the portals of the quiet Wythop dale, which lies alongside and behind, hidden and unsuspected, but is overshadowed by the higher western ridge of Kirk Fell coming down from Lord's Seat. In spite of its inferior height the Ordnance Survey have recognised its worth as a triangulation station and erected a stone column on the summit. This is almost the only feature of note, although the attention of geologists may be directed to a scattering of handsome white stones on the steeper southwest flank overlooking the little valley of Tom Rudd Beck, which has the function of draining the morass of Wythop Moss, a job it performs ineffectively. An insignificant spring on this side rejoices in the name of Bladder Keld — which is more than it deserves.

ASCENT FROM WYTHOP MILL
850 feet of ascent : 1½ miles

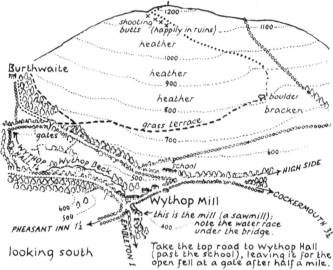

looking south

Take the top road to Wythop Hall (past the school), leaving it for the open fell at a gate after half a mile.

A simple and enjoyable walk, which ought to be, but isn't, a popular ramble for Cockermouth folk.

THE SUMMIT

Cockermouth folk haven't even marked their infrequent visits to the summit by building a cairn; but the Ordnance surveyors obviously have a greater regard for the highest point in this sea of heather and have selected it as a trigonometrical station.

THE VIEW

Broom Fell, rising just across Wythop Moss, severely circumscribes the view inland, but the Skiddaw group is impressive and the skyline of the Grasmoor fells is good —otherwise this is not a favourable station for viewing the hills of Lakeland and the main interest is found by looking away from it, to Criffell and the Galloway hills.

Ling Fell, however, is the best Lakeland height for seeing the town of Cockermouth.

Principal Fells

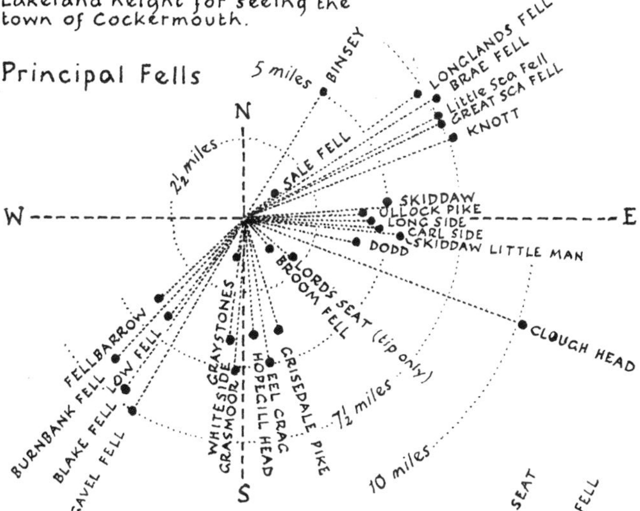

5 miles — BINSEY
LONGLANDS FELL
BRAE FELL
Little Sea Fell
GREAT SCA FELL
KNOTT

2½ miles

SALE FELL

N

SKIDDAW
ULLOCK PIKE
LONG SIDE
CARL SIDE
DODD SKIDDAW LITTLE MAN

W

E

LORD'S SEAT
BROOM FELL

CLOUGH HEAD

FELLBARROW
BURNBANK FELL
LOW FELL
BLAKE FELL
GAVEL FELL

WHITESIDE
GRAYSTONES
GRASMOOR
HOPEGILL HEAD
EEL CRAG
GRISEDALE PIKE

BROOM FELL (tip only)

7½ miles

10 miles

S

Lakes and Tarns
NE : Bassenthwaite Lake (foot of)

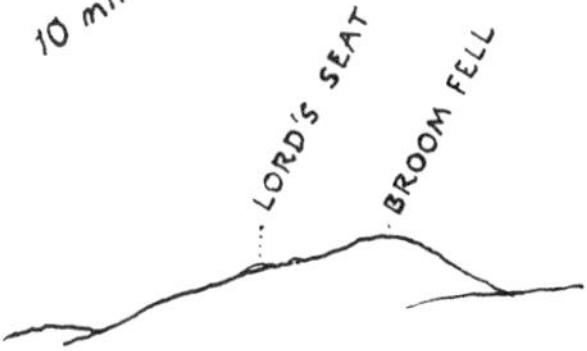

RIDGE ROUTES

Ling Fell is dome-shaped, like the top of a Christmas pudding. A Christmas pudding, in its pristine state, has no ridges. Neither has Ling Fell.

LORD'S SEAT
BROOM FELL

looking southeast

Lord's Seat

BROOM
FELL ▲

BARF ▲

LORD'S ▲
SEAT

● High
Lorton

● Swan
Hotel

Thornthwaite ●

Whinlatter
Pass ●

Braithwaite ●

MILES

0   1   2   3   4

*from a forest road
in Comb Plantation*

NATURAL FEATURES

Some mountains have better names than they deserve and some deserve better names than they have. Lord's Seat is a fine title for any ultimate peak amongst the clouds, and while the modest Lakeland fell of this name hardly aspires to the nobility it suggests it is a pleasing recognition of the commanding position and superior height of this central point in the distinctive group of hills comprising Thornthwaite Forest, between Bassenthwaite Lake and Whinlatter Pass. It is the pivot of this upland area, having four ridges radiating from the summit that enclose streams flowing north, south, east and west—all of which join later in the Derwent. Within the last forty years the fell has been given a dark overcoat of timber by the Forestry Commission, an operation that has detracted from its native appearance, but added to its interest. Once a fashionable climb, Lord's Seat is now out of favour — yet the heathery top is a pleasant lunching-place no less than of yore, retaining the indefinable charm of Lakeland in spite of the advancing march of the Norwegian and American spruces in all directions.

Two elevations on the descending ridges, Barf and Seat How, overlook the Vale of Keswick and are excellent viewpoints.

1 : The summit
2 : Barf
3 : Seat How
4 : Whinlatter Pass
5 : Comb Beck
6 : Comb Gill
7 : Chapel Beck
8 : River Derwent
9 : Beckstones Gill
10 : Bassenthwaite Lake
11 : Thornthwaite

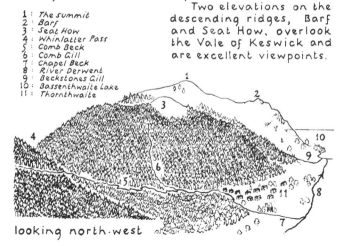

looking north-west

Lord's Seat 3

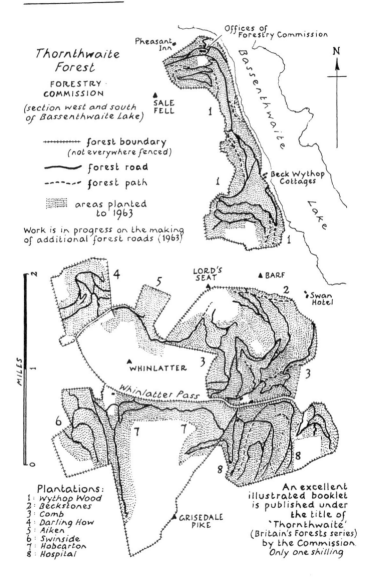

Thornthwaite Forest

FORESTRY COMMISSION

(section west and south of Bassenthwaite Lake)

++++++ forest boundary
(not everywhere fenced)

———— forest road

– – – – – forest path

▨ areas planted to 1963

Work is in progress on the making of additional forest roads (1963)

Pheasant Inn

Offices of Forestry Commission

Bassenthwaite

▲ SALE FELL

Beck Wythop Cottages

Lake

N

LORD'S SEAT

▲ BARF

2

Swan Hotel

4

5

3

3

▲ WHINLATTER

Whinlatter Pass

6

7

7

8

8

MILES

▲ GRISEDALE PIKE

Plantations:
1: Wythop Wood
2: Beckstones
3: Comb
4: Darling How
5: Aiken
6: Swinside
7: Hobcarton
8: Hospital

An excellent illustrated booklet is published under the title of 'Thornthwaite' (Britain's Forests series) by the Commission. Only one shilling

Lord's Seat cannot be ascended from any direction without an increasing awareness of the vast areas of this and neighbouring fells now under timber as a result of the operations

Thornthwaite Forest

of the Forestry Commission. Lord's Seat is the geographical centre of their activities south of Bassenthwaite Lake; on all sides there are plantations. Except for the slopes of Barf the full length of this side of the lake is now afforested, the old-established Wythop Wood being adopted and extended to a new forest fence along the top of the declivity, and further south the Beckstones and Comb Plantations cover the flanks of Lord's Seat, while round to the west the new Darling How and Aiken Plantations are creeping up to the skyline. Over Whinlatter Pass the Hobcarton and Hospital Plantations are firmly entrenched on the northern slopes of Grisedale Pike, and Swinside Plantation clothes the foothills of Hopegill Head. It is interesting to note that the tops of both Lord's Seat and Grisedale Pike are reached by the forest boundary, but not yet planted. All this wealth of timber is, for administrative purposes, known as Thornthwaite Forest, the name including also Dodd Wood across Bassenthwaite Lake and plantations nearer Cockermouth.

The newer plantings are coniferous, spruce predominating, and dense on the ground to promote upright growth. Approach to all parts of the forest, and removal of the timber harvest, is facilitated by a well-planned network of forest roads. The roads generally have a good dry surface and are excellent to walk upon, but one's sense of direction is soon at fault in these dark cuttings, which 'hairpin' and spiral considerably to gain height. This maze has largely come into being since the last revision of the Ordnance maps, but the author's map on the opposite page, compiled after a score of expeditions in the forest (without meeting a soul) corrects this deficiency and is complete to the end of 1961. Road extensions and new links are made from time to time as required.

A forest road
Comb Plantation

There is no objection to the public use of the forest roads (on foot) but (a) the gloom of the plantations, (b) the silence, (c) lack of views, and (d) the close confinement between evergreens, are more than many people can stand. The roads are occasionally, but rarely, useful in ascents of the fells, but, however, the forest has the advantage of being cool on hot days and sheltered on cold days and may then provide good walking when conditions on the open fells may not be tolerable. The forest should be avoided, especially the older parts, in high winds, when the veterans creak and sway alarmingly, and in gales, when dozens come toppling to earth — a circumstance in which the danger lies not in being knocked down and squashed by a trunk but in being pinned to the ground by a tangle of branches. Another *don't* is to wander off the roads, into the forest, where ghastly privations in dense jungle can be suffered before emerging (if at all) in rags. And *don't don't* for heavens' sake start fires, or there'll be hell to pay.

MAP

Thornthwaite Mine

An area of some acres of sterile, spoil-covered ground between the road and the railway north of the village of Thornthwaite is almost all that remains to be seen of the once-valuable and extensive Thornthwaite Mine. The head of the engine-shaft, which went down about 500 feet, well below sea-level, and served several long galleries at different depths, is amongst trees by the roadside further north. Other shafts and adits at higher points on the side of the fell have been engulfed by the Beckstones and Comb Plantations. The workings were far-reaching, following the line of mineral veins up to Seat How and beyond, and they were in use, with few interruptions, for hundreds of years until the early decades of the present century. A variety of ores was extracted but the mine was usually referred to as a lead mine.

A Forest Walk

At the end of the straight lane beyond the farm of Darling How, and also at the entrance to the forest road at the top of Whinlatter Pass, there are notices permitting access to the forest by the public but not in vehicles. It may be noted from the map that these two points are connected by a continuous forest road. This is a route of exceptional interest for walkers.

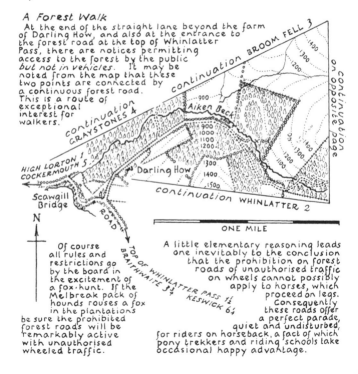

ONE MILE

Of course all rules and restrictions go by the board in the excitement of a fox-hunt. If the Melbreak pack of hounds rouses a fox in the plantations be sure the prohibited forest roads will be remarkably active with unauthorised wheeled traffic.

A little elementary reasoning leads one inevitably to the conclusion that the prohibition on forest roads of unauthorised traffic on wheels cannot possibly apply to horses, which proceed on legs. Consequently these roads offer a perfect parade, quiet and undisturbed, for riders on horseback, a fact of which pony trekkers and riding schools take occasional happy advantage.

MAP

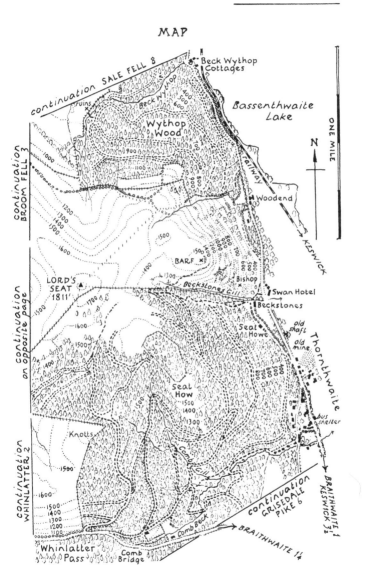

continuation SALE FELL 8

Beck Wythop Cottages

Bassenthwaite Lake

ONE MILE

N

ruins

Beck Wythop

Wythop Wood

continuation BROOM FELL 3

railway

Woodend

KESWICK

BARF ×

LORD'S SEAT 1811'

Beckstone Gill

Bishop ×

Swan Hotel

Beckstones

continuation on opposite page

Seat Howe

old shaft

old mine

Thornthwaite

Seat How

Knotts

bus shelter

continuation WHINLATTER 2

Comb Beck

continuation GRISEDALE PIKE 6

BRAITHWAITE 1½ KESWICK 3½

Whinlatter Pass

Comb Bridge

Comb Beck

BRAITHWAITE 1½

ASCENT FROM THORNTHWAITE
1550 feet of ascent : 2½ miles

The public footpath climbing through Beckstones Plantation is of long standing, though not now used as much as in years gone by, when the combined ascent of Lord's Seat and Barf was one of the fashionable tours. The path can still be followed, and is no less pleasant, but it has suffered some disturbance by the cutting of forest roads, two of which now terminate exactly on the line of the path. Although the fence indicates a possible route in the later (pathless) section of the climb, trees and thick heather on one side and a swamp on the other make it desirable to use one or other of the forest roads (it doesn't matter which) to gain another that doubles back at a higher level above the trees with the summit of Lord's Seat directly ahead across a rising slope of heather (rough going).

LORD'S SEAT

looking west

old fence

heather

1700

1600

heather

1500

forest fence

The forest fence is surmounted (not easily) to reach the top. A stile is needed here.

1400

new forest road

new forest road

1300

new forest road

1200

1100

1000

Beckstones
Plantation

900

800

old forest road

this road ends 15 yards short of the path, and may be passed unnoticed

600

Take the path rising through the wood

500

400

Beckstones

BARF

1300

1200

falls

Zigzag across small crag, right then left, to rejoin path above.

The bumpy summit across here is BARF

900

800

The Bishop

600

500

400

Beckstones Gill

MAIN ROAD

An enjoyable climb, full of interest all the way, but rather rough on the ankles in thick heather towards the end.

PHEASANT INN 3¾
COCKERMOUTH 8½

THORNTHWAITE ½
KESWICK 4¼

Swan Hotel
Bus route 34 (Keswick-Whitehaven)
or 37 (Keswick-Thornthwaite terminus)

ASCENT FROM HIGH LORTON
1550 feet of ascent : 4 miles

looking east-north-east

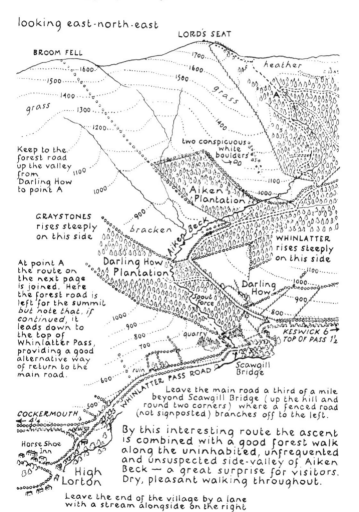

LORD'S SEAT

BROOM FELL

1700
1600
1500
1400
heather

grass

1600
1500
1400
1300
1200

grass

1100
1000

Keep to the forest road up the valley from Darling How to point A

two conspicuous white boulders

A

1100
1000

Aiken Plantation

GRAYSTONES rises steeply on this side

900
bracken

Aiken Beck

WHINLATTER rises steeply on this side

Darling How Plantation

Darling How

1100
1000
900
800

At point A the route on the next page is joined. Here the forest road is left for the summit but note that, if continued, it leads down to the top of Whinlatter Pass, providing a good alternative way of return to the main road.

Spout Force

1000
900
800
700

quarry

KESWICK 6 →
TOP OF PASS 1½

600
500

ruin

Scawgill Bridge

WHINLATTER PASS ROAD

COCKERMOUTH 4

Horse Shoe Inn

High Lorton

Leave the main road a third of a mile beyond Scawgill Bridge (up the hill and round two corners) where a fenced road (not signposted) branches off to the left.

By this interesting route the ascent is combined with a good forest walk along the uninhabited, unfrequented and unsuspected side-valley of Aiken Beck — a great surprise for visitors. Dry, pleasant walking throughout.

Leave the end of the village by a lane with a stream alongside on the right

ASCENT FROM WHINLATTER PASS
800 feet of ascent : 2 miles

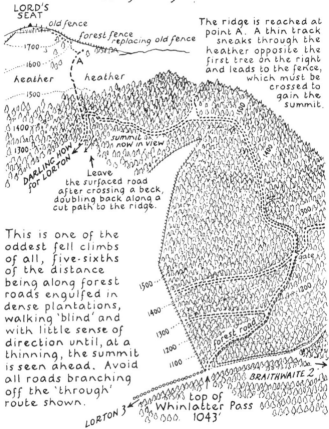

The ridge is reached at point A. A thin track sneaks through the heather opposite the first tree on the right and leads to the fence, which must be crossed to gain the summit.

Leave the surfaced road after crossing a beck, doubling back along a cut path to the ridge.

This is one of the oddest fell climbs of all, five-sixths of the distance being along forest roads engulfed in dense plantations, walking 'blind' and with little sense of direction until, at a thinning, the summit is seen ahead. Avoid all roads branching off the 'through' route shown.

A delightfully easy ascent — but silent gloomy forests aren't everybody's cup of tea!

looking nor'nor'east

Two forest roads (both with notice boards) leave the level top of the Pass. Be sure to start along the right one (i.e. the *left* on the diagram), just where the fence between the plantation and the open fell comes down to the main road.

THE SUMMIT

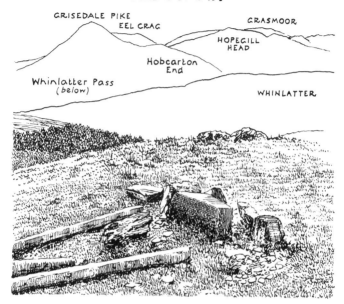

The summit is bare and open to the sky, refreshingly so if the ascent has been made through the plantations. There are a few stones and the scattered remains of three fences that formerly met on the highest point but which have been superseded by a new forest fence, which, out of deference for the freedom of the summit, crosses the top of the fell a hundred yards distant.

It is said that the name of the fell derives from a natural rock seat just below the top on the north-west side — but anyone who spends time trying to identify the place will question the legend, for not even the commonest commoner could instal himself in any of the few rocky recesses hereabouts with the standard of comfort his lordship would surely have demanded.

THE VIEW

The pleasantest scene is eastward, where there is a view down to the Vale of Keswick and beyond, in the distance, the far Pennines, with Cross Fell appearing on the skyline between Blencathra and Great Mell Fell. Southeast is the long line of the Helvellyn range; the little green oasis and white farmhouse seen in this direction is Ashness Farm. But note especially the nearby Wythop valley, north-west, rising as a green shelf and then plunging suddenly down a wooded declivity to Bassenthwaite Lake: an unusual geographical arrangement; above and beyond is an excellent view of the Solway Firth and Criffell. The Grasmoor fells conceal many of the central heights, which are revealed only in unfamiliar fragments above the skyline of Scar Crags.

Principal Fells

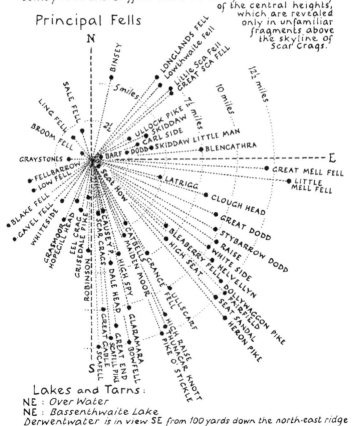

Lakes and Tarns:
NE : Over Water
NE : Bassenthwaite Lake
Derwentwater is in view SE from 100 yards down the north-east ridge

RIDGE ROUTES

To BROOM FELL, 1670' : ⅞ mile : NW
Depression at 1586' : 120 feet of ascent
Easy, uninteresting walking on a wide ridge

There is no path. Go down north-west from Lord's Seat to the obvious connecting ridge, which is marshy in patches, wide, and gently undulating for half a mile, without any definite col, before rising to the flat top of Broom Fell, where a wall identifies the highest point. *In mist, there may be indecision as to route but there is no danger in straying from the course.*

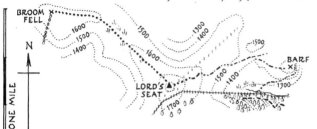

To BARF, 1536' : ¾ mile : ENE, then E
Depression at 1400' : 150 feet of ascent
Rough walking; best left alone in mist

Patches of thick heather impede progress, but sections of an intermittent track may be found by following the line indicated. Note that the far side of Barf's summit is craggy, and leave it by a path on the south flank.

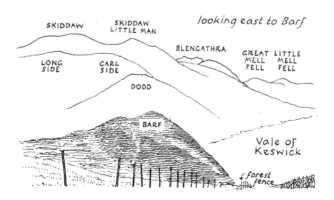

looking east to Barf

Maiden Moor

1887'

from Rigg Beck

- • Stair
  - ▲ CATBELLS
- • Little Town
  - ▲ MAIDEN MOOR
    - • Grange
- ▲ HIGH SPY
- Rosthwaite

MILES

0   1   2   3

from Scope End

NATURAL FEATURES

From mid-Newlands, Maiden Moor is seen to rise in three tiers: the lowest, rock-crowned, behind the hamlet of Little Town; the second, also craggy, above but some distance back; and finally the summit, set at the edge of a steep fall to the upper reaches of the valley. To the left of these successive steps is the wide hollow of Yewthwaite Combe, formerly a scene of mining activity but now a quiet sheep-pasture, below the slow decline of the summit-slope eastwards across a tilted plateau.

On the opposite side of the fell is the parallel valley of Borrowdale, to which Maiden Moor presents a steep slope of undistinguished appearance and a high level skyline, this being not the ridge but the plateau edge, the summit itself being out of sight.

Maiden Moor is the middle section of a very popular fellwalk, starting with Catbells and ending at Honister, along the spine of the ridge forming the Newlands and Borrowdale watershed. Both flanks are scarped — that facing Newlands almost continuously — so that, while the walk along the top is simple and pleasant, on grass, direct access from either valley is possible only in a few places without encountering rock.

The streams are small and insignificant; they drain into the River Derwent to the east and Newlands Beck to the west, joining, however, in the flat country before Bassenthwaite Lake.

1: The summit
2: High Crags
3: Knott End
4: Yewthwaite Combe
5: Yewthwaite Mine
6: Newlands Beck
7: Yewthwaite Gill
8: High Spy
9: slope of Catbells

looking south

The entrance to Little Mine — one of two small mines opened on the lower slopes above Newlands, in view from the old road leading up the valley.

MAP

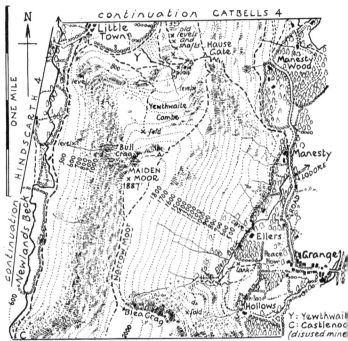

continuation   CATBELLS 4

Little Town

old levels and shafts

House Gate

Manesty Wood

Y

Pools

level

level

Yewthwaite Combe

x fold

level

Bull Crag

x fold

MAIDEN x MOOR 1887'

Manesty

LODORE

Narrow Moor

Ellers

Peace How

ROAD

Grange

Blea Crag

x fold

Hollows

Y: Yewthwaite
C: Castlenook
(disused mine)

ONE MILE

HINDSCARTH 4

continuation   Newlands Beck

continuation   HIGH SPY 4

In the vicinity of Ellers.......

Peace How

Ellers Beck flows alongside the grounds of Ellers, a natural boundary being provided by a long wall of rock bordering the stream. In this rockface is an attractive cave, directly behind the house of Ellers —evidence of old mining activity, as is a cutting in the nearby fellside

Bedecked with rhododendron and watered by a sweet stream this is Lakeland's most exotic cave

ASCENTS FROM GRANGE

via MANESTY
1600 feet of ascent
2½ miles

MAIDEN MOOR
best viewpoint
path goes on to High Spy
1700
1600
pools
1500
1400
Hause Gate
1300
1100
Black Crag
900
800
700

The path to Hause Gate is a popular one, but more commonly used for the ascent of Catbells (*turn right*) or the crossing of the ridge into Newlands (*straight on*). A track to the left soon becomes more distinct, with cairns, and leads up a curving ridge to Maiden Moor.

This is a beautiful climb, very suitable for those who prefer to have an unloseable path under their feet.

looking west

Manesty Band
500
400

Manesty

GRANGE ⅔
ROAD
ROAD
HAWSE END (for NEWLANDS or KESWICK)

---

via PEACE HOW : 1600 feet of ascent : 2 miles

HIGH SPY
Narrow Moor
MAIDEN MOOR
grass
Blea Crag
1800
sheep track
1600
heather
1300

There is no path above the falls. The final heathery slope is very much longer than it appears to be from below

Greenup
900
bracken
waterfalls
700
600
weir
500
Ellers Beck
400
cave

For further details of this route see High Spy 6

As far as the waterfalls this walk is delightful, but then follows a tiring trudge up a steepening, uninteresting slope.

water tank x
Swanesty How
Ellers
x seat
Peace How
Grange
school
MANESTY
ROAD
Hotel

looking west

Waterfalls above Ellers Beck

ASCENT FROM LITTLE TOWN
1250 feet of ascent : 1½ or 2 miles

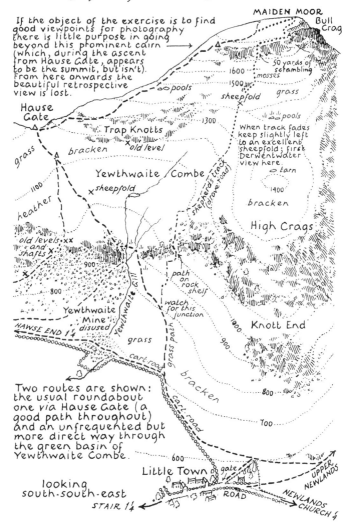

MAIDEN MOOR

Bull Crag

If the object of the exercise is to find good viewpoints for photography there is little purpose in going beyond this prominent cairn ⟶ (which, during the ascent from Hause Gate, appears to be the summit, but isn't). From here onwards the beautiful retrospective view is lost.

50 yards of scrambling

1600

1500

mosses

grass

sheepfold

pools

Hause Gate

Trap Knotts

1300

old level

When track fades keep slightly left to an excellent sheepfold; first Derwentwater view here.

tarn

1400

Yewthwaite Combe

sheepfold

shepherds track (drove road)

bracken

High Crags

grass

bracken

1100

heather

1000

old levels and shafts

900

path on rock shelf

watch for this junction

800

Yewthwaite Mine disused

Yewthwaite Gill

HAUSE END 1¼

grass

grass path

1000

Knott End

900

cart road

bracken

800

700

Two routes are shown: the usual roundabout one via Hause Gate (a good path throughout) and an unfrequented but more direct way through the green basin of Yewthwaite Combe.

cart road

600

Little Town

gate

UPPER NEWLANDS

looking south-south-east

STAIR 1¼

ROAD

NEWLANDS CHURCH 4

THE SUMMIT

Short of lying down with eyes at ground level and taking a few elementary perspectives, there is no way by which a layman can determine the highest point of the fell — and although the Ordnance Survey have been on the spot with instruments and arrived at their own expert conclusions they have left no sign of their visit, and there is no cairn. The actual top could be anywhere within a twenty-yard radius. All is grassy and uninteresting here, without as much as a stone to sit on or an outcrop to recline against, but those who feel the ascent has merited a rest can take their reward on the edge of the steep drop into Newlands, just west of whatever is decided as the summit. A track follows this edge, but the main path across the moor runs some 200 yards to the east.

DESCENTS : Join the path referred to (in mist, watch for it closely: in places it is little more than a flattened trail in the grass) and follow it *left* down to Hause Gate for Newlands, *left*, or Borrowdale, *right*.

Bull Crag is bull-nosed, i.e. in profile it appears as a rounded overhang

The Newlands edge from the top of Bull Crag, looking south-west

THE VIEW

A dreary foreground detracts from the view and unfortunately hides Derwentwater and Borrowdale. In other respects the scene is satisfactory, and especially good looking north. A cairn on the edge of the plateau where the descent to Hause Gate commences commands a much more beautiful though less extensive view.

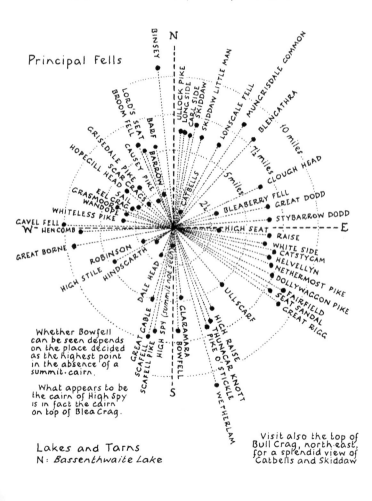

Principal Fells

Whether Bowfell can be seen depends on the place decided as the highest point in the absence of a summit-cairn.

What appears to be the cairn of High Spy is in fact the cairn on top of Blea Crag.

Lakes and Tarns
N: *Bassenthwaite Lake*

Visit also the top of Bull Crag, north-east, for a splendid view of Catbells and Skiddaw.

RIDGE ROUTES

To CATBELLS, 1481': 1½ miles : N.E, then N.
Depression (Hause Gate) at 1180': 310 feet of ascent
It must be something like this in Heaven

Cross to the cairn on the north-east edge of the plateau (this is a notable viewpoint), reaching this preferably by keeping to the rim of the crags. A good cairned path now goes down in a curve to Hause Gate, whence a broad grass path leads easily upwards to Catbells. Beautiful views.

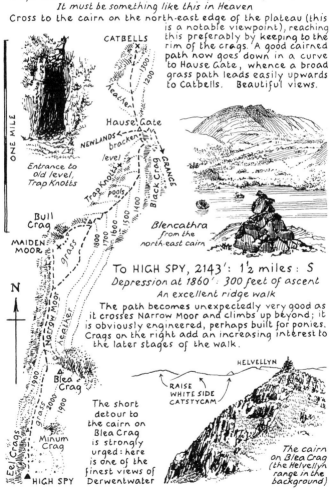

Entrance to old level, Trap Knotts

CATBELLS

Hause Gate

NEWLANDS   bracken   GRANGE
level
Trap Knotts   pools   Black Crag

Bull Crag

MAIDEN MOOR   grass

N

Blencathra from the north-east cairn

To HIGH SPY, 2143': 1½ miles : S
Depression at 1860': 300 feet of ascent
An excellent ridge walk

The path becomes unexpectedly very good as it crosses Narrow Moor and climbs up beyond; it is obviously engineered, perhaps built for ponies. Crags on the right add an increasing interest to the later stages of the walk.

Narrow Moor   heather

Blea Crag

Minum Crag

Eel Crags   grass

HIGH SPY

The short detour to the cairn on Blea Crag is strongly urged: here is one of the finest views of Derwentwater

HELVELLYN

RAISE
WHITE SIDE
CATSTYCAM

The cairn on Blea Crag (the Helvellyn range in the background)

Outerside

1863'

The
Abominable
Snowman?

No, only
the author

(Not that
there's much
difference)

Braithwaite
GRISEDALE ●
▲ PIKE
OUTERSIDE ▲ BARROW
▲
SAIL ● Stair
▲ ▲
EEL CAUSEY PIKE
CRAC

MILES

0   1   2   3

from Coledale

NATURAL FEATURES

The valley of Coledale, coming down straight as an arrow to Braithwaite, is deeply enclosed by a continuous horseshoe rim of high summits, from Causey Pike round to Grisedale Pike, but while the latter descends uncompromisingly in a very steep and unbroken slope, the opposite ridge of Causey Pike is accompanied by a lower and parallel ridge like an inner balcony, the fall to the valley being thereby interrupted. The main eminence on this subsidiary ridge is the abrupt summit of Outerside, and its position is such that it looks *down* into the vast pit of the head of Coledale and *up* to the exciting skyline of the surrounding ring of peaks. This secondary ridge ends in Barrow, overlooking Newlands, and above a thousand feet has a rich heather cover, which gives to the upper expanses a gloomy and forbidding appearance that is belied by a close acquaintance. Between Outerside and Barrow, but out of alignment like a dog's back leg, rises the lesser height of Stile End, which, seen from the Braithwaite approach, forms a noble pyramid.

Outerside springs quite steeply from the abyss of Coledale, and in a less distinctive company it would attract much attention. As it is, visitors rarely tread its pleasant summit.

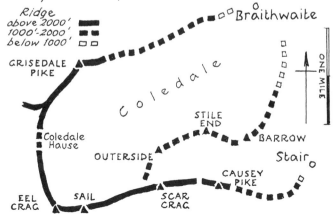

Ridge
above 2000'
1000'–2000'
below 1000'

GRISEDALE PIKE

Coledale

Braithwaite

ONE MILE

Coledale Hause

STILE END

OUTERSIDE

BARROW

Stair

CAUSEY PIKE

EEL CRAG

SAIL

SCAR CRAG

MAP

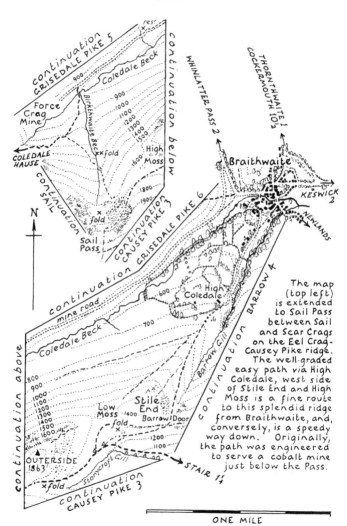

The map (top left) is extended to Sail Pass between Sail and Scar Crags on the Eel Crag-Causey Pike ridge. The well-graded easy path via High Coledale, west side of Stile End and High Moss is a fine route to this splendid ridge from Braithwaite, and, conversely, is a speedy way down. Originally, the path was engineered to serve a cobalt mine just below the Pass.

ONE MILE

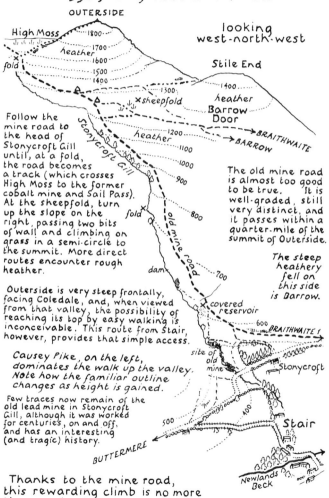

ASCENT FROM STAIR
1550 feet of ascent : 2¼ miles

OUTERSIDE

High Moss

looking
west·north·west

fold

Stile End

sheepfold

heather

Barrow
Door

→ BRAITHWAITE
→ BARROW

heather

Follow the mine road to the head of Stonycroft Gill until, at a fold, the road becomes a track (which crosses High Moss to the former cobalt mine and Sail Pass). At the sheepfold, turn up the slope on the right, passing two bits of wall and climbing on grass in a semi-circle to the summit. More direct routes encounter rough heather.

Outerside is very steep frontally, facing Coledale, and, when viewed from that valley, the possibility of reaching its top by easy walking is inconceivable. This route from Stair, however, provides that simple access.

Causey Pike, on the left, dominates the walk up the valley. Note how the familiar outline changes as height is gained.

Few traces now remain of the old lead mine in Stonycroft Gill, although it was worked for centuries, on and off, and has an interesting (and tragic) history.

The old mine road is almost too good to be true. It is well-graded, still very distinct, and it passes within a quarter-mile of the summit of Outerside.

The steep heathery fell on this side is Barrow.

fold

dam

old mine road

covered reservoir

BRAITHWAITE

site of old mine

Stonycroft

Stair

BUTTERMERE

Newlands Beck

Thanks to the mine road, this rewarding climb is no more than a simple uphill walk for nine-tenths of the way.

ASCENT FROM BRAITHWAITE
1650 feet of ascent : 2½ miles

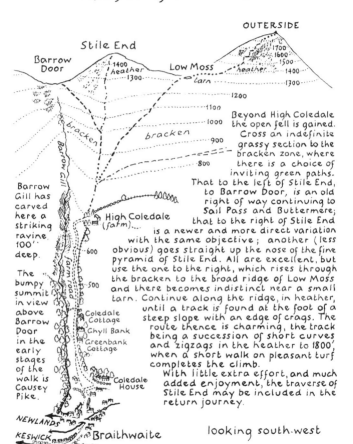

OUTERSIDE

Stile End

Barrow Door

Low Moss

Beyond High Coledale the open fell is gained. Cross an indefinite grassy section to the bracken zone, where there is a choice of inviting green paths. That to the left of Stile End, to Barrow Door, is an old right of way continuing to Sail Pass and Buttermere; that to the right of Stile End is a newer and more direct variation with the same objective; another (less obvious) goes straight up the nose of the fine pyramid of Stile End. All are excellent, but use the one to the right, which rises through the bracken to the broad ridge of Low Moss and there becomes indistinct near a small tarn. Continue along the ridge, in heather, until a track is found at the foot of a steep slope with an edge of crags. The route thence is charming, the track being a succession of short curves and zigzags in the heather to 1800', when a short walk on pleasant turf completes the climb.

With little extra effort, and much added enjoyment, the traverse of Stile End may be included in the return journey.

Barrow Gill has carved here a striking ravine, 100' deep.

The bumpy summit in view above Barrow Door in the early stages of the walk is Causey Pike.

High Coledale (farm)

Coledale Cottage
Chyll Bank
Greenbank Cottage

Coledale House

NEWLANDS

KESWICK   Braithwaite

bus shelter

looking south-west

Here is a simple climb that few walkers ever bother to do; and by this omission they deny themselves a lot of pleasure and a rewarding introduction to the grand circle of hills around Coledale.

THE SUMMIT

From the east the highest point is reached at the end of a gradual incline; from the west it appears abruptly at the top of a rising pavement of embedded rocks: here a few loose stones form a small cairn. The Coledale edge is close by, falling away sharply in an escarpment, and in mist this edge may be followed as a guide to a track down the eastern ridge, the only path off the top.

DESCENTS: The escarpment can be negotiated, with care, on initially steep ground if a direct way down into Coledale is desired, but there is little point in this since Coledale leads only to Braithwaite, which is more quickly and attractively reached by the eastern ridge (watch for a track in the heather) and then by a good path slanting down to the left below the rise to Stile End. For Stair, too, the eastern ridge is best, turning down to the right at the depression to join the Stonycroft mine road.

Sail Pass (left), Sail and Eel Crag from Outerside

THE VIEW

Outerside is severely circumscribed by the mountains around Coledale, which maintain a consistently higher skyline, and only between north and south-east is there an open prospect. The view lacks charm, but its intimate detail of the tremendous declivities amongst which the head of Coledale is so deeply inurned — a fine mountain scene — is very impressive. Who dare tackle Grisedale Pike direct from the beck after seeing its 2000 feet of near-verticality from this viewpoint? Only the brave!

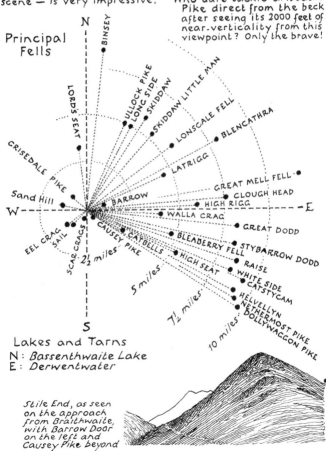

Principal Fells

N

BINSEY

LORD'S SEAT

ULLOCK PIKE

LONG SIDE

SKIDDAW

SKIDDAW LITTLE MAN

LONSCALE FELL

BLENCATHRA

GRISEDALE PIKE

LATRIGG

GREAT MELL FELL

Sand Hill

CLOUGH HEAD

BARROW

HIGH RIGG

W — — — — — — — E

WALLA CRAG

GREAT DODD

EEL CRAG

SAIL

CATBELLS

BLEABERRY FELL

STYBARROW DODD

SCAR CRAGS

CAUSEY PIKE

HIGH SEAT

RAISE

2½ miles

WHITE SIDE

CATSTYCAM

5 miles

HELVELLYN

NETHERMOST PIKE

7½ miles

DOLLYWAGGON PIKE

10 miles

S

Lakes and Tarns
N: *Bassenthwaite Lake*
E: *Derwentwater*

Stile End, as seen on the approach from Braithwaite, with Barrow Door on the left and Causey Pike beyond

RIDGE ROUTE

To BARROW, 1494': 1¼ miles: ENE, then SE and ENE
Depressions at 1380' and 1270'
400 feet of ascent

Rough walking in heather. Avoid Stile End in mist.

If the ridge is to be followed conscientiously, the traverse of Stile End must be included in this walk, although this middle height can more easily be bypassed between Low Moss and Barrow Door. Starting down the eastern ridge, keep always to the highest ground ahead; on Stile End this means a sharp turn to the right.

Outerside from Stile End

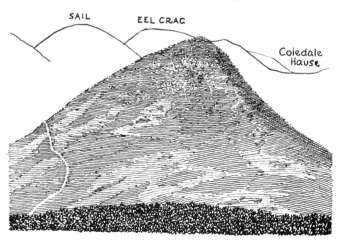

Rannerdale Knotts 1160'

● Rannerdale
▲ RANNERDALE
   KNOTTS
● Buttermere

ONE MILE

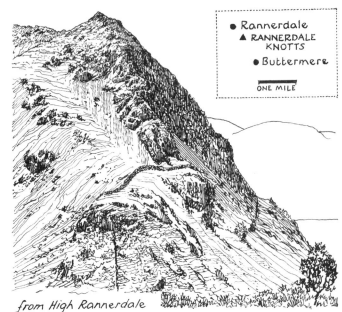

from High Rannerdale

Rannerdale is seen by most visitors to Buttermere —— but only as a farm and a cottage and a patchwork of fields on the shore of Crummock Water : a pleasant green oasis in the lap of shaggy fells, but unremarkable.   Passers-by sometimes tarry in the limpid coves of Crummock, or stroll along convenient paths in the bracken, but most hurry past, to or from Buttermere, unsuspecting that these few acres, now peaceful pastures, were once a scene of violent strife. Rannerdale has a lasting place in history as the setting of a fierce battle in which the Norman invaders were ambushed and routed by the English in the years after the Conquest.

Alongside the fields, and thrusting as a headland into the lake, is the abrupt and rugged end of a low fell that extends south-east for a mile, gradually declining to Sail Beck. All the excitement is concentrated in the dark tower of rock above the lake. Behind, a quiet valley isolates the fell from the greater heights in the rear.

This is Rannerdale Knotts, a mountain in miniature, and a proud one. Not even Gable has witnessed a real battle ! And, what's more, our side won !!

MAP

The name *Buttermere Hause*, indicated on Ordnance maps near Hause Point, has by this time almost lost its significance. It must originally have applied to the top of the old road (now a pedestrian path on grass) climbing over the headland, but the present motor-road closely follows the side of the lake, having been cut out of the rock, and is quite level. As far as users of the road are concerned, no longer is there a hause to climb on the journey to Buttermere from Rannerdale.

CONTINUATION GRASMOOR 3

CONTINUATION WHITELESS PIKE 2

LORTON

Crummock

Rannerdale Farm

fold

RANNERDALE KNOTTS 1160

WHITELESS PIKE 2

N

Hause Point

Water

ROAD

Low Bank

Squat Beck

fold

fold

fold

quarry

Sail Beck

SAIL PASS or RIGG BECK

ONE MILE

Church

KESWICK 8

HONISTER PASS

Buttermere

ASCENT FROM RANNERDALE
*800 feet of ascent
¾ mile*

looking north-east

RANNERDALE KNOTTS

Low Bank

1000

900

800

700

600

500

400

Rannerdale Farm

Hause Point

bracken

A green path starts up the fell from the top of the old road, keeping to a direct line along a rake with crags on the left. The path fades to nothing en route — more people start this climb than finish it!

BUTTERMERE ¾

Crummock Water

ASCENT FROM BUTTERMERE
850 feet of ascent : 1½ miles

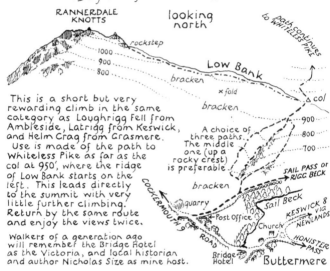

looking north

RANNERDALE KNOTTS

path continues to WHITELESS PIKE

rockstep

1000
900
800

Low Bank

bracken

× fold

bracken

△ col

A choice of three paths. The middle one (up a rocky crest) is preferable

900
800
700

SAIL PASS or RIGG BECK

bracken

COCKERMOUTH 9 ROAD

quarry

Post Office

Sail Beck

Church ⊞

KESWICK 8 VIA NEWLANDS

HONISTER PASS

Bridge Hotel

Buttermere

This is a short but very rewarding climb in the same category as Loughrigg Fell from Ambleside, Latrigg from Keswick, and Helm Crag from Grasmere.

Use is made of the path to Whiteless Pike as far as the col at 950', where the ridge of Low Bank starts on the left. This leads directly to the summit with very little further climbing. Return by the same route and enjoy the views twice.

Walkers of a generation ago will remember the Bridge Hotel as the Victoria, and local historian and author Nicholas Size as mine host.

THE SUMMIT

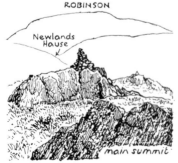

ROBINSON

Newlands Hause

main summit

second summit

A succession of rocky tors athwart the narrow crest gives a fine distinction to this modest fell. Glorious views in addition make this a place for leisurely exploration. Rock formations and striations are interesting.

DESCENTS : The best way off is along the ridge of the fell, Low Bank, to Buttermere, and, after an initial rockstep just beyond the second summit, is a very easy stroll indeed. In mist, the road may be safely reached by a straight descent to Crummock Water from the depression between the two summits, but not elsewhere.

THE VIEW

The view is confined to a distance of a few miles only, but makes up in charm what it lacks in extensiveness; indeed the scene southeast, over Buttermere, is of classical beauty. Crummock Water is much better viewed from a rocky tower 80 yards west, beyond a natural dyke. A feature of interest is the 'hidden' upper course of Rannerdale Beck, directly opposite, the four bends greatly accentuated by foreshortening.

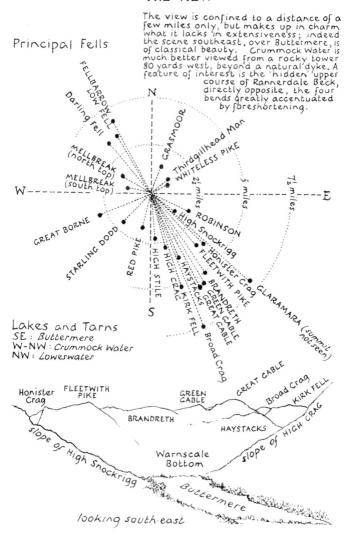

Principal Fells

FELLBARROW
LOW FELL
Darling Fell
MELLBREAK (north top)
MELLBREAK (south top)
GREAT BORNE
STARLING DODD
RED PIKE
HIGH STILE
HIGH CRAG
HIGH KIRK FELL
HAYSTACKS
GREEN GABLE
BRANDRETH
GREAT GABLE
Broad Crag
Honister Crag
FLEETWITH PIKE
High Snockrigg
ROBINSON
CLARAMARA (summit not seen)
GRASMOOR
Thirdgillhead Man
WHITELESS PIKE

N

W — — — — — E

S

2½ miles
5 miles
7½ miles

Lakes and Tarns
SE: Buttermere
W-NW: Crummock Water
NW: Loweswater

Honister Crag
FLEETWITH PIKE
GREEN GABLE
GREAT GABLE
Broad Crag
KIRK FELL
BRANDRETH
HAYSTACKS
slope of High Snockrigg
Warnscale Bottom
slope of HIGH CRAG
Buttermere

looking south-east

Robinson

2417'

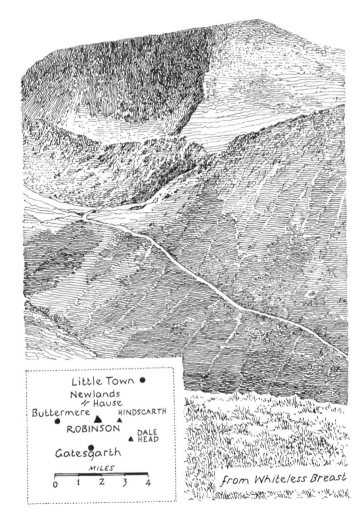

Little Town ●
Newlands
// Hause
Buttermere ● ▲ HINDSCARTH
● ROBINSON
▲ DALE
HEAD
Gatesgarth ●

MILES
0   1   2   3   4

from Whiteless Breast

NATURAL FEATURES

This fell with the prosaic name is, to look at, the least attractive of the group around Buttermere, a defect largely due to its position on the sunny side of the valley. Lack of shadow always reduces the visual appeal of mountain scenery, and on Robinson the steep slopes rise blandly to the sky with nothing in particular to attract the eye, nothing to exercise curiosity and imagination — in complete contrast to the darkly mysterious and more challenging heights across the lake. Robinson's summit lies back, out of sight, beyond a wide shelf at mid-height that serves as an effective gathering ground for Keskadale Beck: this wet expanse is Buttermere Moss, a bad place for walkers. Except for the neat apex of a lower summit, High Snockrigg, and a rough cleft above the woods of Hassness, Robinson contributes little to the scenic value of the Buttermere picture, and one must see it from Newlands to appreciate its distinctive skyline and the long ridge that characterises this aspect, its finest; while from Newlands Hause, too, where passing motorists are excited by a close view of Moss Force, it is strongly in evidence, here fringed by the half-mile precipice of Robinson Crags.

Robinson descends to Newlands in the close company of Hindscarth, which is almost a twin, and between them is the unfrequented valley of Little Dale, which tumbles to a lower level in a gorge thunderous with waterfalls that put many better-known ones to shame; here, too, is a small reservoir, built for mining operations long ceased and now a quiet pool.

Streams join the Cocker, and the Derwent *via* Newlands Beck.

1 : The summit
2 : Ridge continuing to Hindscarth
3 : Robinson Crags
4 : Buttermere Moss
5 : Moss Force
6 : Newlands Hause
7 : High Snab Bank
8 : Keskadale Beck
9 : Scope Beck
10 : Newlands Beck

grass

waterfalls

bracken

reservoir

bracken

pastures

looking south

It's a pity about the name, which derives from a Richard Robinson who purchased estates, including this unnamed fell, at Buttermere many centuries ago; thereafter it was known as 'Robinson's Fell'. But it could have been worse: this early land speculator might have been a Smith or a Jones or a Wainwright.

Robinson 3

MAP

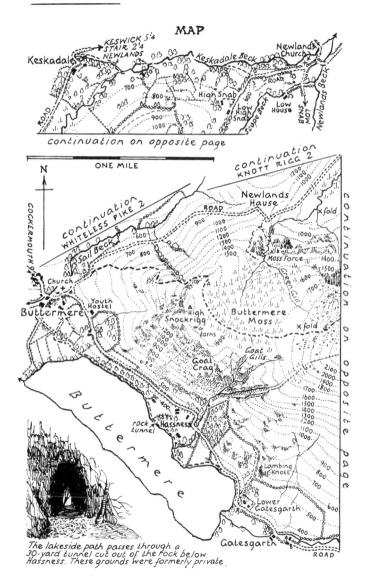

continuation on opposite page

Keskadale

KESWICK 5¼
STAIR 2¼
NEWLANDS

Keskadale Beck

Newlands Church

High Snab

Low High Snab

Low House

Scope Beck

Newlands Beck

LOW SNAB

ROAD

700

800

900

1000

ONE MILE

N

continuation KNOTT RIGG 2

1200
1000

COCKERMOUTH 9½

continuation WHITELESS PIKE 2

Newlands Hause

× fold

ROAD

900
1000
1100
1200
1300
1400
1500

Sail Beck

600
700
800

1000

Moss Force

1400
1500

Church

Buttermere

Youth Hostel

High Snockrigg

1200
1000

tarns

Scope Beck Gill

1600
1700

Buttermere Moss

× fold

continuation on opposite page

Goat Crag

Goat Gills

800
900
1000

2000
1900
1800
1700
1600
1500
1400
1300
1200
1100
1000

Buttermere

rock tunnel

Hassness

Lambing Knott

900
800
700
600

Lower Gatesgarth

500

400

Gatesgarth

ROAD

The lakeside path passes through a
30-yard tunnel cut out of the rock below
Hassness. These grounds were formerly private.

MAP

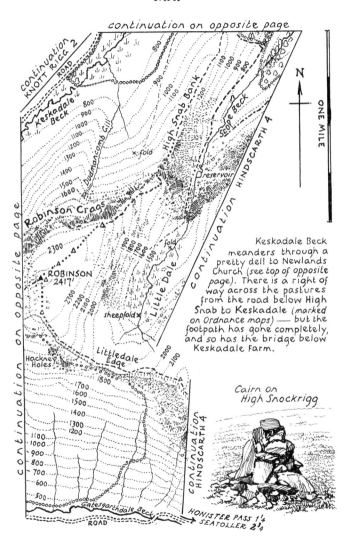

continuation on opposite page

continuation KNOTT RIGG 2

Keskadale Beck

High Snab Bank

Scope Beck

continuation HINDSCARTH 4

ONE MILE

N

reservoir

fold

Dudmancomb Gill

Robinson Crags

2300

ROBINSON 2417'

1900 1800 1700 1600 1500

fold

Little Dale

sheepfold

continuation on opposite page

2000 2100

Littledale Edge

Hackney Holes

1700 1600 1500 1400 1300 1200 1100 1000 900 800 700 600 500

continuation HINDSCARTH 4

Gatesgarthdale Beck

ROAD

HONISTER PASS 1¼
SEATOLLER 2¼

Keskadale Beck meanders through a pretty dell to Newlands Church (see top of opposite page). There is a right of way across the pastures from the road below High Snab to Keskadale (marked on Ordnance maps) — but the footpath has gone completely, and so has the bridge below Keskadale Farm.

Cairn on High Snockrigg

ASCENT FROM NEWLANDS CHURCH
2000 feet of ascent
3 miles

ROBINSON

looking south-west

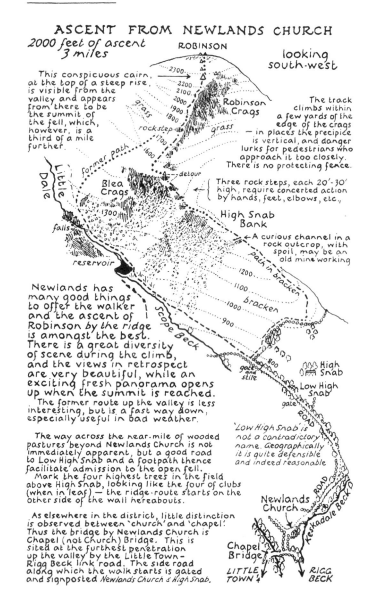

This conspicuous cairn, at the top of a steep rise, is visible from the valley and appears from there to be the summit of the fell, which, however, is a third of a mile further.

2300
2200
2100
2000
1800

Robinson Crags

grass

rockstep

1700
1600

former path

Little Dale

Blea Crags

1300

falls

reservoir

← detour

grass

The track climbs within a few yards of the edge of the crags — in places the precipice is vertical, and danger lurks for pedestrians who approach it too closely. There is no protecting fence.

Three rock steps, each 20'-30' high, require concerted action by hands, feet, elbows, etc.,

High Snab Bank

← A curious channel in a rock outcrop, with spoil, may be an old mine working

1200
1100
1000
900

path in bracken

bracken

Scope Beck

Newlands has many good things to offer the walker and the ascent of Robinson by the ridge is amongst the best. There is a great diversity of scene during the climb, and the views in retrospect are very beautiful, while an exciting fresh panorama opens up when the summit is reached.
The former route up the valley is less interesting, but is a fast way down, especially useful in bad weather.

The way across the near-mile of wooded pastures beyond Newlands Church is not immediately apparent, but a good road to Low High Snab and a footpath thence facilitate admission to the open fell.
Mark the four highest trees in the field above High Snab, looking like the four of clubs (when in leaf) — the ridge-route starts on the other side of the wall hereabouts.

As elsewhere in the district, little distinction is observed between 'church' and 'chapel'. Thus the bridge by Newlands Church is Chapel (not Church) Bridge. This is sited at the furthest penetration up the valley by the Little Town - Rigg Beck link road. The side road along which the walk starts is gated and signposted Newlands Church & High Snab.

800
gate and stile

High Snab

Low High Snab

gate

ROAD

'Low High Snab' is not a contradictory name. Geographically it is quite defensible and indeed reasonable

ROAD

Newlands Church

Keskadale Beck

Chapel Bridge

LITTLE TOWN 4

RIGG BECK

ASCENT FROM NEWLANDS HAUSE
1400 feet of ascent : 1¼ miles

Except for two short sections, the full length of the route is clearly in view from the Hause. The wife, left in the car, will be watching every move!

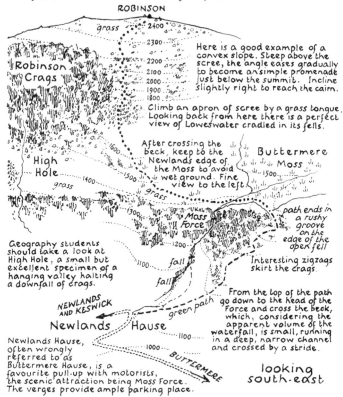

ROBINSON

grass 2400

2300
2200
2100
2000
1900
1800

Robinson Crags

Here is a good example of a convex slope. Steep above the scree, the angle eases gradually to become an simple promenade just below the summit. Incline slightly right to reach the cairn.

Climb an apron of scree by a grass tongue. Looking back from here there is a perfect view of Loweswater cradled in its fells.

After crossing the beck, keep to the Newlands edge of the Moss to avoid wet ground. Fine view to the left.

Buttermere Moss

1500

High Hole

grass 1400

1600
1500
grass

1300
Moss Force
path ends in a rushy groove on the edge of the open fell

Geography students should take a look at High Hole, a small but excellent specimen of a hanging valley halting a downfall of crags.

1100 fall
1200
fall

Interesting zigzags skirt the crags.

NEWLANDS AND KESWICK

green path

Newlands Hause

From the top of the path go down to the head of the Force and cross the beck, which, considering the apparent volume of the waterfall, is small, running in a deep, narrow channel and crossed by a stride.

Newlands Hause, often wrongly referred to as Buttermere Hause, is a favourite pull-up with motorists, the scenic attraction being Moss Force. The verges provide ample parking place.

1100
1000
BUTTERMERE

looking south-east

Motorists, having less energy than walkers, may be attracted by this opportunity of starting 1100 feet up and so shortening the climb. The ascent does not live up to its early promise, however, becoming very dreary at the level of the Moss. Wet ground cannot be avoided entirely, but the walk is generally better in this respect than the direct route from Buttermere across the Moss. Try to do it in one hour.

ASCENT FROM BUTTERMERE
2100 feet of ascent
2½ miles

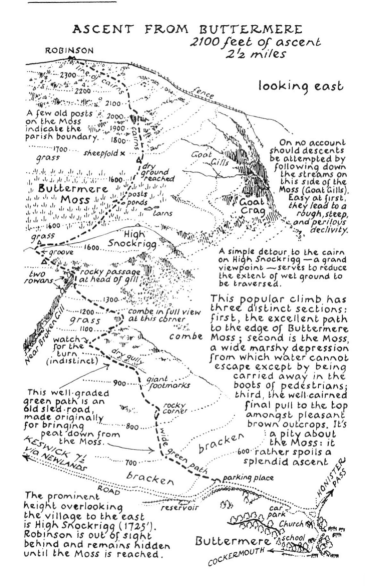

ROBINSON

looking east

2300 · line of cairns
2200
2100
2000
A few old posts · 1900
on the Moss · 1800
indicate the
parish boundary.

fence

1700 · grass
sheepfold ×
1600 · dry ground reached

Goat Gills

On no account
should descents
be attempted by
following down
the streams on
this side of the
Moss (Goat Gills).
Easy at first,
they lead to a
rough, steep,
and perilous
declivity.

Buttermere
Moss
posts
ponds
tarns

Goat
Crag

grass
1600

High
Snockrigg

A simple detour to the cairn
on High Snockrigg — a grand
viewpoint — serves to reduce
the extent of wet ground to
be traversed.

groove
two
rowans
rocky passage
at head of gill

1300

combe in full view
at this corner

grass
1200
1100

combe

watch
for the
turn
(indistinct)

dry gully

giant
footmarks

900

This well-graded
green path is an
old sled-road,
made originally
for bringing
peat down from
the Moss.

rocky
corner

800

This popular climb has
three distinct sections:
first, the excellent path
to the edge of Buttermere
Moss; second is the Moss,
a wide marshy depression
from which water cannot
escape except by being
carried away in the
boots of pedestrians;
third, the well-cairned
final pull to the top
amongst pleasant
brown outcrops. It's
a pity about
the Moss: it
rather spoils a
splendid ascent.

bracken

600

wide green path

700

bracken

KESWICK 7½
VIA NEWLANDS

ROAD

parking place

reservoir

car
park
Church
school

HONISTER
PASS

Buttermere

COCKERMOUTH

The prominent
height overlooking
the village to the east
is High Snockrigg (1725').
Robinson is out of sight
behind and remains hidden
until the Moss is reached.

ASCENT FROM HASSNESS
1900 feet of ascent : 1½ miles

ROBINSON

This approach is indicated as a right of way on the footpath map at Buttermere, but there is little evidence of anybody exercising the right, the start being pathless and uncertain and the walking both rough and steep up to 1600 feet.

looking north-east

2300
grass
2200
2100
2000
line of cairns
route from Buttermere
outcrops
grass
1900
1800
1700
grass

Buttermere Moss

The fence continues almost to the summit but to avoid wet ground ahead cross it here and ascend by a line of pleasant rocks. At the top of these a short traverse to the left leads to the usual cairned route from Buttermere.

1600

1500
Goat Gills
fall

Here the steepness ends and there is an open view ahead to the top.

1500
1400
A young rowan has secured a precarious roothold on this crag. Can it survive? Will some kind reader write to the author in 1970 and say it is still alive and well?

1400
1300
1200
Goat Crag
1100
1000
900
weir
800
700

feather

1100

A useful bit of vandalism has lowered the height of the wall and made it easy to climb.

900
800
700

600

There are striking views here of the tremendous ravines of Goat Gills.

Hassnesshow Beck
ROAD
BUTTERMERE
600
500

There is little sign of a path in the bracken of the first section by the stream. The upper end of the wall is rounded at a broken fence.

A small hurdle at the point where fence and wall meet indicates the place to leave the road.

lake Hassness →GATESGARTH ¾; HONISTER PASS

ASCENT FROM GATESGARTH
2050 feet of ascent : 3 miles

ROBINSON

HINDSCARTH

Hackney
Holes

Robinson
Crag

Littledale Edge

On this route there is little of immediate interest to see, but a short detour (100 yards) across the fence on the final slope of Robinson is worth doing to inspect the curious formations of Hackney Holes and Robinson Crag. Watch for the conspicuous end of a broken wall (which looks like a cairn from the road below) — this stands on the rim of the main hole. Some care is needed in exploration.

Littledale Edge has five features in a regular pattern. On the ridge is the PATH, bounded by a FENCE, over which is a shallow ESCARPMENT with a fringe of SCREE contained by a ruined WALL. All these — path, fence, escarpment, scree and wall — occur in a narrow strip over a considerable distance.

Turn half-left at the bend in the stream, keeping above the bracken.

bracken

The stream is subterranean in places, but its course is well-defined.

bracken

Keep to the Honister Pass road to the bridge, one mile from Gatesgarth. Nothing is gained by fording the stream earlier. From the bridge go immediately up the pleasant slope above. There are good views of the Pass as height is gained.

Hackney
Holes

end of wall

heather

TOP OF
HONISTER
PASS 1½

Gatesgarthdale Beck

ROAD

BUTTERMERE 2

farm

Gatesgarth

looking
north-north-
east

Those sojourners at Buttermere who would fain make the ascent of Robinson but shrink from the wet crossing of Buttermere Moss may well consider the route given above — it involves three miles walking along the Honister road, but is simple, pleasant, moderately interesting and bone-dry.

THE SUMMIT

Two long low outcrops of rock run parallel across the summit, the width of a road apart, almost like natural kerbstones or parapets — the westerly is slightly the higher and has the main cairn. The 'road' between is surfaced with loose stones. The top of the fell is a broad plateau with nothing of interest and no hazards.

DESCENTS: A line of cairns heads northeast for the Newlands descent: there is no path until the ground steepens suddenly beyond a superior cairn after a third of a mile. The Buttermere (direct) route goes off southwest: cairns and a track are soon found.

In mist, the top is confusing and bad conditions may make it advisable to find the ridge-fence as a preliminary to descent. For Newlands, go left alongside the fence to the first depression, where turn down left into Little Dale. For Buttermere, if the usual track cannot be located, the fence is a good guide to the intake wall above Hassness, the last part being very steep and slippery, and having dangerous ground immediately to the right.

Moss Force,
Newlands Hause

Goat Gills, Hassness

THE VIEW

The broad, nearly-flat summit detracts from the quality of the view, but although the valleys are hidden the surround of fells is excellent. Honister Pass, with the motor road snaking over it, is an interesting feature. It is odd to find Scafell Pike's towering summit for once missing from a view, especially as all its satellites are there in force: the Pike is exactly covered by the top of Great Gable, but its south-west slope going down to the gap of Mickledore is clearly visible. Robinson is one of the few fells that has the shy Floutern Tarn in its sights.

Principal Fells

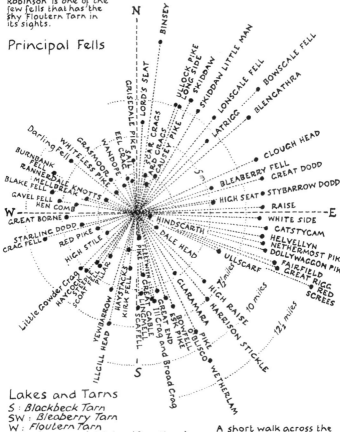

Lakes and Tarns

S : *Blackbeck Tarn*
SW : *Bleaberry Tarn*
W : *Floutern Tarn*
NW : *Crummock Water* (2 sections)
NW : *Loweswater*

A short walk across the summit northeast brings Derwentwater into sight NE.

RIDGE ROUTE

To HINDSCARTH, 2385': 1½ miles: S, ESE and NNE
Depression at 1880': 520 feet of ascent
A linking of two lateral spurs

Little Dale lies deeply between the two summits and can only be circumvented by using the fenced ridge to the south. There is a moderate track alongside the fence down to, across, and beyond a grassy depression. At the top of the rise leave the path on the right and bear left over the gravelly top of Hindscarth.

The north-east ridge of Robinson, from Scope End

Sail

2530'

Braithwaite

CRISEDALE ▲ PIKE

Stair

GRASMOOR   SAIL

▲   ▲   ▲   CAUSEY
        EEL   PIKE
        CRAG   ▲
              ARD CRAGS

● Buttermere

MILES

0   1   2   3   4

from Sail Beck

NATURAL FEATURES

Sail is the least obtrusive of the 2500-footers, being completely dominated by its vaster and more rugged neighbour, Eel Crag, and an absence of attractive or interesting features adds to its inferiority complex.

Sail is, however, an unavoidable obstacle on the way to or from the bigger fell by the fine east ridge rooted in Newlands, and the well-trodden path to its summit is invariably used for this purpose and not with Sail as the main object of the walk; indeed, the path does not even trouble to visit the cairn. The flanks of the fell are steep, excessively so to the south, above Sail Beck, with much scree and heather; northwards they fall more gently to Coledale, where, low down, they are traversed by the rising path from Force Crag Mine.

MAP

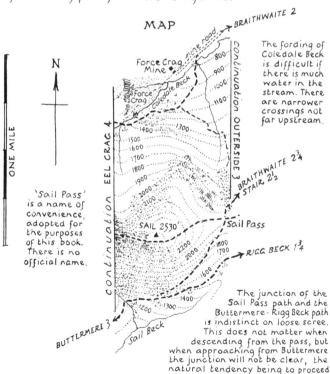

The fording of Coledale Beck is difficult if there is much water in the stream. There are narrower crossings not far upstream.

'Sail Pass' is a name of convenience, adopted for the purposes of this book. There is no official name.

The junction of the Sail Pass path and the Buttermere-Rigg Beck path is indistinct on loose scree. This does not matter when descending from the pass, but when approaching from Buttermere the junction will not be clear, the natural tendency being to proceed too far along the Rigg Beck path.

ASCENT FROM STAIR

2200 feet of ascent
3 miles

looking west-south-west

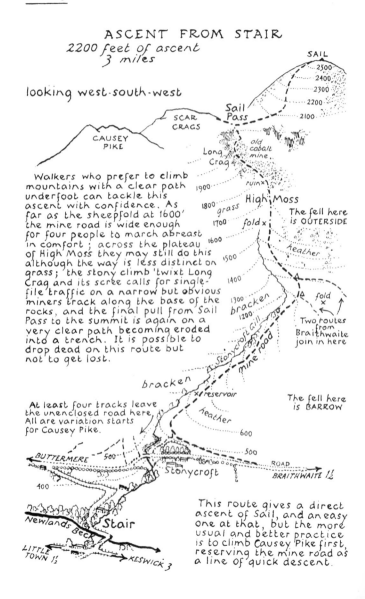

SAIL
2500
2400
2300
2200
2100

Sail Pass

SCAR CRAGS

CAUSEY PIKE

Long Crag

old cobalt mine

ruins x

1900

1800   grass

1700   fold x

1600

1500

1400

1300   bracken

1200

High Moss

The fell here is OUTERSIDE

heather

fold x

Two routes from Braithwaite join in here

Stonycroft Gill

mine road

bracken

x reservoir

heather

600

The fell here is BARROW

500

ROAD

BRAITHWAITE 1½

500

400

BUTTERMERE

Stonycroft

Newlands Beck

Stair

LITTLE TOWN 1½

KESWICK 3

Walkers who prefer to climb mountains with a clear path underfoot can tackle this ascent with confidence. As far as the sheepfold at 1600' the mine road is wide enough for four people to march abreast in comfort; across the plateau of High Moss they may still do this although the way is less distinct on grass; the stony climb 'twixt Long Crag and its scree calls for single-file traffic on a narrow but obvious miners track along the base of the rocks, and the final pull from Sail Pass to the summit is again on a very clear path becoming eroded into a trench. It is possible to drop dead on this route but not to get lost.

At least four tracks leave the unenclosed road here. All are variation starts for Causey Pike.

This route gives a direct ascent of Sail, and an easy one at that, but the more usual and better practice is to climb Causey Pike first, reserving the mine road as a line of quick descent.

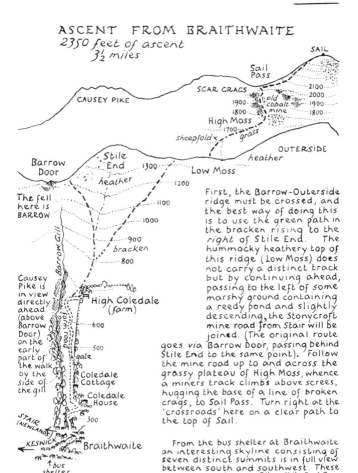

ASCENT FROM BRAITHWAITE
2350 feet of ascent
3½ miles

looking southwest

First, the Barrow-Outerside ridge must be crossed, and the best way of doing this is to use the green path in the bracken rising to the *right* of Stile End. The hummocky heathery top of this ridge (Low Moss) does not carry a distinct track but by continuing ahead, passing to the left of some marshy ground containing a reedy pond and slightly descending, the Stonycroft mine road from Stair will be joined. (The original route goes via Barrow Door, passing behind Stile End to the same point). Follow the mine road up to and across the grassy plateau of High Moss, whence a miners' track climbs above screes, hugging the base of a line of broken crags, to Sail Pass. Turn right at the 'crossroads' here on a clear path to the top of Sail.

From the bus shelter at Braithwaite an interesting skyline consisting of seven distinct summits is in full view between south and southwest. These are Barrow, Causey Pike, Stile End, Scar Crags, Outerside, Sail and Eel Crag.

This route coincides with that from Stair beyond a subsidiary ridge linking Barrow and Outerside, but is more attractive initially, being easier to the feet and having wider views. All gradients are moderate and this is the simplest way of getting a high footing on the Coledale 'horse-shoe' from Braithwaite.

THE SUMMIT

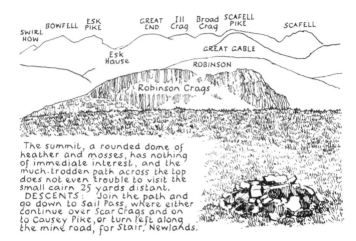

The summit, a rounded dome of heather and mosses, has nothing of immediate interest, and the much-trodden path across the top does not even trouble to visit the small cairn 25 yards distant.

DESCENTS: Join the path and go down to Sail Pass, where either continue over Scar Crags and on to Causey Pike, or turn left along the mine road, for Stair, Newlands.

RIDGE ROUTES

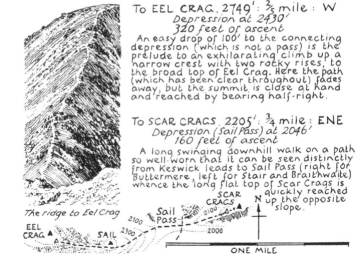

The ridge to Eel Crag

To EEL CRAG, 2749': ⅖ mile : W
    Depression at 2430'
    320 feet of ascent
An easy drop of 100' to the connecting depression (which is not a pass) is the prelude to an exhilarating climb up a narrow crest with two rocky rises, to the broad top of Eel Crag. Here the path (which has been clear throughout) fades away, but the summit is close at hand and reached by bearing half-right.

To SCAR CRAGS, 2205': ¾ mile : ENE
    Depression (Sail Pass) at 2046'
    160 feet of ascent
A long swinging downhill walk on a path so well-worn that it can be seen distinctly from Keswick leads to Sail Pass (right for Buttermere, left for Stair and Braithwaite) whence the long flat top of Scar Crags is quickly reached up the opposite slope.

ONE MILE

THE VIEW

Few walkers will hesitate long over this panorama, with the better viewpoint of Eel Crag so near (or just visited), but those who cannot go a step further without a rest may settle down to enjoy what is really a very fine prospect, although unbalanced by the disproportionate bulk of Eel Crag filling the western sky.

Principal Fells

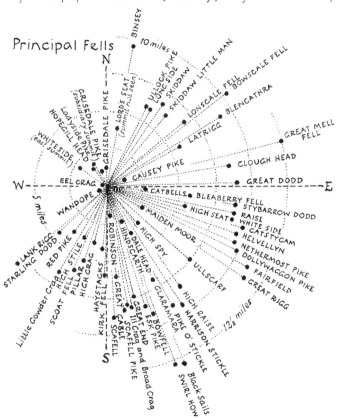

Lakes and Tarns

NNE : *Bassenthwaite Lake and Over Water*
ENE : *Derwentwater* } in view 10 yards from the cairn.
SSW : *Buttermere*
SSW : *Bleaberry Tarn*   SE : *Blea Tarn (Ullscarf)*

Sale Fell

1170'

from the Wythop valley

Embleton
•

Bassenthwaite
• Lake
Station

Wythop
Mill •

▲ SALE FELL

LING ▲
FELL

• Beck
Wythop

BROOM ▲
FELL

▲ LORD'S
SEAT

• High
Lorton

Thornthwaite

MILES

0   1   2   3

NATURAL FEATURES

Sale Fell is the extreme corner-stone of the North Western Fells, with an outlook ranging far across the Cumberland plain to the Scottish coast. It is a familiar sight on the busy Keswick-Workington road, of which it has an oversight for several miles; going west along this road, Sale Fell marks the end of Lakeland.

It is a pleasant eminence of low altitude, not remarkable in itself (although of some interest to geologists) and its main attraction to walkers will be as an easy promenade providing an aerial survey of the hidden Wythop valley. The fell is grassy, with bracken, but the eastern slopes, going down sharply to Bassenthwaite Lake, are within the boundary of Thornthwaite Forest, and thickly planted. This is an old part of the forest, long known as Wythop Wood, and there is a welcome blend of its natural growth of deciduous trees with the more-favoured evergreens introduced commercially in recent decades.

There is a significance in the name of the olde hostelry, the Pheasant Inn, at the foot of the fell. At one time this neighbourhood was actively engaged in the rearing of game birds. There were pheasantries at Lothwaite Side and in the Wood itself, within easy memory.

One very delightful feature of Wythop Wood is the presence of the lovely little roe deer, shyest of creatures. The new plantations are fenced off against them, but they have freedom to roam in the older woodlands, and the men of the Forestry Commission deserve a very good mark for tolerating and harbouring these gentle animals in their preserves.

Baby roe deer

born to be free? or to be hunted and snared and shot by brave sportsmen?

Roe buck

The Wythop Valley

The name is pronounced *With-up* locally. This quiet valley, almost unknown to Lakeland's visitors, is unique, not moulded at all to the usual pattern, a geographical freak.

The opening into it at Wythop Mill, between Sale Fell and Ling Fell, is so narrow and so embowered in trees that it might well pass without notice but for a signpost indicating a byway to Wythop Hall. Following this through a richly-wooded dell, the view up the valley opens suddenly beyond the farm of Eskin to reveal a lofty mountain directly ahead a few miles distant — a sight to stop explorers in their tracks. Of course all valleys run up into hills..... but what can this towering height be ?.... Hearts quicken.... have we discovered an unknown 3000' peak ? Wainwright's map on page 8 indicates no mountain ahead.... Get out a *decent* map, the Ordnance Survey one-inch — and the truth slowly dawns..... why, of course ....it's dear old Skiddaw, of course, not immediately recognisable from this angle...... But how odd! What an illusion! The valley certainly *appears* to lead directly to the mountain, *but*, completely out of sight and unsuspected from this viewpoint, the wide trench containing Bassenthwaite Lake profoundly interrupts the rising contours in the line of vision. The fact is that the Wythop valley, like all others, has hills along both sides, but instead of the normal steepening of ground at its head there occurs a sharp declivity to another (and major) valley system, the Derwent, occupied here by the unseen lake with Skiddaw rising from its far shore. The Wythop valley, elevated 600 feet above that of the Derwent, drains *away* from it, and the unobtrusive watershed (a meeting of green pastures and dark forest) may therefore be likened to a pass. The whole arrangement is unusual and remarkable.

Having described the valley as a freak, it is important to say also, and emphasise, that its scenery is in no way freakish. Here is a charming and secluded natural sanctuary in an idyllic setting, a place of calm, where a peaceful farming community husband the good earth now as for centuries past. Every rod, pole and perch of it is delightful and unspoilt. Motorcars can penetrate as far as Wythop Hall but happily are unaware of this. The valley is undisturbed and quiet; men still travel on horseback. There are five scattered farmsteads and, at the head, Wythop Hall, rich in story and legend. In days gone by the valley maintained a larger population and a church.

The Wythop Valley

The Great Illusion
(see opposite page)

Looking up the Wythop Valley to Skiddaw, from the slopes of Ling Fell. The furthest line of trees marks the end of the valley and Skiddaw rises beyond the unseen Bass Lake.

In this view from Lord's Seat, the Wythop Valley is seen sloping up gently from the left to the plantations of Wythop Wood, which fall steeply to Bass Lake. The distant hill on the right is Binsey.

Ladies Table

In Wythop Wood

Ladies Table is a little peak at the head of the Wythop Valley above the declivity to Bassenthwaite Lake and within the forest boundary. Now wooded to the top, at 950', it has lost its former reputation as a viewpoint. A flat boulder, probably used by Victorian picnickers, may have given the place its name, but more likely it is a gentle parody on Lord's Seat nearby.

Much tree-felling of late has cluttered up and partly concealed the paths in the vicinity, and a visit is not recommended. Former paths giving access to the Table from private woods adjoining are now fenced off. The place is forgotten and only the name remains.

The Walton Memorial

Perched on the edge of a crag in the heart of the forest, with a splendid vista of Skiddaw, is a memorial seat in native green stone, with a tablet inscribed "Thornthwaite Forest. In memory of WILFRED WALTON, Head Forester 1948-1959. In appreciation."

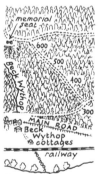

Bassenthwaite Lake looking southwest

Putting out pipes and cigarettes, follow the forest roads from the cottages as indicated, watching for the first turn left in 250 yards. *Don't let the children go on ahead : DANGER!*

Looking across the Wythop Valley to Lord's Seat, from Lothwaite

Lothwaite is the eastern shoulder of Sale Fell. A grassy alp, it is a pleasant sheep pasture and in summer is a floral garden. Apart from a solitary boulder and two strange circular heaps of stones like small tumuli — not cairns, and possibly (but incredibly) collected to keep the grass tidy — it is featureless. The suffix 'thwaite' is unusual for an open upland.

MAP

St.Margarets

At the side of a public footpath beyond Kelswick is the crumbled masonry of a small building that would be passed without notice but for a tablet inscribed SITE OF WYTHOP OLD CHURCH against the inner wall. (On Ordnance maps it is indicated by 'Chapel—Remains of')

This old church has been replaced by a new one — St. Margarets — on the road between Wythop Mill and Routenbeck, but once a year a public service (necessarily open-air) is held in the ruins.

Wythop Beck and Beck Wythop
— a clever distinction in names.
These are separate streams following widely different courses. The map has been extended in the south (next page) to illustrate how they come down from Lord's Seat together, side by side and almost arm in arm, until an insignificant watershed causes them to part company. Thereupon *Wythop Beck* proceeds to act as main drain for the Wythop Valley, escaping through a narrow gap at Wythop Mill to enter the broad strath of Embleton, and here it meanders, contrary to expectations, 'backwards' to Bassenthwaite Lake, joining it just north of the railway station (that's it at the top of the map, next page) after a circular tour around the base of Sale Fell. *Beck Wythop* has a much briefer passage, falling rapidly in its wooded gorge to join Bass Lake at Beck Wythop cottages.

Failure of an Enterprise
There is a story behind the ruins on the edge of the wood (south of Wythop Hall, map next page). Here are substantial foundations of buildings, and it is a great surprise to find them in so remote a place and in such rural surroundings. In the 1930's modern plant was installed here for the manufacture of silica bricks, a mineral railway laid, the road to Wythop Hall improved and re-routed and scores of workmen engaged. The product was not of sufficiently good quality. The buildings and plant were dismantled and taken away, the men dismissed and the site vacated. Today only the road-extension to Wythop Hall remains in use.

MAP

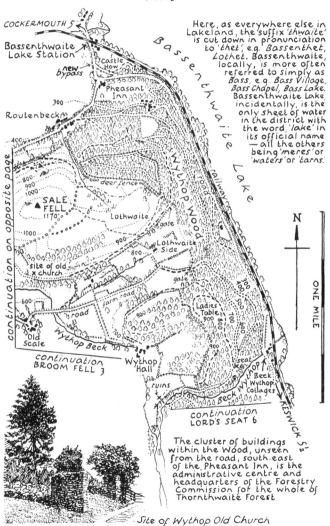

COCKERMOUTH 5

Bassenthwaite Lake Station

new bypass

Castle How

Pheasant Inn

Routenbeck

300

400

Bassenthwaite Lake

Wythop Wood

road

railway

deer fence

SALE FELL
1170

Lothwaite

800
900
1000

gate

Lothwaite Side

site of old church

farm road

600

road

800

900

gate

Ladies Table
900

700

Old scale

Wythop Beck

Wythop Hall

ruins

Beck

Wythop Beck

Lseat

Wythop Cottages

KESWICK 5½

continuation on opposite page

continuation BROOM FELL 3

continuation LORD'S SEAT 6

N

ONE MILE

Here, as everywhere else in Lakeland, the suffix 'thwaite' is cut down in pronunciation to 'thet', e.g. Bassenthet, Lothet. Bassenthwaite, locally, is more often referred to simply as Bass, e.g. Bass Village, Bass Chapel, Bass Lake. Bassenthwaite Lake, incidentally, is the only sheet of water in the district with the word 'lake' in its official name — all the others being 'meres' or 'waters' or 'tarns'.

The cluster of buildings within the Wood, unseen from the road, south-east of the Pheasant Inn, is the administrative centre and headquarters of the Forestry Commission for the whole of Thornthwaite Forest.

Site of Wythop Old Church

ASCENT FROM BASSENTHWAITE LAKE STATION
930 feet of ascent : 2 miles

SALE FELL

Upon reaching a broken wall turn right up the fell

At the highest point of the path, alongside a wall, turn left up the fell

1100

grass

sheep tracks

1000

heaps of stones

900

800

bracken

700

white cross on rock

deer fence

bracken

600

500

gate

gate

Church

WYTHOP MILL ¾

Wythop Wood
(a habitat of roe deer)

ROAD

400

Leave the road at a gate where an ancient (1911) iron signpost indicates 'Public footpath.'

Routenbeck

looking south

The Pheasant Inn is on Bus Route 34 (Keswick·Whitehaven)

Pheasant Inn

KESWICK 7½

Castle How (traces of fort)

Bass Lake Station is served by diesel trains (Keswick·Workington line) but scheduled for closure.

Bassenthwaite Lake Station

railway

Bassenthwaite Lake

COCKERMOUTH 5

White cross painted on rock (visible from the road). Origin and purpose unknown.

A pleasant little climb. Make a traverse of the fell by using both routes; preferably that on the left for ascent, that on the right as a way down. The round journey can be done in an hour from the gate at the roadside. Good views.

ASCENT FROM WYTHOP MILL
750 feet of ascent : 1½ miles

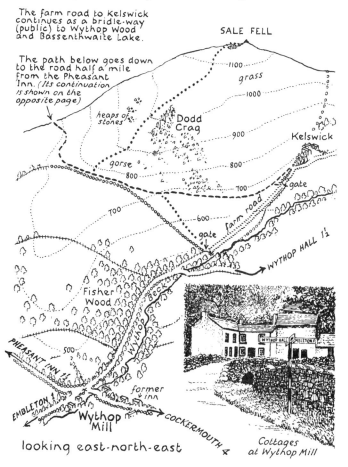

The farm road to Kelswick continues as a bridle-way (public) to Wythop Wood and Bassenthwaite Lake.

The path below goes down to the road half a mile from the Pheasant Inn. (Its continuation is shown on the opposite page)

SALE FELL

1100

grass

1000

heaps of stones

Dodd Crag

900

Kelswick

gorse

800

800

700

gate

700

600

farm road

gate

WYTHOP HALL 1½

Fisher Wood

WYTHOP BECK

500

PHEASANT INN 1½

former inn

Wythop Mill

EMBLETON 1½

COCKERMOUTH 4

looking east-north-east

WYTHOP HALL HILLTOP

Cottages at Wythop Mill

A sylvan approach gives added pleasure to this simple climb. As an introduction to the Wythop Valley (an introduction warmly to be commended) this route is excellent and instructive.

THE SUMMIT

SKIDDAW
ULLOCK PIKE
LONG SIDE
SKIDDAW LITTLE MAN
CARL SIDE
DODD

Lothwaite (subsidiary ridge)

Valley of the Derwent
(Bassenthwaite Lake below, unseen)

The top is a pleasant grassy pasture populated by sheep but unfrequented by man — which makes it a desirable objective on a summers day for anyone who would like to visit a summit for quiet meditation without, however, incurring the expenditure of much energy on the ascent.

For ordinary mortals there is nothing of interest in the vicinity of the cairn, but visitors with geological knowledge might add to it by doing a little exploring. John Postlethwaite's excellent *Mines and Mining in the Lake District* contains this impressive paragraph:— "Near the summit of Sale Fell, there is a small mass of very beautiful rock. It consists of a pink crystalline felspathic base, in which there are numerous crystals of dark-green mica. The base is chiefly composed of orthoclase, but some triclinic, probably oligoclase, is also present. There is no quartz visible to the naked eye, but small crystals may be detected under the microscope. There is also a little hornblende present. The rock is very hard and tough, and in lithological character is unlike any other rock in the Lake Country." (with acknowledgments)

All this is Greek to the poor layman, and he would be no wiser after an inspection of three possible sites: (1) a rockface in view from the cairn, (2) a collection of upstanding boulders, and (3) a scattering of 'white' stones, although he might notice that some of the latter appear to have been chipped by hammers. There is no other rock in sight, and one of these must be Mr.P's 'small mass', but, in spite of his liberal detail, which? What is 'orthoclase'? Or, worse still, 'oligoclase'? Resuming his meditations at the cairn after this abortive tour, let him now reflect on the poverty of his education. How much there is to learn about this fair earth and how little we know! How much beauty is never seen!

stones
boulders
rockface
grass
N
100 YARDS

THE VIEW

The Skiddaw group is the best thing in the view, the top being displayed, not as the usual pyramid but as a long, level skyline. The Helvellyn range is also well seen as a tremendous wall running across the district, but elsewhere the prospect towards Lakeland is disappointing, the higher Lord's Seat nearby concealing the mountains of the interior. The Wythop valley below is very pleasant, a restful hollow of woodlands and green fields.   Criffell is conspicuous on a Scottish horizon extending west to the hills of Galloway.

Lakes and Tarns
NE : *Bassenthwaite Lake*

Principal Fells

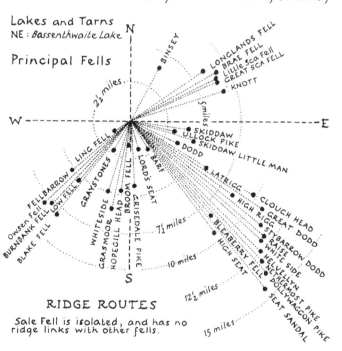

RIDGE ROUTES

Sale Fell is isolated, and has no ridge links with other fells.

A note for sheep fanciers :

The oldest strain of sheep in Lakeland is the Herdwick, a small, ragged but very hardy breed, tough enough to winter on the tops, and producer of the best mutton.   Latterly, the Swaledale and the Rough Fell varieties, bigger animals with a heavier crop of wool but needing the shelter of the valleys in winter, have been increasingly introduced.   The sheep on Sale Fell are a cross between Herdwick and Swaledale and so combine the best qualities of each — but only in half-measure.

Scar Crags

2205'

the eastern ridge

Scar Crags is the big brother of Causey Pike, topping the latter by 170 feet, but it is the lesser height that captures the fancy, that provides the challenge, that steals the picture and is the better known by far. Scar Crags continues the line of the ridge towards Eel Crag, and does so in rather striking fashion, having a ragged edge of broken heathery crag throughout its length, and, below, an excessively rough slope falls steeply to Rigg Beck. There is a regular and recurring pattern of arete and gully on this southern face, as though the fellside had been scraped by a giant comb: an effect best seen from Ard Crags directly opposite. The north flank has nothing of interest; once however it was the scene of unusual industrial activity, Lakeland's only cobalt mine being situated here in the stony amphitheatre of Long Crag.

West of the summit, the fell drops gently to Sail Pass, a useful crossing between Braithwaite and Buttermere for travellers on foot.

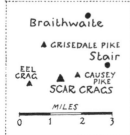

Braithwaite

▲ GRISEDALE PIKE

Stair ●

EEL CRAG ▲

▲ CAUSEY PIKE
SCAR CRAGS

MILES

0   1   2   3

MAP

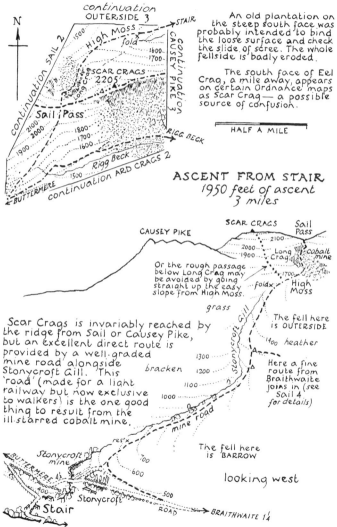

N

continuation
OUTERSIDE 3

STAIR

High Moss
fold

1500

1600
1700

SCAR CRAGS
2205'

continuation SAIL 2

continuation
CAUSEY PIKE 3

Sail Pass

2100
2000

1900

1800
1700
1600

RIGG BECK

2000

Rigg Beck

1500

BUTTERMERE

continuation ARD CRAGS 2

An old plantation on the steep south face was probably intended to bind the loose surface and check the slide of scree. The whole fellside is badly eroded.

The south face of Eel Crag, a mile away, appears on certain Ordnance maps as Scar Crag — a possible source of confusion.

HALF A MILE

ASCENT FROM STAIR
1950 feet of ascent
3 miles

SCAR CRAGS   Sail Pass

CAUSEY PIKE

2100
2000
1900

Long Crag

cobalt mine

1700

fold

High Moss

Or the rough passage below Long Crag may be avoided by going straight up the easy slope from High Moss.

grass

The fell here is OUTERSIDE

Scar Crags is invariably reached by the ridge from Sail or Causey Pike, but an excellent direct route is provided by a well-graded mine road alongside Stonycroft Gill. This 'road' (made for a light railway but now exclusive to walkers) is the one good thing to result from the ill-starred cobalt mine.

Stonycroft Gill

1400 heather

Here a fine route from Braithwaite joins in (see Sail 4 for details)

1300

bracken   1200

1100

mine road

1000

res'x

Stonycroft mine

700

600

The fell here is BARROW

looking west

BUTTERMERE 4½

400

500

Stonycroft

ROAD

BRAITHWAITE 1¼

Stair

THE SUMMIT

looking down to Causey Pike

Unexpectedly the top is flat, and there is no obvious sign of the double breaking wave formed by the summit outline as seen from the Keswick area, although this can be identified after a study of the ground. The largest cairn is not on the highest point, which overlooks Causey Pike (as illustrated). The top is grassy.

DESCENTS: It is usual to descend by the ridge, *via* Causey Pike, but simpler and quicker to go down the north slope (no path) to join the Stonycroft mine road. The south slope is impossible.

RIDGE ROUTES

To SAIL, 2530': ¾ mile : WSW
Depression (Sail Pass) at 2046'
500 feet of ascent
Sail is the next unavoidable obstacle on the ridge to Eel Crag, and calls for a long pull beyond Sail Pass (a walkers' crossroads) on a very distinct path.

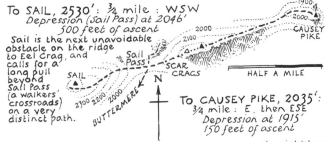

To CAUSEY PIKE, 2035':
¾ mile : E. then ESE
Depression at 1915'
150 feet of ascent

Keeping the steep edge on the right hand, a pleasant track leads down to a depression, beyond which is a short climb and a switchback journey over the several bumps of Causey Pike to the last one.

THE VIEW

The view is good, but its detail is not so well composed as in the panorama from the neighbouring Causey Pike, while the advantage in altitude contributes little extra to the scene; in particular the valley and lake scenery between north and east is less satisfactory. The mountain picture is inspiring, however, especially to the south, and close by in the west the head of Coledale is very well displayed. The more intimate peep downwards to Rigg Beck from the edge of the crags near at hand should not be omitted.

Principal Fells

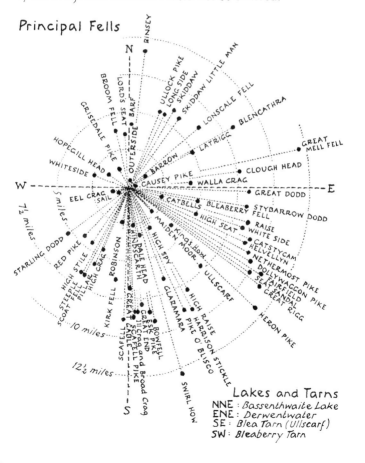

Lakes and Tarns

NNE : Bassenthwaite Lake
ENE : Derwentwater
SE : Blea Tarn (Ullscarf)
SW : Bleaberry Tarn

Wandope

'Wanlope' on recent issues
of Ordnance Survey maps

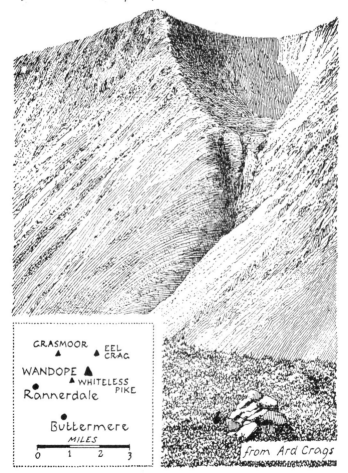

GRASMOOR ▲

EEL
CRAG ▲

WANDOPE ▲
▲ WHITELESS
PIKE

● Rannerdale

● Buttermere

MILES

0   1   2   3

from Ard Crags

NATURAL FEATURES

There is no mountain not worth climbing, and any summit above the magic figure of 2,500 feet might be expected to attract fellwalkers and peakbaggers in large numbers. To some extent Wandope does this, but only because the top almost gets in the way of a popular triangular tour based on Buttermere — Whiteless Pike, Eel Crag, Grasmoor — and the cairn is visited almost as a matter of course (if indeed it is noticed at all) and by the simplest of detours.   The other three, too, feature more prominently in the landscape and are often climbed individually as sole objectives — but rarely Wandope, which is sandwiched between neighbours and too hidden to attract separate attention.   In fact, Wandope is only well seen from the uninhabited valley of Sail Beck, from which it rises in a mile-long wall rimmed a thousand feet above by a line of shattered crags.   The hinterland of the summit is an upland prairie dominated by Grasmoor and Eel Crag, and it is along here that most walkers pass, often without realising that the insignificant swell of grass on the eastern fringe is distinguished both by a name and an altitude above the 2500' contour.

Wandope might be expected to stand out more conspicuously from the greater mass behind, for it is partly severed by two gills which drain from the plateau and immediately form, on either side, deeply carved rifts, one a scree-choked ravine, the other a profound hollow.   These are Third Gill, south, and Addacomb Gill, north, and both go down to Sail Beck. The first is a place to avoid, the second a place to visit or at least look at from the rim of its crater: the profound cwm is Addacomb Hole, a perfect example of a hanging valley, quite the finest in Lakeland, and a remarkable specimen of natural sculpturing. The issuing stream has high waterfalls and the whole scene is a complete geography lesson without words.   Wandope is also a feeder of Rannerdale Beck.

As for the name, many generations of Lakeland walkers have known the fell as Wandope (Wandup a century ago). Now the Ordnance Survey claim good authority for naming it Wanlope and up-and-coming walkers in future will no doubt use this new spelling without question. But old-timers never will.

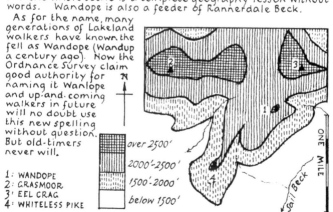

over 2500'

2000'-2500'

1500'-2000'

below 1500'

1: WANDOPE
2: GRASMOOR
3: EEL CRAG
4: WHITELESS PIKE

The Addacomb Ridge,
from Sail Beck

The Thirdgill Ridge,
from Whiteless Breast

MAP

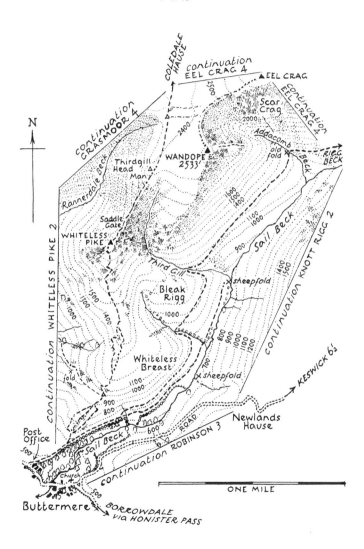

ASCENT FROM BUTTERMERE
via THIRD GILL

2250 feet of ascent
2¾ miles

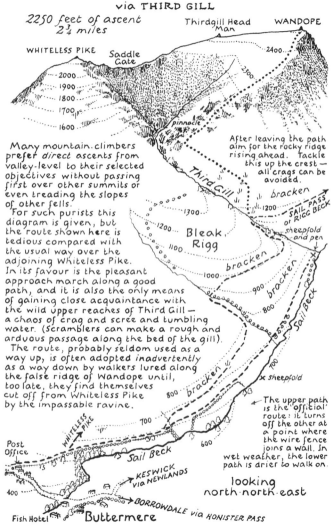

WHITELESS PIKE — Saddle Gate — Thirdgill Head Man — WANDOPE

2400
2000 1900 1800 1700 1600
2300
pinnacle
Third Gill

After leaving the path aim for the rocky ridge rising ahead. Tackle this up the crest — all crags can be avoided.

bracken
SAIL PASS or RIGG BECK
1200
sheepfold and pen

Many mountain climbers prefer *direct* ascents from valley-level to their selected objectives without passing first over other summits or even treading the slopes of other fells.

For such purists this diagram is given, but the route shown here is tedious compared with the usual way over the adjoining Whiteless Pike. In its favour is the pleasant approach march along a good path, and it is also the only means of gaining close acquaintance with the wild upper reaches of Third Gill — a chaos of crag and scree and tumbling water. (Scramblers can make a rough and arduous passage along the bed of the gill).

The route, probably seldom used as a way up, is often adopted inadvertently as a way down by walkers lured along the false ridge of Wandope until, too late, they find themselves cut off from Whiteless Pike by the impassable ravine.

1300
1200
Bleak Rigg
1100
1000
bracken
900
800
bracken
Sail Beck

700
x sheepfold

800 bracken

700
600

The upper path is the 'official' route: it turns off the other at a point where the wire fence joins a wall. In wet weather, the lower path is drier to walk on.

Post Office
WHITELESS PIKE
Sail Beck
400
Fish Hotel
Buttermere

→ KESWICK via NEWLANDS
→ BORROWDALE via HONISTER PASS

looking north-north-east

ASCENT FROM BUTTERMERE
via THE ADDACOMB RIDGE

2250 feet of ascent
3½ miles

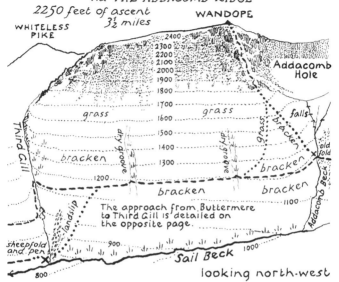

WHITELESS PIKE

WANDOPE

Addacomb Hole

2400
2300
2200
2100
2000
1900
1800
1700
1600
1500
1400
1300
1200
1100
1000
900
800

grass

grass

grass

bracken

falls

dry groove

dry groove

bracken

bracken

bracken

Third Gill

landslip

old fold

Addacomb Beck

sheepfold and pen

Sail Beck

The approach from Buttermere to Third Gill is detailed on the opposite page.

looking north-west

The path across the breast is part of the through-route from Buttermere to Rigg Beck, Newlands — a grand walkers' way among the hills, avoiding the motor road. A branch goes over Sail Pass to link with Braithwaite.

From the sheepfold at the crossing of Addacomb Beck go left straight up the ridge (here ill-defined), or, to avoid overmuch bracken, cut the corner from the second of two rushy grooves. When the first rocks are reached the ridge becomes narrower and a thin track climbs up through heather and bilberry and sundry Alpine flora, with Addacomb Hole sinking ever lower on the right. This section of the ridge is excellent and the route continues first-class to the top, which is reached exactly at the summit-cairn.

If using this route in reverse (or travelling to Buttermere from Newlands by the path) pedestrians hurrying to catch a bus, or desperate for a pint, can save ten minutes by dropping down to the sheepfold at Third Gill and using the lower (straighter) path.

The great feature of this route, apart from the ridge itself (the upper half of which is delightful) is Addacomb Hole — a perfect hanging valley. Only by the gradual gaining of height along the ridge can the proportions of this remarkable half-crater be fully appreciated.

ASCENT FROM BUTTERMERE
2300 feet of ascent : 2½ miles

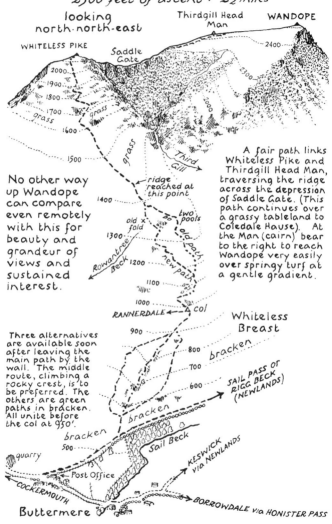

looking
north-north-east

Thirdgill Head Man

WANDOPE

WHITELESS PIKE

Saddle Gate

2400

2000
1900
1800
1700 grass
1600

grass

2300

2000

grass

Third Gill

1500

ridge reached at this point

1400

two pools

old fold

old path

1300

Rowantree Beck 1200

new path

1100

1000

Δ col

RANNERDALE

900

Whiteless Breast

800

bracken

700

SAIL PASS or RIGG BECK (NEWLANDS)

600

bracken

bracken

500

quarry

Sail Beck

Post Office

KESWICK via NEWLANDS

COCKERMOUTH

Buttermere

BORROWDALE via HONISTER PASS

No other way up Wandope can compare even remotely with this for beauty and grandeur of views and sustained interest.

A fair path links Whiteless Pike and Thirdgill Head Man, traversing the ridge across the depression of Saddle Gate. (This path continues over a grassy tableland to Coledale House). At the Man (cairn) bear to the right to reach Wandope very easily over springy turf at a gentle gradient.

Three alternatives are available soon after leaving the main path by the wall. The middle route, climbing a rocky crest, is to be preferred. The others are green paths in bracken. All unite before the col at 950'.

THE SUMMIT

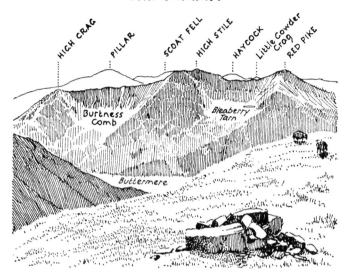

Apart from the view, the summit is unremarkable, being a smooth grassy parade kept neat and trim by grazing sheep. The stones of the cairn, which stand near the brink of the great downfall to Sail Beck, were obviously not provided by the summit itself, and some anonymous enthusiast must, in days gone by, have laboured mightily in bringing them up from the escarpment.

DESCENTS: The quickest way down (for Buttermere) is by the steepening southern slope, keeping the edge of the craggy east face close on the left until the ground falls more abruptly to Third Gill. There are crags below, which can be avoided, but it is best to break out of them to the left to a grassy slope, which can be followed down to join the Sail Beck path for Buttermere. If time permits, the Addacomb ridge should be preferred — this is useful also for Newlands — or the valley may be reached by a detour over Whiteless Pike, this being the usual course. In mist the Addacomb ridge is least likely to lead to trouble.

For destinations north, there is a very fast descent via Coledale Hause to Braithwaite in 1½ hours.

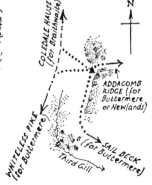

THE VIEW

Pride of place in the view must be conceded to the Scafells, from here looking magnificent, but scarcely less impressive is the scene eastwards, where range after range of tall fells cross the line of vision to culminate finally in the long Helvellyn skyline. The head of Sail Beck is a striking feature far below. Grasmoor and Eel Crag occupy much of the horizon, appearing dreary and shapeless at such close quarters, and Hopegill Head fits neatly into the gap between.

Ingleborough, Cross Fell, and the Isle of Man are all visible on a clear day.

Principal Fells

N

10 miles
7½ miles
5 miles
2½ miles

HOPEGILL HEAD

BOWSCALE FELL
BLENCATHRA
GREAT MELL FELL
CLOUGH HEAD
GREAT DODD
BLEABERRY FELL — — — E
STYBARROW DODD
RAISE
WHITE SIDE
CATSTYCAM
HELVELLYN
NETHERMOST PIKE
DOLLYWAGGON PIKE
FAIRFIELD
RED SCREES
GREAT RIGG

EEL CRAG
GRASMOOR
SAIL CAUSEY PIKE
ARD CRAGS
HIGH SEAT
MAIDEN MOOR
HIGH SPY
KNOTT RIGG
ROBINSON
FLEETWITH
DALE HEAD
HINDSCARTH
GREAT GABLE
HIGH RAISE
ULLSCARF
HARRISON STICKLE

BURNBANK FELL
BLAKE FELL
W —
GAVEL FELL
MELLBREAK
HEN COMB
GREAT BORNE
CRAG FELL
LANK RIGG
STARLING DODD
RED PIKE
CAW FELL
HAYCOCK
SCOAT FELL
PILLAR
HIGH CRAG
KIRK FELL
HAYSTACKS
LINGMELL
GREAT END
ESK PIKE
BOWFELL
GREAT GABLE
SCAFELL PIKE
SCAFELL
CLARAMARA
WETHERLAM

LITTLE GOWDER CRAG
HIGH STILE

12½ miles — S

The Scafell group

B EP G.E.   G.G. SP   S
                          L   KF
      FP   H

Lakes and Tarns
E : Derwentwater
S : Buttermere
SSW : Bleaberry Tarn

RIDGE ROUTES

To GRASMOOR, 2791': 1¼ miles: NW, then W.
Depression at 2375': 430 feet of ascent
An uninteresting journey over wide plateaux

Aim north-west to reach the Coledale-Whiteless Pike path where it skirts the head of Rannerdale. There is a cairn here on a little patch of gravel. Turning towards Coledale, watch for a series of cairns ascending the fellside on the left and do likewise. Along the wide top of Grasmoor, at the head of the slope, the track is more imaginary than real, but the walking, on mossy turf, could not be better; there is a half-mile of it before the top is reached.

To EEL CRAG, 2749': ¾ mile: N, then NE.
Depression at 2420': 340 feet of ascent
A cliff-edge circuit of Addacomb Hole

The only instruction necessary is to follow the semi-circular rim of the crater immediately to the north. There is no path at first, but a thin one is soon picked up and this becomes more distinct on rougher ground as height is gained.

To WHITELESS PIKE, 2159': ⅞ mile: W, then SW.
Depression at 2050': 110 feet of ascent
A good finish along an excellent ridge

Many walkers must have been beguiled by the southern ridge of Wandope into the false assumption that, if they follow it down, it will lead them to Whiteless Pike. Every step along here, however, puts Whiteless Pike further out of reach while bringing it nearer, because of the rough ravine forming between. The southern ridge is, in fact, a snare and a delusion. To gain the true one, aim west from the summit and make for the cairn of Thirdgill Head Man: it comes into view after a few paces. Here a path will be met; turn left along it and go down a narrowing crest to Saddle Gate for the climb to the Pike, now directly ahead.

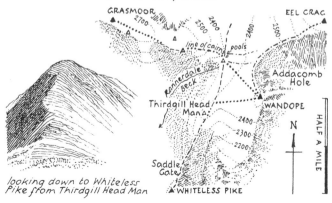

looking down to Whiteless Pike from Thirdgill Head Man

Whinlatter

1696'

from High Lorton

BROOM FELL ▲

CRAYSTONES ▲

LORD'S
SEAT ▲

High ●
Lorton

▲ WHINLATTER

Whinlatter ⚡ Pass

● Braithwaite

▲
GRISEDALE PIKE

MILES

0   1   2   3   4

Whinlatter Pass

NATURAL FEATURES

Whinlatter the Pass, an excellent motor road, is known to many; Whinlatter the Fell, a lonely sheep pasture, is known to few. The abrupt heathery slopes, streaked with long tongues of scree, form an effective northern wall to the pass, and there is little in this rough and forbidding declivity to suggest the pleasant heights above, where an undulating plateau trends downwards to the quiet valley of Aiken Beck. This stream defines the boundaries to west and north; the eastern termination of the fell, among the Thornthwaite plantations, is less distinct. From the top the extent of the afforestation of the surrounding area is appreciated fully: plantations almost encircle the fell, and indeed its own western and northern flanks are under timber. The rough face above the pass, significantly, has not been acquired for forestry, and the solitary sheep-farm of Darling How has retained much of its open range.

MAP

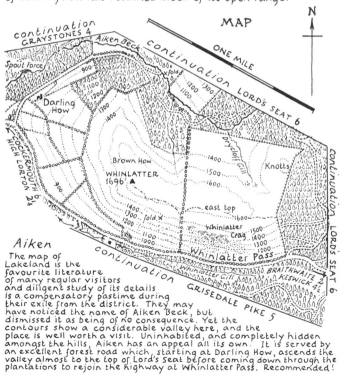

Aiken

The map of Lakeland is the favourite literature of many regular visitors and diligent study of its details is a compensatory pastime during their exile from the district. They may have noticed the name of Aiken Beck, but dismissed it as being of no consequence. Yet the contours show a considerable valley here, and the place is well worth a visit. Uninhabited, and completely hidden amongst the hills, Aiken has an appeal all its own. It is served by an excellent forest road which, starting at Darling How, ascends the valley almost to the top of Lord's Seat before coming down through the plantations to rejoin the highway at Whinlatter Pass. Recommended!

Grisedale Pike, from the east ridge of Whinlatter

ASCENT FROM WHINLATTER PASS
750 feet of ascent : 1¼ miles

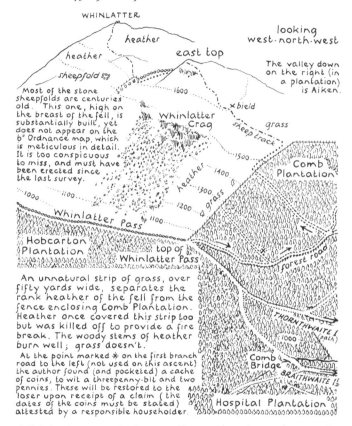

WHINLATTER

heather

heather

sheepfold

east top

looking
west·north·west

The valley down
on the right (in
a plantation)
is Aiken.

1600

×bield

Whinlatter
Crag

sheep track

grass

1500

Comb
Plantation

heather 1400

1300 grass

1200

1000 1100

Whinlatter Pass

1100

Hobcarton
Plantation

top of
Whinlatter Pass

forest road

THORNTHWAITE (path)

1000

Comb
Bridge

BRAITHWAITE 1½

Hospital Plantation

Most of the stone
sheepfolds are centuries
old. This one, high on
the breast of the fell, is
substantially built, yet
does not appear on the
6" Ordnance map, which
is meticulous in detail.
It is too conspicuous
to miss, and must have
been erected since
the last survey.

An unnatural strip of grass, over
fifty yards wide, separates the
rank heather of the fell from the
fence enclosing Comb Plantation.
Heather once covered this strip too
but was killed off to provide a fire
break. The woody stems of heather
burn well; grass doesn't.

At the point marked ✳ on the first branch
road to the left (not used on this ascent)
the author found (and pocketed) a cache
of coins, to wit a threepenny-bit and two
pennies. These will be restored to the
loser upon receipt of a claim (the
dates of the coins must be stated)
attested by a responsible householder.

Whinlatter tempts few walkers, the steep slopes of
heather and scree above the Pass being too rough
to contemplate, but the crest of the fell is entirely
different — a delightfully undulating ridge, a joy
to walk upon. It can be attained, moreover, by the
simplest of gradients if the direct climb alongside
the fence is disregarded in favour of the helpful
forest roads depicted in the diagram, the whole of
the walk then being no more than an hour's ramble.

THE SUMMIT

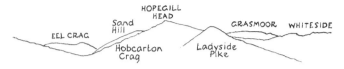

Sand Hill — HOPEGILL HEAD — GRASMOOR — WHITESIDE
EEL CRAG — Hobcarton Crag — Ladyside Pike

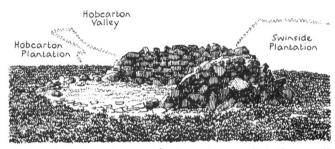

Hobcarton Valley — Swinside Plantation
Hobcarton Plantation

The part of the fell recognised as the summit is the small heathery dome of Brown How at the westerly end of its long undulating top. Here, still in a good state of preservation, is a wall in the form of a crescent, which, if intended as a wind-shelter, seems an extravagance in a place so seldom visited; more probably, considering the ocean of heather all around, it was built to serve as a shooting-hide.

The Ordnance Surveyors had no doubts that this was the highest point of the fell, at 1696', for only here is a 25' contour shown (on their 2½" map) above 1650', yet the eastern top appears from here to be at least equally high.   This may be an illusion of the sort familiar to all who frequent mountain-tops, for subsidiary summits often have a trick of appearing higher than the true summit when viewed from the latter, the eye having no horizontal level to assist in hilly terrain. In this case, however, the illusion is strengthened by the distant background to the eastern top, formed by Stybarrow Dodd (2770') with Sticks Pass (2420') to its right — for the line of vision from the main top to the eastern top strikes the background only a few hundred feet lower than the Pass, say at 2000', and is therefore rising, from which it follows that any

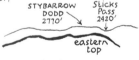

STYBARROW DODD 2770' — Sticks Pass 2420'

eastern top

looking from the summit

intermediate points on that line (including the eastern top) must be at a greater elevation than the viewpoint. Without instruments allowances must be made for defective vision and mental weakness, while refraction of light and curvature of the earth may be factors necessary to correct the judgment of the eye.   The most that one dare bet is that the eastern top should be credited with at least a 1675' contour — an investment worthy of anybody's bottom dollar.

DESCENTS: Routes down to Aiken Beck are easy if the plantation is avoided, down to Whinlatter Pass are exceedingly rough other than by the line suggested as a route of ascent (see page 4).

THE VIEW

The view generally is inferior to those from neighbouring heights, but in one direction it excels, this being to the south, where the supporting buttresses of the lofty Grisedale Pike-Hopegill Head ridge build up magnificently across the depths of Whinlatter Pass and reveal various lines of ascent that have tended to become overlooked as afforestation of the lower slopes has taken place.

The Vale of Lorton also features well, but here is viewed from the side and is less effective than when seen end-on along its full length.

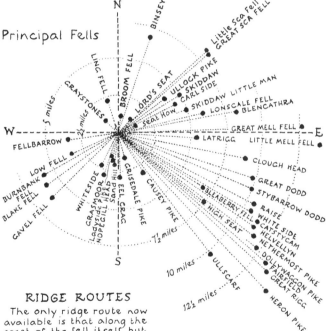

Principal Fells

RIDGE ROUTES

The only ridge route now available is that along the crest of the fell itself, but at one time it was possible to make a high-level way round to Lord's Seat and Broom Fell, keeping above 1500' throughout — a fine circuit of the Aiken valley. Afforestation and fences have put an end to this.

Lakes and Tarns

The Solway Firth is the only sheet of water in sight, but from the eastern top of the fell Derwentwater makes a charming picture above the intervening plantations.

Whiteless Pike

2159'

from Rannerdale Farm

GRASMOOR ▲   ▲ EEL CRAG

▲ WANDOPE

▲ WHITELESS PIKE

● Rannerdale

● Buttermere

MILES

0   1   2   3

The popular concept of a true mountain shape is a pyramid, with steep uniform sides on all flanks and a sharp peak. For a short distance along the road near Rannerdale Farm, on the shores of Crummock Water, it seems that Whiteless Pike has the qualifying attributes. But it fails to present an outline of similar shapeliness and beauty to other angles of view, and so cannot rank for stardom. Yet, seen from Rannerdale, surely it is the Weisshorn of Buttermere.

MAP

ONE MILE

A peculiarity of the streams flowing down to join Squat Beck is that they become subterranean, sinking in their beds at the 700' contour. The largest of these, Rowantree Beck, is crossed by the path on dry stones although there is surface water just above and below.

The face of Whiteless Pike overlooking Rannerdale is too steep to be climbed direct in comfort, but the path of ascent from Buttermere may be joined very pleasantly by following the valley of Squat Beck to its head. (Parts of a former path through the enclosures have gone but the walking is easy). Or, if a drove road slanting across the side of the fell to an old sheepfold near the head of Rowantree Beck is seen, this may be taken instead to cut off a big corner. It may be remarked here that Squat Beck does not occupy the main valley of Rannerdale as it appears to do: note the course of Rannerdale Beck.

ASCENT FROM BUTTERMERE
1800 feet of ascent : 1¼ miles

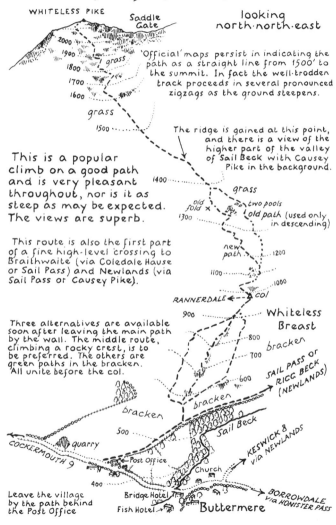

WHITELESS PIKE

Saddle Gate

looking north·north·east

2000
1900
1800
1700
1600
1500

grass

grass

'Official' maps persist in indicating the path as a straight line from 1500' to the summit. In fact the well-trodden track proceeds in several pronounced zigzags as the ground steepens.

The ridge is gained at this point, and there is a view of the higher part of the valley of Sail Beck with Causey Pike in the background.

This is a popular climb on a good path and is very pleasant throughout, nor is it as steep as may be expected. The views are superb.

1400

grass

old fold ✕

two pools

old path (used only in descending)

1300

new path

1200

1100

1000

This route is also the first part of a fine high-level crossing to Braithwaite (via Coledale Hause or Sail Pass) and Newlands (via Sail Pass or Causey Pike).

RANNERDALE ←

COL

900

Whiteless Breast

Three alternatives are available soon after leaving the main path by the wall. The middle route, climbing a rocky crest, is to be preferred. The others are green paths in the bracken. All unite before the col.

800

bracken

700

SAIL PASS or RIGG BECK (NEWLANDS)

600

bracken

bracken

Sail Beck

KESWICK 8 via NEWLANDS

500

COCKERMOUTH 9

quarry

Post Office

Church

400

BORROWDALE via HONISTER PASS

Leave the village by the path behind the Post Office

Bridge Hotel

Fish Hotel

Buttermere

THE SUMMIT

WANDOPE

SAIL

SCAR CRAGS

CAUSEY PIKE

The top is small and exposed, with an untidy accumulation of stones on the highest point. Except as a viewing station it has little of interest.

DESCENTS: The only route of descent is by the path to Buttermere, which turns off to the left sharply and not too distinctly some 20 yards south of the cairn.

Whiteless Pike, from the Thirdgill ridge of Wandope

THE VIEW

Like Causey Pike, its counterpart at the other extreme of the Eel Crag ridge, Whiteless Pike has a great advantage as a viewpoint, by reason of the small uplifted summit and the abrupt downfall therefrom, which together permit a prospect both wide and deep, a view of valleys as well as of mountains. The Scafell mass is most excellently displayed, and is nowhere better seen than from this northern side of Buttermere, the valley scene below the distant, lofty skyline being very beautiful; indeed the whole rich picture in this direction is crowded with lovely detail. Less rugged but not less charming is the appearance of Crummock Water and Loweswater to the west. In contrast, nearby Grasmoor and Wandope fill up the northern horizon unattractively.

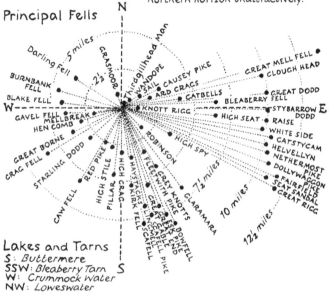

Principal Fells

Lakes and Tarns
S: Buttermere
SSW: Bleaberry Tarn
W: Crummock Water
NW: Loweswater

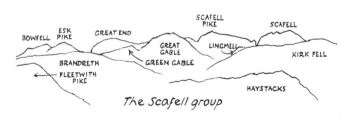

The Scafell group

RIDGE ROUTE

To WANDOPE, 2533' : ⅞ mile : NE, then E.
Depression at 2050' : 500 feet of ascent

A winding path leads down to,
and traverses, the depression of
Saddle Gate before climbing up to
the cairn of Thirdgill Head Man
(which, in mist, should not be
mistaken for Wandope). Here
desert the path and cross the
meadow on the right to its
culminating point.

The illustration below shows the
ridge rising to Thirdgill Head Man
(left skyline). Wandope's summit
is on the right.

Whiteside 2317'

from the road
to Scale Hill

- High Lorton

- Hopebeck

HOPEGILL
▲ HEAD

WHITESIDE ▲
Loweswater

Lanthwaite ▲ GRASMOOR

MILES

0   1   2   3

NATURAL FEATURES

As travellers make their way up the Vale of Lorton, eager for sight of the thrilling Buttermere skyline just around the corner, their enthusiasm is kept in check by the successive buttresses of Whiteside, which descend steeply into the valley on the left and conceal the desired view of lake and mountain ahead. There are three buttresses on this western flank of Whiteside — Dodd, Penn and Whiteside End — and together they form a cornerstone in triplicate to the high fells in the rear, for it is here that Lakeland really leaps into the sky from the flatlands of West Cumberland. These steep acclivities are rough and stony, and bulky rather than graceful — but many a beautiful picture is seen in an unattractive frame, and so it is here, the gaunt, massive portal enhancing the delicate, exciting scene ahead. The three buttresses rise in convex slopes to a sharply-cut summit ridge, and in a matter of yards the immediate dreariness of the grassy top is succeeded by a dramatic view down the other side of the mountain to Gasgale Gill in its ravine below. This south-eastern side presents an entirely different aspect: here are no sturdy buttresses but a vast scoop hollowed out of the fell, the debris of powerful forces of erosion, a place of shattered aretes, a natural quarry. This is Gasgale Crags, which a rich growth of heather is doing its best to make attractive by softening its naked harshness. From the ridge above, or the stream below, the natural architecture of the face cannot be appreciated, and one needs to visit Grasmoor, directly opposite, to observe the remarkable repeated pattern of aretes and scree-runs. This scene is unique. A splendid ridge from the summit eastwards leads on to Hopegill Head and Grisedale Pike. All waters drain into the River Cocker.

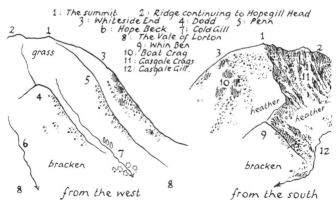

```
1 : The summit      2 : Ridge continuing to Hopegill Head
      3 : Whiteside End    4 : Dodd    5 : Penn
      6 : Hope Beck    7 : Cold Gill
         8 : The Vale of Lorton
            9 : Whin Ben
            10 : Boat Crag
            11 : Gasgale Crags
            12 : Gasgale Gill
```

grass

from the west

heather

heather

bracken

bracken

from the south

Whiteside 3

Gasgale Gill

Between Lorton and Buttermere the only route through the mountains is provided by a rough path along the side of Gasgale Gill, starting from Lanthwaite and leading up to Coledale Hause, at 1900', for Braithwaite. This is an excellent way for walkers in a hurry, Crummock Water and Keswick thereby being linked in a half-day's march. In Gasgale Gill the path runs along the base of Whiteside.

The rockstep

Waterfalls near the head of the gill

Proceeding eastwards, just after rounding the corner of Whin Ben, it is necessary to negotiate an awkward rocky obstacle at a place where a recent landslip has carried away the path. The illustration is of the scene looking back. Shuffling bottoms provide sufficient security here. There is no need for pitons.

The lower section

The middle section

MAP

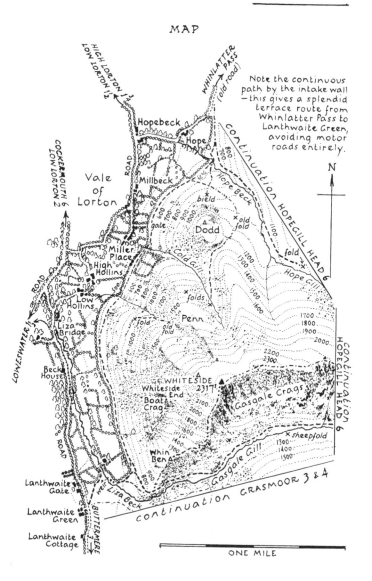

Note the continuous path by the intake wall — this gives a splendid terrace route from Whinlatter Pass to Lanthwaite Green, avoiding motor roads entirely.

N

ONE MILE

Dodd Pass

A pronounced indentation in the ridge of Dodd serves as a pass between Hope Gill and Cold Gill, and is much used by sheep. One side of the pass is a tumble of scree, and it is clear that the rocks still standing here are the remains of what must at one time have been a continuous rampart. A counterpart to this curious gap is to be found at Trusmadoor in the Northern Fells.

Cold Gill

Just above the intake wall, Cold Gill is crossed by a stone bridge carrying a path to a walled enclosure alongside. This is possibly the smallest stonebuilt bridge in Lakeland. Or is it only a culvert?

ASCENT FROM HOPEBECK
1950 feet of ascent : 2¼ miles

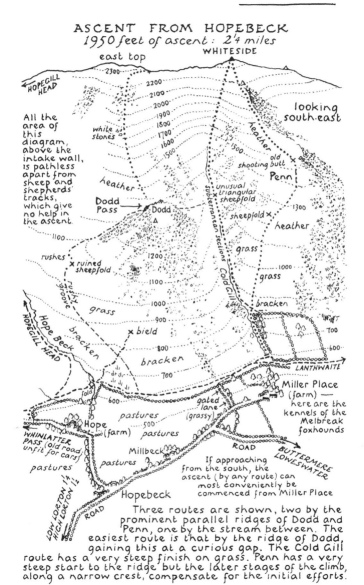

WHITESIDE

east top

2300

HOPEGILL HEAD

2200
2100
2000
1900
1800
1700
1600
1500

white stones

looking south-east

heather

1500

old shooting butt

Penn

All the area of this diagram, above the intake wall, is pathless apart from sheep and shepherds' tracks, which give no help in the ascent.

heather

Dodd Pass

Dodd

unusual triangular sheepfold

subterranean sections   Cold Gill

sheepfold

1300

heather

1100

1200

grass

grass

1000

rushes

ruined sheepfold

1100

grass

1000

bracken

rusty groove

900

bield

700

600

Hope Beck

HOPEGILL HEAD

bracken

800

700

LANTHWAITE

700

600

fold

600

Miller Place (farm) — here are the kennels of the Melbreak foxhounds

WHINLATTER PASS (old road, unfit for cars)

pastures

Hope (farm)

500

pastures

gated lane (grassy)

pastures

Millbeck

ROAD

BUTTERMERE
LOWESWATER

pastures

pastures

If approaching from the south, the ascent (by any route) can most conveniently be commenced from Miller Place

Hopebeck

LOW LORTON 1½
HIGH LORTON 1½

ROAD

Three routes are shown, two by the prominent parallel ridges of Dodd and Penn, one by the stream between. The easiest route is that by the ridge of Dodd, gaining this at a curious gap. The Cold Gill route has a very steep finish on grass. Penn has a very steep start to the ridge but the later stages of the climb, along a narrow crest, compensate for the initial efforts.

ASCENT FROM BECK HOUSE
1950 feet of ascent : 1¼ miles

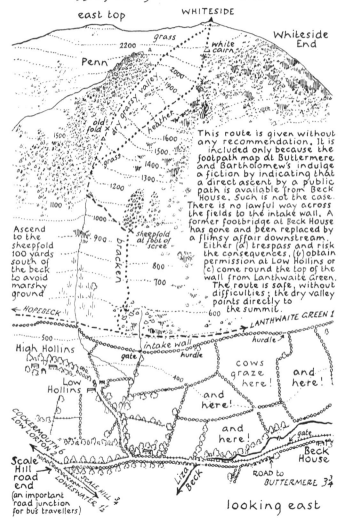

east top

WHITESIDE

Whiteside End

grass

2200

white cairn

Penn

2000

1900

dry grassy valley

heather

1500

old fold ×

1600

1500

1400

1300

1200

1100

grass

1000

This route is given without any recommendation. It is included only because the footpath map at Buttermere and Bartholomew's indulge a fiction by indicating that a direct ascent by a public path is available from Beck House. Such is not the case. There is no lawful way across the fields to the intake wall. A former footbridge at Beck House has gone and been replaced by a flimsy affair downstream. Either (a) trespass and risk the consequences, (b) obtain permission at Low Hollins or (c) come round the top of the wall from Lanthwaite Green. The route is safe, without difficulties; the dry valley points directly to the summit.

Ascend to the sheepfold 100 yards south of the beck to avoid marshy ground

900

sheepfold at foot of scree

800

700

bracken

← HOPEBECK

600

LANTHWAITE GREEN 1 →

500

intake wall

hurdle

High Hollins

gate

hurdle

cows graze here!

and here!

Low Hollins

400

and here!

and here!

COCKERMOUTH 6
LOW LORTON 2

gate

Beck House

Scale Hill road end (an important road junction for bus travellers)

SCALE HILL 3¾

LOWESWATER 12

Liza Beck

ROAD to BUTTERMERE 3¾

looking east

ASCENT FROM LANTHWAITE GREEN
1850 feet of ascent : 1½ miles

When viewed from the road Whiteside looks uninviting and it is difficult to see how a good route can be worked out. The key to the ascent is Whin Ben, reached from the sharp corner on the Gasgale Gill path to Coledale Hause. At this corner Whin Ben appears as a steep dark tower. There is no track at first but a good one materialises in the heather and facilitates the ascent. From the Ben onwards the route keeps to the edge of the crags overlooking Gasgale Gill.

Like Grasmoor and many other fells hereabouts Whiteside is richly vegetated and of special interest to botanists.

WHITESIDE

Whiteside End

Boat Crag

2200
2100
2000

striated rocks and prostrate juniper

1600
1500

heather

Whin Ben

heather

COLEDALE HAUSE
BRAITHWAITE

Gasgale Gill

1000
900

heather

800
700
bracken

600

700

fall

Liza Beck

weir

grass

cattle grid

500

ROAD

LORTON 3½

Lanthwaite Green

BUTTERMERE 3

GRASMOOR rises very steeply on this side

From Whin Ben onwards the views of Gasgale Gill are tremendously impressive.

looking north-east

The first problem is to cross Liza Beck; normally it is better to ford the gravelly shallows just above the weir. The footbridge downstream is now closed to the public and its approaches are defended by barb-wire.

This ascent, which promises nothing but a hard grind, turns out instead to be a delightful and interesting climb. It is incomparably the best route up the fell!

THE SUMMIT

east top   GRISEDALE PIKE   HOPEGILL HEAD   Sand Hill

The cairn is well sited at the end of the ridge, just above the steepening drop to Crummock Water, and on the edge of an abrupt downfall of crags. But there is little doubt that this is not the highest point of the fell: the first pronounced rise on the ridge eastwards certainly seems to have an advantage in altitude — looking back from here the official summit fits into the same horizontal plane as Blake Fell, 1878', four miles in the background, and therefore the view of it is downward.

The top is grassy, away from the rim of crags. The only other cairn is prominently seen 300 yards in a westerly direction.

DESCENTS : The best way down is to Lanthwaite Green via Whin Ben, keeping the steep edge on the left throughout; a fair track soon materialises. In mist, a complete stranger to the mountain would be better advised to aim northwest and descend the grassy valley there found : it has no difficulties, and leads down to the intake wall.   This route is also to be preferred to the Dodd and Penn ridges in bad weather.

The summit rocks

from the south   from the east

THE VIEW

Whiteside is the finest viewpoint for the coastal plain of West Cumberland, the Solway Firth, and the hills of Scotland beyond: a magnificent uninterrupted panorama crammed with detail; it is surprising to find the intervening Fellbarrow range sunk into complete insignificance from this elevation.

In other directions the view is patchy. The Skiddaw and Helvellyn ranges are well seen but the best skyline in Lakeland (south to the Scafells) is completely hidden by Grasmoor.

More intimately, the glimpses down the aretes of Gasgale Crags to the gill far below are very striking.

Principal Fells

Fells shown (clockwise): BINSEY, LONGLANDS FELL, BRAE FELL, Little Sca Fell, GREAT SCA FELL, ULLOCK PIKE, SKIDDAW, SKIDDAW LITTLE MAN, SALE FELL, LING FELL, GRAYSTONES, SWINSIDE, WINLATTER FELL, BROOM FELL, LORDS SEAT, Harrot, FELLBARROW, LOW FELL, GRISEDALE PIKE, HOPEGILL HEAD, Sand Hill, BURNBANK FELL, Carling Knott, BLAKE FELL, CAUSEY PIKE, SCAR CRAGS, EEL CRAG, GAIL, BLEABERRY FELL, STYBARROW DODD, GAVEL FELL, RAISE, WHITE SIDE, CATSTYCAM, HELVELLYN, NETHERMOST PIKE, GRIKE, HEN COMB, GREAT BORNE, MELLBREAK, STARLING DODD, CAW FELL, GRASMOOR, LANK RIGG, Little Gowder Crag, HAYCOCK

Scale circles: 2½, 5 miles, 7½ miles, 10 miles, 12½ miles

Crummock Water (SW) cannot be seen from the summit-cairn; a stroll of 30 yards in the direction of the Whin Ben descent brings it into sight.

The cairn 300 yards west across the grassy top is worth a visit — from this point Loweswater and Crummock Water are both seen in a comprehensive valley view.

Lakes and Tarns

NNE : *Over Water*
   (a faint trace only)
W : *Loweswater*

RIDGE ROUTE

To HOPEGILL HEAD, 2525′ : 1⅛ mile : ENE, then E.
Main depression at 2200′: 360 feet of ascent

An exhilarating high-level traverse with a grand finish.
The path is sketchy, but the sharp rim of the great downfall
to Gasgale Gill is an infallible guide. The best part of the walk
is the final depression, where a narrow heathery crest with
a distinct track leads across to the pyramid of Hopegill Head.
Approach this depression down the grass to the left of the rocks
of the ridge.

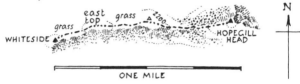

ONE MILE

*Whiteside, with Whin Ben (right)
from Lanthwaite Green*

Gasgale Crags, Whiteside   from Dove Crags, Crasmoor

looking east along the ridge to Hopegill Head and Sand Hill

THE NORTH WESTERN FELLS

Some Personal notes
in conclusion

When concluding Book Five I expressed the opinion that the north western Fells were the most delectable of all, and, after two years in their charming company, I hold to that view.   In other areas I have sometimes tired a little of repeatedly tramping the same tracks, but not here. Times without number I came off the hills faced with a long trudge down Whinlatter, or along the Coledale mine road or Newlands, until every stone and every tree became familiar, but never, rain or shine, did I do so wearily, but only regretting that another day was done, that another week must pass before I could return. always I was lingering, always looking back.

All this territory is wonderful walking country. much of it, south of the Grisedale Pike ridge, is well known and needs no introduction (although I have just completed nearly 300 pages doing that!). Even so, there are many corners rarely visited,   many excellent routes rarely trodden, many interesting features rarely seen.   several of the lines of ascent described in this book are as good as anything else in Lakeland, which is saying a lot, yet the majority of walkers are unaware of them. Searchers after traces of ancient history or old industrial activity will find much of interest. Geologists and botanists are well catered for here. Photographers cannot fail to produce beautiful pictures.

On the whole, the walking is quite excellent. The hills are easier to climb than their abrupt appearance suggests: the secret is to get on the ridges early, because it is the ridges, not the fellsides, that provide the best travelling underfoot and the finest views, and give the area its special appeal.

Newlands is a privileged valley, not only extraordinarily pleasant in itself but ringed by grand fells; for a quiet fellwalking holiday there is no better centre. Borrowdale we all know and love, but this valley is not so well placed for the area, and is nowadays so busy with cars that its joys are best experienced in winter. Buttermere is beautiful, but a better base for the Western

Fells than the North Western. I ought to put in a good word for Thornthwaite Forest, to the north of Whinlatter, which, in spite of much afforestation, is a fascinating place to explore. I never saw a soul here in eight months' weekend wandering, except once when I found myself mixed up in a foxhunt. Nothing in this region pleased me more than the shy Wythop Valley, so easy to walk, so charming and unspoiled, a little tranquil world apart.

Several times I came down to Buttermere, and it was hard to deny myself an occasional excursion to the magnificent mountains on the far side, but now the time has come when I am free to do this, and Book Seven will tell of High Stile and of Great Gable and Pillar and others that yet remain unrecorded. If I say that I start upon the last book in the series with mixed feelings, many of you will know what I mean.

AW

Autumn, 1963.